Physical Infrastructure Development

Physical Infrastructure Development: Balancing the Growth, Equity, and Environmental Imperatives

Edited by
William Ascher and Corinne Krupp

Prepared under the auspices of the
Pacific Basin Research Center,
Soka University of America

First published in 2010 by
PALGRAVE MACMILLAN®
in the United States—a division of St. Martin's Press LLC,
175 Fifth Avenue, New York, NY 10010.

Where this book is distributed in the UK, Europe and the rest of the world,
this is by Palgrave Macmillan, a division of Macmillan Publishers Limited,
registered in England, company number 785998, of Houndmills, Basingstoke,
Hampshire RG21 6XS.

Palgrave Macmillan is the global academic imprint of the above companies
and has companies and representatives throughout the world.

Palgrave® and Macmillan® are registered trademarks in the United
States, the United Kingdom, Europe and other countries.

ISBN: 978–0–230–10030–5

Library of Congress Cataloging-in-Publication Data

    Physical infrastructure development : balancing the growth, equity,
and environmental imperatives / editors, William Ascher and Corinne
Krupp.
      p. cm.
    Includes bibliographical references and index.
    ISBN 978–0–230–10030–5
     1. Infrastructure (Economics) 2. Economic development. I. Ascher,
William. II. Krupp, Corinne.

HC79.C3P59 2009
388—dc22   2009038938

A catalogue record of the book is available from the British Library.

Design by Newgen Imaging Systems (P) Ltd., Chennai, India.

First edition: May 2010

10 9 8 7 6 5 4 3 2 1

Printed in the United States of America.

To Barbara, again, with even more enthusiasm. W.A.

To my parents, Jerry and Rita Krupp, whose lives are a testament to the belief that giving back is a privilege and a responsibility. Thank you for your loving support and encouragement. C.K.

And in memory of John D. Montgomery and Dennis A. Rondinelli, dynamic leaders who built the Pacific Basin Research Center and made innumerable intellectual contributions to the field of development.

Contents

Illustrations

Figures

Tables

Preface and Acknowledgments

This project was the farsighted initiative of the late Professor Dennis Rondinelli, who clearly recognized the crucial if controversial role of physical infrastructure development, in both developing and developed nations. As the Director of the Pacific Basin Research Center (PBRC) of Soka University of America, in addition serving as Research Professor at the Duke Center for International Development, Dr. Rondinelli began to enlist contributors for a comprehensive treatment of the issues of infrastructure development, concentrating primarily but not exclusively on the Pacific Basin. Upon Dr. Rondinelli's very untimely death in 2007, William Ascher became the PBRC Director, and enlisted Professor Cory Krupp of the Duke Center for International Development to join him as co-editor of this volume.

We are indebted to Soka University of America for its stalwart support of the Pacific Basin Research Center for this and many other projects, and especially to Dr. John M. Heffron, who serves as Professor of History, Dean of Students, and Associate Director of the PBRC at Soka. We are also indebted to the Duke Center for International Development for arranging talks and workshop sessions that contributed to shaping this book. Valuable research assistance was provided by Claremont McKenna College students Alexis D'Agostino, Akta Jantrania, and Meredith Willis.

Finally, it is fitting to express gratitude for the leadership of both Dr. Dennis Rondinelli and Dr. John D. Montgomery, the founding director of the PBRC, who also passed away during the time that this book was under preparation. As a professor in Harvard University's Government Department and the Kennedy School of Government for many decades, Dr. Montgomery tirelessly campaigned for a holistic approach to understanding development, based on sharing experiences across the Pacific Basin and beyond. The many books of the PBRC, on compelling topics ranging from the impacts of globalization on Asia to human rights, from the changing meaning of national sovereignty to the development of pioneering economic and social policies, are testimony to the vision and leadership of these sorely missed friends.

Contributors

William **Ascher** is the Donald C. McKenna Professor of Government and Economics at Claremont McKenna College and also serves as the Director of the Pacific Basin Research Center of Soka University of America. He previously served as the Director of the Duke Center for International Development. His research has focused primarily on socioeconomic development and the policy processes in developing countries, particularly in Asia and Latin America. He is the author of seven books and coeditor of five others. His most relevant recent books are *Why Governments Waste Natural Resources: Policy Failures in Developing Countries* (Johns Hopkins University Press) and *Bringing in the Future: Strategies for Farsightedness and Sustainability in Developing Countries* (University of Chicago Press). He currently serves on advisory committees of the World Bank, the U.S. Environmental Protection Agency, and others.

Robert Cervero is Professor in the Department of City and Regional Planning at the University of California, Berkeley. He also directs Berkeley's Institute of Urban and Regional Development and the University of California Transportation Center. He has written extensively on sustainable transportation policy and planning and transit-oriented development worldwide and in recent years has been an advisor and consultant on transport projects in China, Colombia, Brazil, Indonesia, the Philippines, and the United States.

Rosemary Morales Fernholz is Senior Research Scholar and Lecturer at the Duke Center for International Development, Sanford School of Public Policy of Duke University. She has been involved in research, consultancy, and teaching in Asia, the Americas, and Africa for over two decades. Her research interests focus on innovations in public policy and development management to enable disadvantaged groups to participate effectively in development. Her recent research under the auspices of the Pacific Basin Research Center, the Research

Triangle Institute, the UN World Food Programme, and the World Bank has focused on child nutrition and school feeding in Latin America, financial innovations and strategies in the delivery of urban services such as public transport in Latin America and Africa, leadership in Asia, and social and environmental challenges for indigenous peoples. She served as the Director of a Philippine research center in the Philippines and is currently teaching graduate level courses on policy analysis for development, innovative policies, indigenous peoples and human rights, and culture and policy at Duke University. She has a Ph.D. in Political Economy and Government from Harvard University.

M. Julie Kim is Senior Researcher at RAND Corporation, with primary expertise in the transportation sector. Throughout her 25-year career, she worked extensively in the United States and East and Southeast Asia on large-scale infrastructure and real property development projects, examining all phases of development, from project feasibility and planning to construction and operations phases. She was the founding Executive Director of Stanford University's Collaboratory for Research on Global Projects, a research center to advance the science of managing large-scale global projects with complex cultural, organizational, and institutional issues through collaboration among academic, private sector, and government affiliates. Prior to Stanford, she held senior executive positions with large multinational engineering firms. She holds a B.S. in Civil Engineering from MIT and M.S. and Ph.D. degrees in Civil Engineering Infrastructure Planning and Management from Stanford University. She recently led RAND's Asia-Pacific Infrastructure Development Initiative.

Corinne Krupp is Associate Professor of the Practice of Public Policy at Duke University's Terry Sanford School of Public Policy and serves as the Director of Graduate Studies of the Sanford School's Program in International Development Policy. She also holds an adjunct appointment in finance at the Kenan-Flagler Business School at the University of North Carolina-Chapel Hill. Previously she taught at Michigan State University and was a consultant with the trade law group at Wilmer, Cutler, and Pickering. As an economist (Ph.D. from the University of Pennsylvania), her primary fields are international trade and finance, econometrics, and statistics. Her research interests include industrial organization, international trade, international finance, and economic development, and she is currently working on issues of the use and effectiveness of industrial policy as a development strategy.

Richard G. Little is Director of the Keston Institute for Public Finance and Infrastructure Policy at the University of Southern California where he teaches, consults, conducts research, and develops policy studies aimed at informing the discussion of infrastructure issues critical to California and the nation. He has conducted numerous studies dealing with life-cycle management and financing of infrastructure, project management, and hazard preparedness and mitigation and has lectured and published extensively on risk management and decision-making for critical infrastructure. He has been certified by the American Institute of Certified Planners, is a member of the American Planning Association and the Society for Risk Analysis, and is Editor of the journal *Public Works Management & Policy*. He holds a B.S. in Geology and an M.S. in Urban-Environmental Studies, both from Rensselaer Polytechnic Institute. Little was elected to the National Academy of Construction in 2008.

Rita Nangia is a development practitioner with over 30 years of experience. She is currently working as a Senior Advisor in the Asian Development Bank, an international development finance institution based in Manila, the Philippines. She has hands-on experience as a policy specialist working on complex issues in energy and infrastructure sectors in the Asia and Pacific region. She was the ADB's focal point for a joint ADB-World Bank-JBIC study on *Connecting East Asia: A New Framework for Infrastructure."* Recently she has published a regional energy strategy study titled *Building a Sustainable Energy Future: The Greater Mekong Subregion.* She has held senior positions in the Government of India including six years as an economic adviser in the Indian Prime Minister's Office and in research institutions. Nangia is an economist with postgraduate degrees from the London School of Economics and Boston University.

CHAPTER 1

Rethinking Physical Infrastructure Development

William Ascher and Corinne Krupp

The extent and quality of physical infrastructure are among the most crucial characteristics defining development. Any traveler from the First World to the Third World will be struck by the sheer difficulty of getting around, the economic opportunities lost for lack of transport or reliable energy, the flooding during heavy rains, or the stench of untreated sewage. It is almost trite to say that physical infrastructure is the backbone of any developed economy and a pillar of quality of life. For that matter, the quality of physical infrastructure can determine which developed nations maintain this quality of life in their cities and towns by preventing the collapse of bridges, disruption of neighborhoods, emission of toxic fumes, and the loss of touch with nature as rivers disappear under concrete. Countries with very strong physical infrastructure can maintain dense populations in comfort and can move people, goods, and information swiftly and at low cost; countries with weaker infrastructure, whether developed or developing, cannot.

We argue in this chapter—and support this argument in the rest of this book—that the promise of physical infrastructure development has been inadequately realized in both developing and developed nations, largely because of the failure to balance in farsighted ways the three key objectives of growth, poverty alleviation, and environmental protection. To balance these objectives requires planning and execution that acknowledges the complexity of how physical infrastructure fits within the economic tradeoffs—and the politics—faced by each country. Infrastructure planning and decision-making often take short-cut approaches—glossing over the question of who ultimately shares the benefits and the burdens, neglecting the full range of risks, relying on private-sector financing that for a host of reasons may fail to materialize, and ignoring the fact that infrastructure expansion is not necessarily a win-win for all concerned.

More concretely, the huge literature on infrastructure development[1] raises the following troubling points:

First, the performance of major infrastructure projects has often been disappointing despite very promising engineering and economic evaluations. The gaps between plans and results have been glaring in many cases in both developed and developing countries.

Second, the private sector response to government efforts to stimulate private investment and management of major infrastructure development has often been very disappointing. Over the past two decades, privately financed initiatives through "public-private partnerships" have not been the cure-all for underinvestment in physical infrastructure that they were hoped to be. And in many instances the risks to public monies that the privatization initiatives were hoped to eliminate remain, as private companies not infrequently require bailouts, or the public-private partnerships involve some public financing.

Third, the distributional impacts of burdens and benefits in the expansion of physical infrastructure are murky at best. Contrary to the wishful thinking that "a rising tide lifts all boats," it is easy to demonstrate that different designs, financing arrangements, and fee structures will have different consequences for the rich and poor, for different regions of the country, and for different sectors of the economy. This is the most challenging aspect of assessing the consequences of physical infrastructure, because both burdens and benefits have many direct and indirect impacts, which can vary greatly from one context to another. In addition, the outcomes depend on decisions made before, during, and after the infrastructure is in place, such as future user fees, or whether government spending on infrastructure will divert funds from other spending targets (e.g., education and healthcare for the poor).

Fourth, infrastructure planning and execution are often egregiously disconnected from the other aspects of planning and policy-making crucial for infrastructure expansion to make sense. In fact, different subsectors of infrastructure are often developed in isolation. In many instances, land-use planning and regulation are disconnected from transportation planning and execution. For example, new airports are sited where roads are vulnerable to major flooding; factories are sited far from existing electricity generation facilities; dams are built before the government has formulated appropriate plans to accommodate displaced people.

As daunting as these problems often are, it is important to understand that this book is not an argument against physical infrastructure expansion. On the contrary, there is much evidence pointing to the importance of expanding *some* physical infrastructure with *particular* designs and financing arrangements, in conjunction with due attention to the consequences of who gets what.

Under What Circumstances Does Infrastructure Expansion Make Sense? What do we need to know about the advisability of expanding physical infrastructure? First, policy-makers must choose a general strategy regarding how much to promote infrastructure development—for example, how much of the national budget should be devoted to physical infrastructure; how much credit should be made available to private investors for infrastructure. Second, policy-makers and citizens must make specific decisions on particular infrastructure projects, whether the government should undertake the projects directly or should approve private initiatives to proceed.

The question of the general strategy can be approached from different angles. One is to focus on needs assessments: how much do the economy and quality of life suffer from weak physical infrastructure? As of the dawning of the new millennium, a billion people lacked access to all-weather roads; a like number to telephone services; roughly 1.6 billion people lacked electricity; and an astonishing 2.4 billion lacked adequate sanitation (Fay and Yepes 2003). While the shortage of telephone access may be rapidly addressed by cell phone system expansion, the fact that billions of people lack electricity, sanitation, and access to all-weather roads can be addressed only by prioritizing infrastructure development for the benefit of these people—which does not necessarily correspond to the most financially attractive initiatives. World Bank infrastructure experts estimate that for the 2005–2010 period, developing countries would need US$550–650 billion in physical infrastructure development, requiring 6.5–7.7 percent of Gross Domestic Product (GDP), compared to the 3–4 percent currently available.[2] One assessment for Latin America estimated an *annual* economic loss during the 1990s of 1–3 percent of GDP growth because of infrastructure shortfalls (Easterly and Serven 2003). Felix Rioja (2003) estimated that for Latin America, productivity losses due to poor infrastructure *quality* are equivalent to 40 percent of real per capita income. In Africa, underinvestment in power and telecommunications *alone* during the 1980s and 1990s had cost the region an estimated 1.3 percent of annual GDP growth (Briceño-Garmendia, Estache, and Shafik 2004). Lack of access to infrastructure-dependent services is much more prevalent in rural than in urban areas (Briceño-Garmendia, Estache, and Shafik 2004: 12); rural areas often need secondary roads, sanitation systems, and schools. We must also recognize that international competitiveness hinges on the quality of physical infrastructure. Surveys of executives from multinational corporation also show that the quality of physical infrastructure is also an important consideration in deciding where to place foreign investment and locate global or regional headquarters.[3] In terms of international trade, poor transport infrastructure, along with inefficient document processing, can make an enormous difference in the time it takes to ship goods to other countries and the losses resulting from these delays.[4]

However, the needs assessments do not answer the question of whether the resources necessary to fill the needs are best used in that way. Does the expansion of physical infrastructure contribute sufficiently to economic productivity and quality of life, such that infrastructure investment is worth diverting government or private resources away from other targets? After all, people would do better with enhanced healthcare, educational and training opportunities, and other public goods besides physical infrastructure. The most comprehensive approach is to estimate the contribution of particular types of infrastructure to increases in overall output, and then to compare these increases to the costs of the new infrastructure. This would yield the so-called social rate of return—the measure of the net benefits to society as a function of the amount of expenditure put into the activities yielding these benefits.[5] However, the picture is bewildering because of the technical difficulty of assessing the connections. The number of economic assessments on this question exploded after David Aschauer, noting that a decline in U.S. productivity followed a prolonged drop in infrastructure investment, estimated huge rates of return to infrastructure investments. Aschauer (1989: 195) argued: "Dramatically, the fall-off in productivity growth is matched, or slightly preceded, by a precipitous decline in additions to the net stock of public nonmilitary structures and equipment." Yet Aschauer's assessment has been criticized for his methodology by literally hundreds of subsequent assessments. However, the methodologies of these subsequent assessments are also vulnerable, because such assessments are highly sensitive to assumptions that have to be made. Therefore the variation in the estimates of contributions for any given country or locale has typically been huge as well. This is more than just a thorny problem for economists—it is a problem for policy-makers trying to gauge how much investment in infrastructure is warranted.

Nevertheless, we can gain insights from a broad, middle-of-the-road assessment. David Canning and Esra Bennathan (2000) estimated the contribution of investments in paved roads and electricity generating capacity—in many countries the major infrastructure investments—over a 40-year period beginning in 1960. They had sufficient data for 41 countries (including the United States) to estimate the contribution of investments in paved roads. Although cost data for developed countries were not available for electricity generation, there were sufficient data for 52 developing countries. Canning and Bennathan then compared the social rates of return for each of these aspects of physical infra-structure investment with the overall returns on capital. They found a remarkable range of returns. These are discussed below.

For developed countries, with the exception of Japan, the social returns on infrastructure investments over the 40-year period were uni-formly quite low, with the returns consistently below the overall returns on capital (which, for mature economies, are themselves lower than for most developing countries). In the case of Australia and Austria, the returns on investments on paved roads were slightly negative (i.e., the construction and maintenance costs slightly exceed the contribution to economic productivity);[6] for the United States, the returns on road investments were only a quarter of the returns on capital investment as a whole.

However, before taking these results as an indictment against build-ing roads in developed countries, it is important to note that in nearly half of the developed countries, the rates of return were still above the 10 percent "hurdle rate" that development agencies such as the World Bank regard as sufficient to undertake an investment for developing countries, where one would expect that well-placed capital would have more impact than in a developed country that has already benefited from higher overall investment levels.

For all 11 Latin American countries in the sample, the social returns on paved-road investment exceeded the overall returns on capital, with some returns at remarkable levels (e.g., Colombia, Bolivia, and Chile). It is no accident that these happen to be countries faced with the major challenge of integrating their economies physically across difficult terrain.

Of the Asian countries in Canning and Bennathan's sample, the two Southeast Asian nations, Indonesia and the Philippines, revealed high

Table 1.1 Rates of Return to Paved Roads

	Rate of Return to Paved Roads	Rate of Return to Capital	ROR Paved Roads/ ROR Capital
Western developed countries			
Australia	−0.01	0.30	−0.02
Austria	0.00	0.29	−0.02
Belgium	0.06	0.40	0.14
Denmark	0.12	0.30	0.40
Finland	0.15	0.22	0.68
Germany, West	0.16	0.29	0.55
Ireland	0.06	0.36	0.15
Italy	0.26	0.34	0.76
Netherlands	0.15	0.32	0.46
New Zealand	0.08	0.36	0.23
Norway	0.02	0.21	0.08
Sweden	0.06	0.29	0.21
United Kingdom	0.13	0.39	0.32
United States	0.07	0.29	0.26
Latin America			
Argentina	3.85	0.29	13.33
Bolivia	7.96	0.21	37.09
Brazil	0.61	0.57	1.07
Chile	5.24	0.73	7.15
Colombia	9.47	0.54	17.53
Costa Rica	1.96	0.37	5.24
Ecuador	1.97	0.51	3.85
El Salvador	1.11	0.47	2.38
Guatemala	0.76	0.38	2.01
Honduras	0.39	0.34	1.15
Panama	2.18	0.38	5.76
Asia			
India	0.74	0.78	0.96
Indonesia	2.03	0.83	2.45
Japan	0.62	0.20	3.05
Korea, Rep.	15.76	0.43	36.95
Pakistan	0.52	1.17	0.45
Philippines	7.19	0.40	17.99
Turkey	1.58	0.78	2.03
Africa			
Botswana	0.20	0.58	0.34
Cameroon	1.88	0.35	5.31
Liberia	1.04	0.15	6.82
Malawi	0.60	0.40	1.50
Senegal	0.48	0.45	1.07
Tunisia	0.16	0.43	0.36
Zambia	0.65	0.24	2.69
Zimbabwe	0.15	0.45	0.33

rates of return, both in absolute terms and in relation to the overall returns on capital. South Asian rates were considerably lower, especially in light of the higher benchmarks of the rates of return on capital in general. South Korea had the highest return on paved-road investment of all, both in absolute terms and in relation to the relatively low overall returns on capital. Japan, which has twice the per capita public capital stock of the average high-income country after pouring an enormous amount of capital into physical infrastructure in its reconstruction, had three times the return on paved-road investment than on overall returns.

The returns on paved-road investment in the African sample vary greatly from country to country. For Botswana, Zimbabwe, and Tunisia (the only North African country in the sample), the returns on road building contributed less to productivity than overall capital investment did; in the other countries, paved-road investment had more attractive social rates of return than the overall returns on capital.

Canning and Bennathan's analysis of investments in electricity generation in developing countries also shows a thoroughly mixed picture. Most of the sub-Saharan African countries benefited more from investment in electricity generation than from capital investment in general, in large part because the general returns on capital were so low. Yet some sub-Saharan nations had negligible or negative returns on electricity generation expansion; with the exception of Senegal, these are countries that experienced political turmoil in the four-decade period—Mozambique and Zimbabwe. A few sub-Saharan countries had very high returns on electricity generation investment: Congo, Gambia, Kenya, and Uganda.

Among Latin American nations, Bolivia and Honduras, two of the poorest in Latin America, had the highest returns on electricity generation investment; Brazil, which one might assume would have benefited greatly from expanded electricity generation to serve its industrial expansion, had a very modest return on electricity generation investment compared to the overall returns on capital. Yet Mexico, with roughly the same overall returns, had much higher returns on electricity generation expansion. In Asia, China and India had robust returns on electricity generation investment, but not as high as the overall returns on capital.

The most important take-away message from the Canning-Bennathan analysis is that infrastructure investment makes sense when it is complementary to the potential for growth in economy because of synergies with human capital investments and investments in other aspects

Table 1.2 Rates of Return to Electricity Generating Capacity and Capital

	Rate of Return to Electricity Generating Capacity	Rate of Return to Capital	Ratio		Rate of Return to Electricity Generating Capacity	Rate of Return to Capital	Ratio
Algeria	0.63	0.15	4.20	Korea, Rep.	0.31	0.45	0.68
Argentina	0.46	0.29	1.59	Malawi	0.54	0.18	3.00
Bangladesh	0.61	0.80	0.77	Malaysia	0.77	0.44	1.76
Bolivia	0.92	0.19	4.74	Mali	0.51	0.24	2.16
Brazil	0.10	0.58	0.16	Mexico	0.51	0.52	0.98
Central African Rep.	0.40	0.12	3.25	Mozambique	-0.07	0.17	-0.42
Chile	0.41	0.73	0.56	Myanmar	0.34	0.33	1.03
China	0.54	0.41	1.31	Nepal	0.40	0.56	0.72
Colombia	0.28	0.55	0.50	Nicaragua	0.20	0.30	0.67
Congo	1.14	0.25	4.58	Niger	0.12	0.13	0.92
Costa Rica	0.25	0.36	0.69	Pakistan	0.18	0.95	0.19
Cyprus	0.36	0.31	1.19	Panama	0.21	0.38	0.55
Dominican Rep.	0.25	0.61	0.42	Papua N. Guinea	0.06	0.24	0.26
Ecuador	0.45	0.50	0.91	Peru	0.21	0.40	0.51
Egypt	0.45	0.50	0.90	Philippines	0.44	0.35	1.25
El Salvador	0.17	0.42	1.31	Portugal	0.07	0.46	0.14
Fiji	0.32	0.30	0.40	Senegal	0.06	0.24	0.27
Gambia	1.05	0.23	4.49	Sri Lanka	0.27	0.86	0.31
Ghana	0.25	0.18	1.37	Syria	0.35	0.80	0.44
Guatemala	0.18	0.34	0.52	Thailand	0.42	0.61	0.69
Honduras	0.95	0.27	3.56	Tunisia	0.40	0.37	1.07
India	0.24	0.53	0.44	Turkey	0.32	0.72	0.45
Indonesia	1.06	0.62	1.70	Uganda	0.80	0.02	46.26
Jamaica	0.11	0.20	0.54	Uruguay	0.30	0.51	0.59
Jordan	0.40	0.42	0.96	Yugoslavia	0.24	0.34	0.72
Kenya	1.25	0.19	6.63	Zimbabwe	0.05	0.38	0.14

Source: Adapted from Canning and Bennathan (2000: Table 6).

of physical capital (e.g., factory equipment). The unsurprising premise is that impressive returns to infrastructure investment come when the progress in other drivers of economic growth have been increasing but the physical infrastructure to bring economic progress to fruition had been lagging. Thus, they argue that "in a limited number of countries we find evidence of very acute shortages of electricity generating capacity and paved roads, and large excess returns to infrastructure investment. For electricity generating capacity, these excess return countries tend to be low income countries; for paved roads, they are all middle income countries. These excess returns are evidence of sub-optimal investment that, in the case of paved roads, appear to follow from a period of sustained economic growth during which road building stocks has [sic] lagged behind investments in other types of capital." (Canning and Bennathan 2000: 1). This is consistent with the conclusions from a recent survey of over 120 articles and reports on the record of physical infrastructure projects:

> Many studies report that... the effect of public investment differs across countries, regions, and sectors. This is perhaps not a surprising result. After all, the effects of new investment spending will depend on the quantity and quality of the capital stock in place. In general, the larger the stock and the better its quality, the lower will be the impact of additions to this stock. The network character of public capital, notably infrastructure, causes non-linearities. The effect of new capital will crucially depend on the extent to which investment spending aims at alleviating bottlenecks in the existing network. Some studies also suggest that the effect of public investment spending may also depend on institutional and policy factors. (Romp and de Haan 2007: 33)

It is also important to understand what this sort of analysis does not take into account. First, Canning and Bennathan (2000: 6) acknowledge that their estimation cannot take into account the economies of scale afforded by infrastructure. The potential contributions to technological advancement and total productivity are underestimated. This demonstrates that the unavoidable need to simplify the models used to estimate returns will leave some impacts unmeasured.

Second, the assessment is restricted to economic productivity, and thus leaves out other quality-of-life considerations. This encompasses both positive effects, such as more pleasant cities, and negative effects, such as the travails of people displaced by hydroelectric dams. Because the displaced people from the rural areas generally have low market incomes to begin with, their worsening economic situation is unlikely to register in estimates of productivity changes. These negatives are not confined to developing countries: physical infrastructure can make cities less livable as well as more livable. The enormously expensive dismantling of portions of Boston's Interstate 90 and Interstate 93 highways, requiring the US$14.8 billion "Big Dig" to bury portions of the highways, is testimony to the disruption and blight that the highways had imposed. Robert Cervero's chapter in this volume describes a similar initiative to dismantle a major highway in Seoul, Korea. In short, physical infrastructure expansion in both developing and developed countries can have important impacts on the lives of people that cannot be captured in the economic assessments.

Third, the national-level focus does not speak to the local advantages of physical infrastructure in attracting economic activity that otherwise might be sited elsewhere in the country. For example, the excellent road system in Sydney may be one of the factors that has led international and domestic firms to place their Australian headquarters there, as opposed to other sites in that country.

An alternative (though often complementary) explanation for the huge variation in the returns to infrastructure investment is that infrastructure investment has been squandered through some combination of poor design, shoddy or sluggish execution, corruption, and unsound macroeconomic policies. The economic analysis cannot tell us whether low returns reflect the fact that the infrastructure expansion is not needed, or that the expansion has been inadequate in serving the needs despite the investment in it. Nor for the many countries with unsound macroeconomic policies can it tell us whether the problem of low-productivity gains from infrastructure expansion means that this expansion would do no good under sounder macroeconomic conditions. Daniel Kauffman (1991) has demonstrated that the macroeconomic environment must be fairly sound for any sort of investment to prosper. In other words, worthwhile physical infrastructure investment depends not only on finding the "bottlenecks in the existing framework," but also on carrying out the infrastructure development with sound decision processes, and under sound economic policies in general, such that the bottlenecks are actually alleviated.

The social rates of return on carefully screened and monitored infrastructure projects in many developing countries appear to be very high. The World Bank's Independent Evaluation Group estimated that the rates of return to World Bank–funded transport projects approved during the 1995–2005 period averaged at 28 percent.[7] Yet this does not speak to the large number of transport projects that do not have to go through the gauntlet of design that meets approval from the World Bank, procurement restrictions that the World Bank imposes, and the periodic inspections that Work Bank staff perform.

The "institutional and policy factors" on which infrastructure development depends begin with problems in planning and execution. One common institutional problem in designing infrastructure projects is the difficulty of bringing coherence between infrastructure planning and land-use planning. These functions are often in the hands of different agencies within the same level of government, or even in agencies of different levels of government. For example, in Thailand, the provincial government of the Bangkok metropolitan area is responsible for land-use planning, but the national government controls transportation planning.[8] The coordination of transportation and land-use decision-making is typically complicated by the fact that the decisions involve control over huge sums of money, triggering fierce "bureaucratic politics" battles over jurisdiction. Often, as has been the case in Thailand, the national government and the provincial governments are in the hands of rival political parties, making cooperation and coordination even more difficult.

Corruption in the planning, construction, and operation of major infrastructure facilities is another institutional issue of great relevance. Corruption can result in poor project choices, overcharges, incompetence, and plain theft. Briceño-Garmenia, Estache, and Shafik (2004: 25) estimated that over US$100 billion could be saved over the 2005–2010 period for infrastructure development in developing countries if the inefficiencies and diversion of funds resulting from corruption were eliminated. It is important to keep in mind that the costs of corruption are not simply in the magnitude of bribes that government officials may collect—that is simply a transfer—but also in poor designs, sites, construction, and operations that arise out of government officials' corrupt decisions. Everhart and Sumlinski (2001: 9), noting the empirical evidence that the extent of corruption[9] is positively correlated with larger public infrastructure projects, argue:

> Infrastructure projects can be large and the implementation is often carried out by private firms. The incentive for the private enterprise to pay a "commission" to secure the contract is strong, particularly when the contract is large. When the approval of investment projects is influenced by corrupt public officials, rates of return and cost-benefit analyses become mere exercises. The firm paying the "commission" is unlikely to bear the cost of the bribe. It is more likely this cost will be recouped in some inefficient way. Perhaps project costs will be pared by adhering poorly to

plan specifications or by using poor quality materials or workmanship. Perhaps an "understanding" will be reached with the bribed official that the initial low estimate will be revised upward as the project progresses. Or the bid may be padded initially. In the more rare instances of cost-plus contracting, the firm can hide the bribe expense through overpricing. All of these work to make the public investment in infrastructure more costly and less likely to meet specifications.

These problems have led some observers to regard physical infrastructure investment as being particularly prone to corruption, compared with other investments and activities (Rose-Ackerman 1996).

Understanding the "Political Economy" of Physical Infrastructure Development. All of these considerations point to the fact that securing sound infrastructure development depends on institutions and a policy process that can identify the appropriate opportunities and carry them forward competently, coherently, and honestly. This requires overcoming some of the problems that have been given the broad label of "political economy." The interactions between politics and economics of physical infrastructure encompass both the logic of economic maximization through politics and institutional arrangements, and the political uses of economic policy decisions on the part of government.

The economic motive of getting the greatest benefit from physical infrastructure development at the least cost is often expressed through two maneuvers: shedding costs and risks onto others, and appropriating property rights from others. Problems arise when the results of these maneuvers divert resources from the soundest infrastructure development away from the perspective of what is good for the society as a whole.

Individuals and companies conduct their lives and businesses either with the assistance of physical infrastructure provided to them as public goods, or by having to purchase access to infrastructure. From the perspective of infrastructure users, individuals and firms have an incentive to have government pay for free-access infrastructure or at least to reduce the costs of infrastructure use by providing or subsidizing facilities that would reduce the costs of using infrastructure (e.g., building airports, promoting railroad expansion by granting right-of-way easements). Yet these costs are borne by taxpayers, whether individuals or firms. Therefore the efforts to get more for less take advantage of the differences in benefits and burdens across taxpayers. The result is a host of decisions to vote or lobby for particular infrastructure expenditures and to off-load costs of desired infrastructure onto others. The choices to support particular aspects of infrastructure development that benefit some voters or those with the capacity to lobby (or to bribe) may diverge from the soundest infrastructure development for the society as a whole. For example, Haughwout (2002: 426) argues that urban infrastructure has suffered in the United States because the voters represent households, not firms, and therefore increasing residential property values has been more important than making cities attractive to businesses. He emphasizes the underinvestment that occurs when people in the city themselves do not support infrastructure expansion for the metropolitan area as a whole. Similarly, Cadot, Röller, and Stephan (1999) find suboptimal infrastructure investment in France, but they correlate it with lobbying and campaign contributions by French firms that benefit if the infrastructure investments favor their particular locations and needs. One indication of the tendency to respond to these pressures rather than to assess potential infrastructure initiatives on their merit for society as a whole is the practice of earmarking government infrastructure funds for specific purposes and sites, rather than permitting the technical experts in the infrastructure planning units to choose the best projects. In the United States, the Congressional Budget Office complained that according to the Department of Transportation, about 15 percent of the US$36.6 billion appropriated to Federal Highway Administration programs in fiscal year 2006 was earmarked, as was 28 percent of the US$8.6 billion funding for Federal Transit Administration programs. The Congressional Budget Office report criticized its own master by urging that

> the federal government also could encourage efficiency by lowering the costs of supplying infrastructure services. One way to accomplish that is to encourage funding of high-value projects through more systematic use of rigorous analysis, and conversely, to minimize funding of potentially low-value projects—for example, by careful scrutiny of projects initiated by the Congress, which represent significant portions of federal investments in infrastructure.[10]

Thus from the perspective of government officials, we see the mirror-image of political economy implications: the behavior of government officials reflects, to a greater or lesser degree, their calculations of how infrastructure decisions will affect political support. This goes far in explaining what is perhaps the most common weakness in the sustainability of infrastructure systems: the dire shortage of funds for maintenance. For developing countries, a common tragedy is that scarce resources are spent on creating physical infrastructure, which then, for lack of maintenance, becomes nonfunctional. Highways revert to bush, electricity generating plants are shuttered, power lines collapse, and irrigation systems suffer from huge water losses. One indication of the seriousness of the neglect of maintenance is that the estimates of the returns to infrastructure maintenance tend to be far greater than the estimates of returns to construction. As early as the mid-1980s, when the U.S. infrastructure was less developed than it is now, the estimated returns to maintenance of existing highways was 35 percent, compared to 15 percent for new urban construction and 5 percent for upgrading highway sections not meeting minimum standards (U.S. Congressional Budget Office 1988). A European Investment Bank estimate the economic returns on new roads in the Balkans as 5 percent, but the returns on road maintenance as between 20 percent and 70 percent (Hörhager 2006). A 2007 assessment by the World Bank's Independent Evaluation Group (2007: 24) of the transport projects approved by the World Bank during the 1995–2005 period notes:

> Despite the Bank's emphasis on adequate and timely road maintenance, this objective was seldom satisfactorily accomplished. The limited funds allocated to roads were often wasted through inefficient work methods and too much spending on new construction at the expense of the maintenance budget. As a result, a high proportion of the roads in developing countries remained in poor condition.

For Africa, estimates of the rates of return to World Bank–funded road maintenance have averaged around 40 percent (Heggie 1995). At first glance, a high return would seem like a good sign, but in fact such high returns imply that maintenance is so desperately needed that when it can be supplied, it pays off handsomely. A 2006 World Bank assessment reports that of the 18 sub-Saharan African countries that have established road-maintenance funds and provide enough data to assess the degree to which maintenance is accomplished, only four countries are meeting the full routine maintenance; none is fully meeting the periodic maintenance needs; and the median level of meeting periodic needs is less than 40 percent (Benmaamar 2006: 13). Without investment in maintenance and rehabilitation, infrastructure can actually shrink. For Africa, Njoh (2008: 152) reports that "at least three countries, Burkina Faso, Ethiopia and Mozambique, recorded a negative change in their road inventory between 1963 and 1997. This suggests that although road construction is an additive process, some of the roads that existed in these countries in 1963 had in fact disappeared by 1997."

Maintenance is also frequently neglected in developed countries. Because developed countries typically already have extensive infrastructure systems, the challenges to traditional physical infrastructure arise primarily from the deterioration of existing structures, in many cases reflecting decades of neglect. The investment in physical infrastructure in the United States averaged around 0.7 percent of the GDP in the 1960s and 1970s, but then suffered a fairly steady decline, dropping down to 0.03 percent in 2007 (Baker 2008: 4–5). From 1990 to 2006, vehicle travel in the United States increased by 41 percent, whereas the miles of roads in the United States increased by only 4 percent (U.S. Department of Transportation 2006: Chapters 6 and 7), putting much greater strain on the existing road system. According to the U.S. Federal Highway Administration, road *maintenance* from all levels of government in the United States requires an annual expenditure of US$79 billion, and US$132 billion is needed to adequately maintain and improve them to meet increased traffic demand; however actual spending as of 2006 was only US$70 billion (U.S. Department of Transportation 2006: Chapter 7). The United States is not alone; for example, in 2003, the Conference Board of Canada estimated the infrastructure investment shortfall in Quebec Province at $17.9 billion (Conference Board of Canada 2003). It is too early to see whether the "shovel-ready" projects funded as part of the stimulus packages around the world will significantly raise the funding for maintenance and rehabilitation.

In what respects is the neglect of maintenance a reflection of political economy considerations? Insofar as political leaders feel compelled to calculate the support they will receive by providing goods and services to voters and campaign contributors, they would find the infrastructure initiatives that have the greatest "political returns." Generally, providing the infrastructure itself—the road, the irrigation channel, the electricity generator, and transmission lines—are regarded as a gift or a boon to the previously underserved area, often with impressive political payoff. The appreciation for providing the infrastructure is all the greater to the degree that the financing comes from beyond the local area. In many instances, the more grandiose the project, the more political capital government leaders can count on.[11] In contrast, maintenance has little political allure and often requires local people and local government to bear a large portion of the costs.

Another political economy effect on government behavior is that in order to get support for expensive infrastructure projects, government officials have an incentive to exaggerate the benefits and underestimate the costs of these projects. Flyvbjerg, Bruzelius, and Rothengatter (2003) shocked the European infrastructure-planning establishment by recounting the huge cost overruns and poor performance of what they call "megaprojects," and attributing the results to the motivation of infrastructure promoters, both within and outside of government, to cultivate support for projects that otherwise might be recognized as too costly and insufficiently productive to undertake. Their indictment is harsh:

> At the same time as many more and much larger infrastructure projects are being proposed and built around the world, it is becoming clear that many such projects have strikingly poor performance records in terms of economy, environment and public support. Cost overruns and lower-than-predicted revenues frequently place project viability at risk and redefine projects that were initially promoted as effective vehicles to economic growth as possible obstacles to such growth. (*Flyvbjerg, Bruzelius, and Rothengatter 2003: 3*)

To be fair to infrastructure planners, it is often very difficult to take into account the myriad things that can go wrong with a major infrastructure project.[12] However, one indication that infrastructure project evaluators tend to neglect the negatives and accentuate the positives is that when they are aware that parallel assessments will challenge their exaggerations, their ex ante (i.e., preapproval) evaluations tend to have more accurate estimates of rates of return.[13]

Yet another political economy dynamic arises from the discrepancy between the appropriate time horizon for society as a whole and the time horizons of government decision-makers. The obligation of government is to take both current and future generations into account in the planning and execution of infrastructure development. Yet some government officials, particularly those who stand for reelection, must weigh more heavily the shorter-term consequences, and the impact of these consequences on the public's assessment of the leaders' performance. Infrastructure projects that will gain immediate or nearly immediate appreciation and political credit will tend to be favored. Adding to the discrepancy is that accountability for long-term consequences erodes as these consequences are further and further into the future. This does not mean that leaders will tend to choose infrastructure projects that will come to fruition quickly, but rather that leaders are more likely to choose short-term or long-term projects that will have immediate popularity.

The Private Sector as the Great Hope? Is it possible to "get more for less" by promoting public-private partnerships, through which private sector financing and management of infrastructure facilities would bring in appropriate investment, select infrastructure initiatives that can withstand "market discipline," and contribute greater efficiency? Here we are not referring to the traditional practice of the government hiring private firms to construct or manage infrastructure, but rather involving private firms that essentially own or co-own the infrastructure temporarily or permanently. Much of the history and politics of infrastructure development over the past two decades has focused on how to reduce governments' financial burdens for this, with the consequence of greatly increasing complexity of partnering with the private sector and of devising financial instruments and fee structures to reduce or redistribute the immediate burdens of paying for infrastructure development.

For developed countries, the prospects of budget relief spawned a huge number of efforts to attract private financing and management for infrastructure. As governments encountered the difficulties of financing infrastructure through taxes, they tried to go back to the future with private toll roads and bridges. This is not the simple question of how much capital is available within the country or region, but rather how much willingness exists to capture capital for infrastructure. Some of the wealthiest countries, including the United States, are miserly in terms of devoting public capital to infrastructure. Indeed, governments have been selling off existing infrastructure to private investors as much to fill government coffers as to lay off the responsibility for infrastructure maintenance. American cities and states have been selling off iconic structures, such as the initiative of the State of California to sell the Los Angeles Memorial Coliseum.

This enthusiasm is increasingly shared in developing countries, where, despite the daunting challenges of policy instability and political risk, many governments have expected private investment to overcome the shortage of government funds to finance major infrastructure expansion. Although a few governments, most notably those of China and the Emirates, have poured part of their huge hard currency reserves into massive expansion of transport and energy, most developing country governments have also largely put their hopes on the private sector.

As this volume's chapter by Richard G. Little elaborates, there are many public-private partnership arrangements, but they all share the core characteristics that private companies provide capital and stand to gain profits from the operations of the infrastructure. In principle, there is much to be said for public-private partnerships: when capital is short and yet highly productive, infrastructure development is possible, and public-private partnerships can bring in the capital. Contractors that will profit from the operations of the infrastructure have more incentive to build well and to maintain infrastructure because their profits depend on it. Firms with experienced planners, engineers, financial analysts, and managers may increase the competence at all phases of infrastructure development and operation. When the private partners are international firms, their diversification can permit them to take on risks that otherwise would have to be borne by the public. If the government might otherwise be pressured into unsound infrastructure development by special interests or a shortsighted citizenry, partnerships with profit-maximizing firms will impose a "market test" on infrastructure development, and increase the chances that the construction and operations will strive to reduce costs and risks. No wonder Everhart and Sumlinski (2001: 9) assert that "[t]here is a growing consensus that private investment is more efficient and productive than public investment."

From a political economy perspective, government leaders would typically have an easier time selling major infrastructure projects to the public if their financing does not entail raising taxes or diverting public funds from other uses. The public still pays ultimately, but it is not in the up-front costs of construction, but rather in the drawn-out payments of user fees.[14] There is a logic of fairness to having the users of infrastructure bear the ongoing costs, rather than the general public, parts of which are not using the infrastructure to the same degree as others.

Several pitfalls of public-private partnerships exist, although they are rarely voiced against the tide of enthusiasm for off-loading the immediate construction costs onto the private sector. For one thing, public-private partnerships are not completely free of the risk of corruption, because suborned officials may accept lower concession bids, or permit higher user fees, than are appropriate for the project. Additional risks arise from the difficulty of projecting infrastructure use, opening up the possibility that the private firms will be unwilling or unable to proceed with the projects.

A less obvious but possibly more important problem is that the political attractiveness of bringing in private financing often induces infrastructure plans to overestimate the amount of private financing that will actually materialize. The government can reduce its budgetary commitments to infrastructure development, and the tax effort needed to cover these commitments. Thus the fond hope that private funds will be abundant is convenient when government leaders do not want to suffer the political costs of increasing taxes. Yet when the private response is lower than anticipated, the government finds itself in a difficult position of having to choose between scaling back the infrastructure plans and redirecting budget resources away from other spending targets. Insofar as the budget allocations for these other expenditures are typically anticipated by their beneficiaries, the government will face opposition to these budget changes. Often the political path of least resistance is to cut back on services to the poor.

The reductions in government spending on infrastructure in the expectation of private financing have been seen in many different contexts. In India, despite the infrastructure needs required for the take-off of the Indian economy, the public infrastructure investment declined to 3 percent from 4 percent from 1990 to 1998, with the expectation that the private sector would fill the gap, resulting in a total infrastructure investment decline to 4.6 percent from 5.4 percent.[15] Indian economists and policy-makers bemoan this decline, and yet India's Eleventh Five-Year Plan 2007–2012 insists that "[a]ll contracts on provision of road services for high density corridors to be taken up under [the National Highway Development Programme] onwards would be awarded only on BOT [Build, Operate, Transfer] basis" (Government of India 2007: 42). This, despite the warning in the very same report:

> However, considerable work is needed to create an enabling environment which should not only attract private investment but must also be seen to be in the public interest and this is best assured if the process is seen to provide services at reasonable cost and in a transparent manner. If we adopt best practices, it will be possible to create credible [Public-Private Partnership] projects that evoke a positive public response and do not require re-negotiation or payment of unforeseen liabilities by the government or the users. (Government of India 2007: 41)

This reliance on public-private partnerships, notwithstanding the recognized risks, is consistent with the relatively sluggish transportation infrastructure in India compared to China, as documented in the Kim and Nangia chapter in this volume.

This vulnerability to overreliance on private infrastructure investment is by no means unique. One assessment of investment in eight

Latin American countries found that public infrastructure investment declined from an average of 3 percent of GDP to 0.8 percent
over the course of the 1990s (Calderon and Serven 2004), despite the
fact that the 1990s was a decade of growth following the "lost decade"
of the 1980s. Kitchen (2003: 76) reports the lower than expected private sector investment in major infrastructure in Canada; Koppenjan
(2005: 135) in the Netherlands; Bayliss (2009) in sub-Saharan Africa;
Szalai (2001) in urban infrastructure in the former Soviet Union; and
Hall and Lobina (2006) in water infrastructure in developing countries.
In assessing urban water and sanitation infrastructure, Tremolet et al.
(2007) conclude that "[t]he international private sector also plays a role
but its ability to bring in financing has been lower than expected and
somewhat disappointing."

If public-private partnerships are to remain a great hope for sound
infrastructure development, policy-makers need to understand and
address the reasons why private investment has been disappointing. Explaining this outcome is undoubtedly complicated, but many
(not mutually exclusive) possibilities come to mind. Most optimisti-
cally, it may be that the mechanisms of public-private partnerships for
public-access infrastructure (e.g., toll roads) had not been sufficiently
developed and tested to the point that governments and private investors could be confident of their success. Robert Cervero's chapter on
Tokyo and Hong Kong in this volume describes how complicated it
is to arrange public-private partnerships that meet both public needs
and private investors' requirements for sufficient risk-adjusted profit.
If these lessons can be learned and the mechanisms for public-private
partnerships refined, it is possible that the private sector's role can grow
impressively in the future.

It may also be that the potential for public dissatisfaction over the
full or partial privatization of infrastructure prevented governments
from offering arrangements that were sufficiently attractive to private
investors and construction firms. It is unclear whether public attitudes
toward privatization have become more or less favorable over the past
decade, given the mixed experience both within and among countries.
We have just witnessed a potentially important shift from viewing public
expenditures on infrastructure as a fiscal drag, to the reliance on public
infrastructure spending as a major part of economic stimulus plans.
"Shovel-ready" projects have been targeted as the quickest way to jump-
start stagnant economies, not only in the United States via the 2009
Economic Recovery Act, but also in Western Europe (Commission of
the European Communities 2008). However, this may or may not cause
a long-lasting change in public attitudes.

From the private firms' perspective, it may be that, beyond the technical soundness of available public-private partnership mechanisms, private sector investors and construction firms found the "policy risk" that governments would renege on agreements to be too great to ensure a sufficient risk-adjusted profit. As firms try to take political and policy risk into account, the exciting opportunities that governments think they are offering are frequently not what private investors regard them to be. The government's calculations of profitability are unlikely to reflect the full range of risks. The role of the government analyst who assesses the potential profitability of an infrastructure project is decidedly not to factor in the possibility that the government will renege on its commitments, fall prey to corruption, or alter other policies that would turn a sound investment into a disaster. In 1993, the Japanese-led consortium Kumagai Gumi saw the Thai government seize the consortium's control over the ring road expressway around Bangkok, just before the highway was to open, in the dispute over whether the consortium could charge the previously agreed-upon tolls (Levy 1996: 372). Private investors must build in a cushion to safeguard their investments from these possibilities. Therefore a partnership offer that the government regards as attractive may not be so in the eyes of the private investors. If the private investors demand better terms, government officials tend to presume that the private investors are colluding or otherwise trying to take unfair advantage. If the government does not offer better terms, the private investors may stay away. When private actors try to hedge against these risks by insisting on a higher profit margin in the formal contract, public dissatisfaction is likely to be even higher. Overcoming the concern over policy risk would require that governments make credible commitments to maintain their contractual obligations.

It is also possible that in some instances government leaders are appropriately motivated to try to promote infrastructure expansion for a combination of economic and social benefits (i.e., the social rates of return are sufficiently high), but the arrangements offered to potential private investors ask them to provide the infrastructure services with insufficient financial returns. For example, Bayliss (2009: 23) observes that in Sub-Saharan Africa "many end-users cannot afford to pay prices for services that would allow a commercial rate of return." This may reflect an insufficient rate of return overall, but it may also reflect the inability or unwillingness of the government to subsidize the user fees or to use the shadow toll approach to compensate private operators if the social rates of return justify these expenditures. More cynically, we may consider that the public-private partnership offers may reflect politically motivated efforts on the part of government officials to demonstrate commitments to infrastructure development without true commitment to make the initiatives attractive to the private sector.

Four of the chapters in this book address aspects of this complicated challenge of settling on terms with private sector partners that are attractive, fair, and politically acceptable. Robert Cervero's chapter on infrastructure development in Tokyo and Hong Kong points out that private mass transit projects are often unattractive unless strong linkages to property development are built into the initiatives. This takes particularly strong coordination among the relevant government agencies to ensure that transportation and land-use planning are consistent, and it takes a political climate in which it is acceptable for private transportation providers to gain what might appear to be "windfall" profits when the routes bring commuters close to the properties that the providers have developed. Richard G. Little's chapter on public-private partnerships enumerates the numerous uncertainties and risks involved in such partnerships, which have to be addressed if the private sector is to opt for involvement, *and* this involvement does not later lead to a backlash against the private investors because of a perception that they are unfairly benefiting. Little emphasizes the crucial importance of balancing the risk exposure of the government and the private investors/operators. By the same token, in tracing out who benefits and who bears the burdens of infrastructure expansion under the many variations of financial arrangements, our chapter on financial instruments and distribution highlights that infrastructure planners and policymakers may not be in a position to understand these distributional consequences, which can lead to a backlash against the public-private partnership arrangements. Finally, Rosemary Morales Fernholz's chapter on the plight of people negatively impacted by infrastructure expansion reminds us that private sector initiatives to build dams, highways, generating plants, and other infrastructure in remote areas require vigilant oversight to avoid maltreatment of these people. How to build safeguards into the arrangements, and ensure that they are enforced, is a significant challenge.

Infrastructure and Equity. Beyond the question of whether enough investment can be mobilized for sound physical infrastructure development, distributional questions arise concerning both the burdens and the benefits. On the one hand, the poor often bear the brunt of infrastructure weakness. In their advocacy of greater infrastructure investment, World

Bank and Asian Development Bank analysts have painted a rosy picture of both the long-run growth and equity advantages of physical infrastructure development.[16] The overall rates of return, if calculated sensibly, tell the story of potential growth, but the fact that eventually everyone benefits from stronger infrastructure does not necessarily mean that low-income people will be better off from a comprehensive perspective. Public-private partnerships run the risk of excluding the poor from access because of unaffordable user fees, even if there are promising approaches like shadow tolls to address this risk.

We have to ask first whether the infrastructure will be *fairly* financed, in terms of the burden on both current and future generations. As chapter 2 in this volume explores, every infrastructure financing mechanism has particular distributional implications. If increased levels of infrastructure investment are financed through higher taxes, the burden can be placed upon taxpayers, which in many (though not all) situations would be progressive in terms of burden.[17] If increased financing of infrastructure comes from public funds that are diverted from other categories of public spending, the distributional impact would obviously depend on which income groups would be receiving smaller benefits. Infrastructure investment may increase the productivity of the poor and alleviate poverty, but that does not mean that it accomplishes these goals more effectively than would other targets for the investment. If the financing is through standard bonds, the development-cost burden on the taxpayers would be delayed, and may have an impact through increased interest rates that borrowers would face. Revenue bonds (i.e., bonds paid off from tolls or other user fees) impose the burden on users.[18]

In addition, physical infrastructure development frequently poses the additional challenge that it is often the poorest segments of society—in developing countries, typically rural, indigenous populations—who are adversely affected by major infrastructure projects that are sited, or go through, the areas where they live. Roads that cut through fragile forest ecosystems can threaten the livelihoods of local people trying to make a living from the forest.[19]

The displacement of villagers to make way for large dams can threaten the economic and cultural bases of their lives. In developed nations, the challenge that only recently has been addressed is the need to alter the physical structures that have undermined the environmental and social conditions where they have been erected. Infrastructure initiatives are as likely to be redevelopment efforts as new development. Multilane highways have cut through neighborhoods, eroding community life and creating isolated ghettos. Low-income urban areas are more likely to be exposed to the blight and pollution of transport infrastructure, especially rail- and highways. Children living near major U.S. highways have highly unhealthy exposure to air pollutants (American Academy of Pediatrics 2004). Housing markets virtually guarantee that low-income people will populate the areas most adversely affected by these problems. Therefore the concern for environmental justice calls for infrastructure development that minimizes these problems.

Distribution also has a spatial dimension that will be affected by the macrodesign of the infrastructure networks. From a political economy perspective, the regions targeted for infrastructure development may be those with the greatest potential for disruption if the government does not provide more infrastructure, or perhaps the infrastructure is intended to provide the government with greater capacity to exert its authority within particular regions. In neither case would the infrastructure development necessarily be optimal for alleviating poverty, or, for that matter, increasing productivity. As Rosemary Morales Fernholz's chapter in this volume reveals, physical infrastructure expansion can have very different impacts on the poor, depending on both design and the doctrines for addressing the disruptions that infrastructure expansion can create.

Infrastructure and the Environment. The exposure of low-income people to pollution caused by the use of physical infrastructure is hardly the only environmental issue. The physical structures themselves can cause environmental damage, disrupting natural waterways and encroaching into marshlands and other delicate ecosystems. Yet the expansion of transport infrastructure also brings people into areas where they may threaten ecosystems. Large-scale dams have eroded ecosystems as well and in some countries, including the United States, have provoked movements demanding the dismantling of existing dams.

This is not to say that physical infrastructure development is necessarily harmful to the environment, but rather that it has a complicated relationship with the environment. The development of mass transit can reduce automobile pollution, and a new emphasis of infrastructure development is to restore ecosystems, at least partially, through dismantling or otherwise modifying structures responsible for severe environmental damage. Robert Cervero's chapter on the dismantling of a major highway in Seoul is a gripping case in point.

Coping with the Challenges. Our review and diagnosis of the obstacles to sound infrastructure development highlight intrinsic challenges that must be addressed: long time horizons, complex distributional impacts, perverse incentives growing out of political economy considerations, and the necessity of having multiple government agencies involved in the decision-making processes. While these are facts of life that will not go away, there are ways to minimize the problems they can create.

The policies and specific decisions that determine the growth, efficiency, and fairness of physical infrastructure depend on the processes and institutions that generate them. Therefore, it is important to ask whether the *decision-making process* for designing and executing infrastructure development will be appropriate for balancing the sometimes conflicting challenges of achieving coherent, competent technical design, gaining enough support for the financial sacrifices that large-scale physical infrastructure requires, and representing stakeholder interests.

Major infrastructure projects such as highways, power plants, and ports are enormously complicated engineering feats. It is extremely difficult to assess the full set of risks to the on-time, successful completion of a major infrastructure project. Uncertainties abound in terms of construction challenges (Will hard rock be encountered where it is not expected? Will seismic activity require unanticipated retrofitting?), demand estimates (Will highway traffic materialize sufficiently to generate enough toll revenue?), and environmental consequences. Yet another difficulty is anticipating future technological advances: the dilemma is whether to use today's technology or to wait until more advanced technologies are available. These thorny technical issues will naturally provide crucial, if not always dominant, roles to planners, engineers, and economists. Unless their technical expertise is heeded, the inefficiencies of infrastructure design, construction, and maintenance can have drastic consequences for the entire economy. Once a major infrastructure project is constructed, the costs of retrofitting and upgrading can be enormous.

Yet despite the fact that empowering highly qualified technical experts is important, they must be directed to pursue projects that meet the needs and preferences of stakeholders. And while stakeholder involvement is now generally considered obligatory, it is challenging to do meaningfully for major infrastructure projects. Such projects typically impact huge geographical areas that encompass many local communities. Different communities will have different interests, and often interests will clash within communities as well. Nevertheless, involving stakeholders is often crucially important, both to take advantage of essential local knowledge and to fulfill genuine needs of the local communities. Public scrutiny and involvement is also important to deter governments from adopting unsound infrastructure strategies, whether in design, financing, or operations. Government officials have to be able to work with the private sector without succumbing to the temptations of corruption, or simply evading their responsibilities to provide public goods in just and sustainable ways.

Preview of the Chapters. The following chapters address the wide variety of the issues discussed in this introduction, including the challenges of financing and maintaining infrastructure projects, regulatory policy that improves access to the poor and underserved populations, comparative experiences with private-sector participation in infrastructure planning and investment across different countries, and the strategic challenges faced in addressing infrastructure needs as a country develops, modernizes, and becomes more urbanized.

In the next chapter, William Ascher and Corinne Krupp assess the "Distributional Implications of Alternative Infrastructure Financing Instruments." The chapter elaborates on how the choice of financing instruments for infrastructure projects can have significant implications for the poor and for future generations, both in terms of burdens and benefits. The authors analyze a wide range of infrastructure financing instruments, including different types of bonds, direct budget expenditures, user fees, and public-private partnerships in assessing both the intra- and intergenerational distribution implications of each, as well as who bears the risk associated with each type of financing instrument. The authors also discuss the issue of cross-subsidies (subsidizing low tariffs for some users by charging higher rates to other users), their distribution and risk effects, and whether some financing instruments lend themselves more to cross-subsidies than others.

Richard G. Little's chapter, "Beyond Privatization: Rethinking Private Sector Involvement in the Provision of Civil Infrastructure," discusses the impetus for attempting to privatize the provision of civil infrastructure in many countries: primarily to relieve pressure on the federal budget and to improve efficiency. He examines past struggles with the efficiency/equity tradeoff in developing countries that led to a rejection of privatization experiments, notably in Bolivia over water services. He reviews the newer models of public finance initiative/ public private partnerships that have been applied in Great Britain, the United States, and Canada, and he suggests ways in which safeguards can be put in place to protect the poorer members of society in designing, building, and financing civil infrastructure in developing countries.

M. Julie Kim and Rita Nangia coauthored the chapter on comparative infrastructure investment titled "Infrastructure Development in India and China: A Comparative Analysis." They describe the infrastructure planning, investment, and implementation processes in China and India over the past fifteen years, and they vividly describe the vast differences between the experiences of these two huge emerging market countries. While they focus most of their detailed analysis on the road and highway networks, they also compare the infrastructure investments in railroads, telecommunications, energy, and water sectors between these two countries. The strategy of "building before demand" has propelled China onto a path of remarkably rapid infrastructure expansion, while India's ambivalence about whether transport expansion should concentrate on connecting metropolitan areas or extend roads to remote villages has held back the infrastructure needed to ensure India's continued economic growth.

In "Physical Infrastructure as a Challenge for Farsighted Thinking and Action," William Ascher diagnoses why governments often fail in long-term infrastructure planning and maintenance, choosing instead to divert expenditures to immediate needs. The analysis of root causes of short-term planning (impatience, selfishness, analytical limitations, and vulnerability) point to internal and external variables that influence how political and economic incentives derail long-term planning. He presents a prescriptive framework to enable governments to ensure adequate funding and commitment to infrastructure investment and operation over time.

In his chapter "Transit Transformations: Private Financing and Sustainable Urbanism in Hong Kong and Tokyo," Robert Cervero reviews the technical and financial challenges faced by these cities as they sought to improve mass transit railway systems. He shows how private profit-driven investment combined with public sector planning and influence led to the provision of highly efficient mass transit railway networks in Hong Kong and Tokyo. While the infrastructure approaches differed somewhat between these two cities, the author draws lessons from both cases that may be useful for rapidly industrializing developing countries, like China, in their urban development planning.

Professor Cervero's chapter on "Urban Reclamation and Regeneration in Seoul, South Korea" assesses a very different sort of transformation: the dismantling of a major highway to restore nature amenities in the midst of the heavily congested Korean capital. He demonstrates the potential for public support, effective traffic re-routing, and enhanced property values from environmental restoration.

In "Electrifying Rural Areas: Extending Electricity Infrastructure and Services in Developing Countries," Corinne Krupp addresses the issues of extending access to electricity to rural areas and to the poor in developing countries. She discusses a wide range of issues, including the technical requirements of electricity provision, the cost and feasibility of extending the grid, regulatory issues of pricing and allocation, and the historical experiences of several countries in their attempts to expand access to electricity, especially to the poor and to those in remote rural areas. She ends with the consideration of other possible technologies that would enable off-grid electrification and a discussion of some of the more creative and cheaper ideas to address the demand for power in rural areas.

Finally, the treatment of indigenous people in the face of massive infrastructure projects and planning has been poor in many cases, and guidelines to protect the interests of these people need to be enforced. In her chapter "Infrastructure and Inclusive Development through 'Free, Prior, and Informed Consent' of Indigenous Peoples," Rosemary Morales Fernholz describes the motivation for infrastructure development in remote areas in developing countries, and how the process of planning and construction often ignores the needs and desires of the indigenous people who inhabit these areas. As a result, in many cases, infrastructure construction has led to environmental degradation and displacement of these people. She discusses the current protections in place for these indigenous peoples, and offers suggestions for ways in which these projects can involve community participation during the planning phases in order to balance the push for development and modernization with the sustenance of these indigenous communities and their ways of life.

There are several overarching themes that appear in this book. While all of the chapters focus on the issue of physical infrastructure in promoting economic growth, they also illustrate that the impact of these projects on poverty alleviation is much less straightforward. One must consider issues of how the projects are chosen and designed to assess the ways in which they will impact local groups that are living in the affected areas, for good and bad. One must also recognize that different methods of paying for the infrastructure, not only the initial construction but also maintenance and operations over time, will have differential effects on the poor. There are opportunity costs of pursuing particular projects that must also be considered; while building rural roads using local labor may be seen as a pure win-win, a proper accounting of the full cost must reflect the other projects that were foregone as a result of the expenditure. The same types of considerations must be taken into account when analyzing grid extensions for electricity provision, building rail networks, and providing water treatment and distribution systems.

Thus, it has become clear to us that while physical infrastructure investment is an important component in spurring economic growth in developing countries, its impact on poverty alleviation is much more complicated and dependent on the context in which the building takes place. We have endeavored to provide careful consideration of some of these issues in this book, and we hope it will spur the development community to work harder to make infrastructure investments more "pro-poor."

Notes

1. Romp and de Haan (2007) provide a thorough survey of the econometric estimates of the contributions of physical infrastructure, updating the earlier surveys by Gramlich (1994) and Sturm, Kuper, and de Haan (1998).
2. See Briceño-Garmendia, Estache, and Shafik (2004).
3. See, for example, A.T. Kearney (2004); IMD (2006); Lin, Chiu and Chu (2006); United Nations Conference on Trade and Development (2005).
4. Djankov, Freund, and Pham (2006) report a range of shipping delay times for Asia Pacific nations from six days for Singapore to 23 days for Thailand.
5. Measures of "social profitability" or "social rate of return" (akin to a company's economic rate of return) are intended to gauge the productivity of a project for the society as a whole, by accounting not just for the economic gains as narrowly defined in a business sense for the funded operation, but comprehensively to encompass both the economic gains for the society as a whole and the social gains, such as increased access to healthcare, of all stakeholders. By the same token, the costs that must be deducted from the gains include both comprehensive economic costs and adverse impacts such as environmental degradation. Naturally, such estimates inevitably have a significant degree of uncertainty.
6. The seemingly anomalous negative ratio to overall returns on capital for Austria, which has a 0.0 figure for the return on infrastructure, is presumably because of the latter figure having been rounded off from a slightly negative result that is not given in Canning and Bennathan (2000); hence the negative ratio to overall returns on capital.
7. World Bank Independent Evaluation Group (2007: 24).

8. See Ascher and Rondinelli (2006).
9. They base this premise on research by Tanzi and Davoodi (1997). The extent of corruption can be gauged by any number of survey-based ratings or rankings of the need and magnitude of bribes that private sector individuals believe are required to do business with, or get approvals from, the government; Tanzi and Davoodi use the Political Risk Service's *International Country Risk Guide*.
10. Cited in U.S. Congressional Budget Office (2008: 22).
11. Ascher and Healy (1990) document a number of these grandiose projects, including highways, irrigation systems, and hydroelectric dams.
12. See Ascher (1993) for some of the technical reasons why accurate assessments of risks and costs are difficult.
13. This was the experience at the World Bank, where the establishment of a "Quality Assurance Group" with the mandate to review project work on a selective basis led to sounder project evaluations and approvals. See Ascher (2009: 109–111).
14. An alternative to a fee paid by actual users is the "shadow toll," which is a payment to the operator, usually from the government, based on the extent of use of the infrastructure. Thus a shadow toll for a road would be based on the distances traveled by vehicles on the road, perhaps differentiated according to the type of vehicle. Shadow fees save on the cost and inconvenience of physically collecting tolls from users. Compared to actual toll or fee collection, they subsidize those using the infrastructure. It is still the case, though, that the public pays ultimately, in the form of higher taxes or diversions of funds from the goods and services that the government would provide to them. The United Kingdom has had the most experience with shadow tolls, which remain controversial in terms of their effectiveness, risk-sharing implications, and fairness. See Bonar and Fuss (1997).
15. Cited in Briceño-Garmendia, Estache, and Shafik (2004).
16. See Estache (2003); Fay and Yepes (2002); Briceño-Garmenia, Estache, and Shafik (2004); Cook et al. (2004); Estache and Fay (2007).
17. This outcome depends, of course, on whether the increased taxes are (1) imposed on individuals through direct taxes (such as income taxes) at higher rates for higher-income individuals; or if, through indirect taxes such as value-added tax or sales tax, exclude items consumed by the poor; and/or (2) are imposed on firms that do not pass the burden onto the poor through higher prices of items that the poor consume.
18. Some revenue sources require excluding infrastructure use, for example through road tolls that make the toll roads too expensive for some potential users; other revenue sources, such as fuel levies, do not have such a direct exclusionary impact, but do make general infrastructure use less affordable for the poor.
19. Ascher and Healy (1990) review several Asian and Latin American cases.

References

A.T. Kearney. 2004. Making offshore decisions: A.T. Kearney's 2004 offshore location attractiveness index. Chicago, IL: A.T. Kearney.

American Academy of Pediatrics Committee on Environmental Health. 2004. Ambient air pollution: Health hazards to children. *Pediatrics* 114: 1699–1707.

Aschauer, David A. 1989. Is public expenditure productive? *Journal of Monetary Economics* 23: 177–200.

Ascher, William. 1993. The ambiguous nature of forecasts in project evaluation. *International Journal of Forecasting* 9(1): 109–115.

_____. 2009. *Bringing in the future: Strategies for farsightedness and sustainability in developing countries.* Chicago: University of Chicago Press.

Ascher, William and Robert Healy. 1990. *Natural resource policymaking in developing countries: Environment, economic growth, and income distribution.* Durham, NC: Duke University Press.

Ascher, William and Dennis Rondinelli. 2006. "Bangkok as a regional center: Strengthening greater Bangkok as an economic hub in Asia," for the Bangkok Metropolitan Administration, Bangkok, December.

Baker, Dean. 2008. The public investment deficit: Two decades of neglect threaten 21st century economy. Washington, DC: Economic Policy Institute Briefing Paper.

Bayliss, Kate. 2009. Private sector participation in African infrastructure: Is it worth the risk? Working Paper No. 55. London: International Policy Centre for Inclusive Growth, May.

Benmaamar, Mustapha. 2006. Financing of road maintenance in Sub-Saharan Africa: Reforms and progress towards second generation road funds. Sub-Saharan Africa Transport Policy Program. RMF Series Discussion Paper No. 6. Washington, DC: Road Management and Financing, September.

Bonar, Mary and Stephen Fuss. 1997. *The use of private finance for infrastructure investment in Western Europe.* London: Wilde Sapte.

Briceño-Garmendia, C., A. Estache, and N. Shafik, 2004. Infrastructure services in developing countries: Access, quality, costs and policy reforms. World Bank Policy Research Working Paper No. 3468. Washington, DC: World Bank Institute.

Cadot, Olivier, Lars-Hendrik Röller, and Andreas Stephan. 1999. A political economy model of infrastructure allocation: An empirical assessment. Berlin: FS IV 99–15, Wissenschaftszentrum Berlin, October.

Calderon, C. and L. Serven. 2004. *The effects of infrastructure development on growth and income distribution.* Washington, DC: World Bank.

Canning, David and Esra Bennathan. 2000. The social rate of return on infrastructure investments. World Bank Research Paper. Washington, DC: World Bank.

Commission of the European Communities. 2008. Communication from the Commission to the European Council: A European economic recovery plan. Brussels, November 26.

Conference Board of Canada. 2003. *Performance and potential 2003–04: Defining the Canadian advantage.* Ottawa: Conference Board of Canada.

Cook, Cynthia, Tyrrell Duncan, Somchai Jitsuchon, Anil K. Sharma, and Wu Guobao. 2004. Assessing the impact of transport and energy infrastructure on poverty reduction. Manila: Asian Development Bank Regional Technical Assistance Report 5947, June.

Djankov, Simeon, Caroline Freund, and Cong Pham. 2006. Trading on time. *Doing Business,* January 2006. http://www.doingbusiness.org/documents/trading_on_time_full_report.pdf

Easterly, William and L. Serven. 2003. *The limits of stabilization: Infrastructure, public deficits and growth in Latin America.* Washington, DC: Stanford University Press and World Bank.

Estache, Antonio. 2003. On Latin America's infrastructure privatization and its distributional effects. World Bank Working Paper. Washington, DC: World Bank.

Estache, Antonio and Marianne Fay. 2007. Current debates on infrastructure policy. World Bank Policy Research Working Paper No. 4410.Washington, DC: World Bank.

Everhart, S.S. and M.A. Sumlinski. 2001. The impact on private investment of corruption and the quality of public investment. International Finance Corporation. Discussion Paper No. 44. Washington, DC: World Bank Group.

Fay, M. and T. Yepes 2002. *Investing in infrastructure: What is needed from 2000 to 2010?* Washington, DC: World Bank.

Flyvbjerg, Bent, Nils Bruzelius, and Werner Rothengatter. 2003. *Megaprojects and risk: An anatomy of ambition.* Cambridge: *Cambridge University Press.*

Government of India Planning Commission. 2007. *Eleventh five year plan (2007–2012).* New Delhi: Government of India.

Gramlich, Edward M. 1994. Infrastructure investment: A review essay. *Journal of Economic Literature* 32: 1176–1196.

Hall, David and Emanuele Lobina (2006). Pipe dreams: The failure of the private sector to invest in water services in developing countries, World Development Movement Website. http://www.wdm.org.uk/resources/reports/water/pipedreamsreport01032006.pdf. Accessed July 25, 2009.

Haughwout, Andrew. 2002. Public infrastructure investments, productivity and welfare in fixed geographic areas. *Journal of Public Economics* 83: 405–428

Heggie, I. 1995. Management and financing of roads: An agenda for reform World Bank Technical Report 275. Washington, DC: World Bank.

Hörhager, Axel. 2006. Financing investment in transport infrastructure: The European Investment Bank [Power Point presentation]. Luxemburg: European Investment Bank. December. http://www.seetoint.org/site/pdf/20-ddf7.pdf. Accessed November 18, 2007.

IMD. 2006. *The world competitiveness yearbook.* Gland, Switzerland: IMD.

Kaufmann, Daniel. 1991. The forgotten rationale for policy reform: The productivity of investment. Background study for the World Bank's World Development Report 1991. Washington, D.C.

Kitchen, Harry. 2003. Physical infrastructure and financing. Research paper prepared for the Panel on the Role of Government in Ontario. Ottawa, December 4.

http://www.law-lib.utoronto.ca/investing/reports/rp44.pdf. Accessed July 29, 2009.

Koppenjan, J.F.M. 2005. The formation of public-private partnerships: Lessons from nine transport infrastructure projects in the Netherlands. *Public Administration* 83(1): 135–157.

Levy, Sidney. 1996. *Build, operate, transfer: Paving the way for tomorrow's infrastructure.* New York: John Wiley & Sons.

Lin, C.-T., H. Chiu, and P.-Y. Chu. 2006. Agility index in the supply chain. *International Journal of Production Economics* 100(2): 285–299.

Njoh, Ambe J. 2008. Implications of Africa's transportation systems for development in the era of globalization. *Review of Black Political Economy* 35: 147–162

Rioja, Felix. 2003. The penalties of inefficiency infrastructure. *Review of Development Economics* 7(1): 127–137.

Romp, Ward and Jakob de Haan. 2007. Public capital and economic growth: A critical survey. *Perspektiven der Wirtschaftspolitik* 8(Special Issue): 6–52.

Rose-Ackerman, Susan. 1996. Second-generation issues in transition: Corruption. Annual World Bank Conference on Development Economics 1995, pp. 373–378.

Sturm, J.E., G.H. Kuper, and J. de Haan. 1998. Modelling government investment and economic growth on a macro level: A review. In *Market behaviour and macroeconomic modelling*, ed. S. Brakman, H. van Ees and S.K. Kuipers. London: Macmillan.

Szalai, Akos. 2001. New models of privatizing public utilities: Highlights of reform in post-soviet countries. *Local Government Brief: The Quarterly Journal of Local Government and Public Service Reform Initiative.* Budapest, Hungary, 18–24.

Tanzi, Vito and Hamid Davoodi. 1997. Corruption, public investment, and growth. IMF Working Paper No. WP/37/139. Washington, DC.

Tremolet, Sophie, Rachel Cardone, Carmenda Silva, and Catarina Fonseca. 2007. Financing shelter, water and sanitation: Innovations in financing urban water & sanitation. New York: Center for Sustainable Urban Development, July. http://www2.gtz.de/Dokumente/oe44/ecosan/en-Innovations-financing-urban-water-sanitation-2007.pdf. Accessed July 29, 2009.

United Nations Conference on Trade and Development. 2006. *World investment report 2005.* FDI Performance Indices

U.S. Congressional Budget Office. 1988. New directions for the nation's public works. Washington, DC: U.S. Congress, September.

_____. 2008. Issues and options in infrastructure investment. Washington, DC: U.S. Congress, May.

U.S. Department of Transportation. 2006. *Status of the nation's highways, bridges, and transit: 2006: Conditions and performance; Chapter 7; Capital investment scenarios: Highways and bridges.* Federal Highway Administration. March 14, 2007. http://www.fhwa.dot.gov/policy/2006cpr/es07h.htm. Accessed July 5, 2008.

World Bank Independent Evaluation Group 2007. *A decade of action in transport.* Washington, DC. World Bank.

CHAPTER 2

Distributional Implications of Alternative Financing of Physical Infrastructure Development

William Ascher and Corinne Krupp

Introduction

As argued in the introductory chapter of this volume, there is a compelling economic growth argument for much greater investment in physical infrastructure in virtually all developing countries and in many developed countries. Yet asserting a need to expand physical infrastructure does not directly engage the issues of poverty alleviation and equity. In addition to the question of the volume of investment are the questions of who bears the burdens of financing these investments, and who reaps the benefits. These questions are important because, in any given context, the available modes of financing can make a substantial difference in the distribution of burdens and benefits. Although the consequences of different financing options are too context-specific to permit broad generalizations about the distributive superiority of one option over another, outlining the taxonomy of these modes, and the considerations that determine their distributive implications, can be very helpful for planners and policy-makers.

Despite the many efforts to gauge the contributions of physical infrastructure to poverty alleviation, typically arguing the case for expanding physical infrastructure, our analysis is necessary because existing studies rarely explore the burdens of funding the expansion or distributional consequences of particular designs, access restrictions, and geographic location. Because the financing approach dictates both the burdens of payment and risk-bearing, and the characteristics of the project, the mode of financing an infrastructure project has major implications for the distributional impacts of both costs and benefits:

> It should be underscored that important social and environmental concerns are also interlaced with infrastructure decisions regarding technology choice, coverage, and charges. For example, although toll roads can serve to reduce traffic congestion, and water metering can promote greater conservation, both will have distributive effects that will be a greater burden on low-income households. (Inter-American Development Bank 1995: 2)

The boosters of infrastructure development, most prominently within the World Bank, have expressed very positive views on the win-win nature of infrastructure expansion, regarding both its contributions to economic growth and its impact on poverty alleviation and reducing income inequality. The logic is as follows:

1. Improvements in physical infrastructure increase the productivity of the poor as well as the rich.
2. Infrastructure improvements that enable people working in the low-productivity traditional sector to move into the higher pro-ductivity sector and therefore higher-compensated modern-sector jobs will narrow the income gaps.
3. Improvements in physical infrastructure provide the poor as well as the rich with greater access to educational, healthcare, and other social services, improving their quality of life as well as their productivity.
4. Comparing countries with high or low infrastructure quantity and quality shows that those with more impressive infrastruc-ture development tend to have both higher economic growth and greater declines in income inequality.

This has led Estache (2003: 2) to argue that "the main combined message from . . . research . . . is that infrastructure is good for growth, that since growth is good for the poverty reduction, infrastructure is good for poverty reduction."

However, this seems to be based more on fond wishes than on rigor-ous analysis. As compelling as the logic of the first three points seem, they reflect partial analysis that ignores other dynamics. Doesn't a rising economic tide lift all ships? Unfortunately, the answer could be no, depending on the country, the nature, and the location of the infrastructure. The geographic location of infrastructure investment may draw other investments away from the poorest areas. This was the pattern in Italy, with the much more developed infrastructure of the North attracting industrial investment; the South, despite lower wages, had (and probably still has) too large an infrastructure gap to compete with the North for this investment. In 2003, Coppin estimated that if the overall infrastructure level of Italy is scored as 100, the "industrial heartland" of Northwest Italy should be rated as 118 and the South as only 77. He pointed out that "between 1990 and 1996, the average annual government investment in infrastructure projects per capita stood at €141 for the central and northern parts of Italy, whilst the amount was only €115 for the South. The gap between northern and southern Italy was growing ever wider" (Coppin 2003: 130). Northern Brazil, northern Argentina, northern Thailand, and the noncoastal areas of many African countries have faced the same disadvantage. Only when the Argentine and Brazilian governments made a concerted effort to redress the regional imbalance in roads and sanitation did a convergence in income levels across regions occur (Estache and Fay 1997).

Doesn't investment in infrastructure provide greater capacity for the poor to increase their productivity? Not if infrastructure development is financed by beggaring the budgets for health, education, and training. India is currently at a crossroads, with the government stating the need to secure some US$150 billion in physical infrastructure investment over a seven- or eight-year period, relying on both government investment and private investment through public-private partnerships. As noted in the introduction of this book, in the past, private infrastructure investment levels hoped for in India and other countries have been disappointing. Insofar as the Indian government feels compelled to meet this commitment, if private investment continues to disappoint, the Indian budget for social service may be drained to make up the difference.

The statistical assessments that are used to try to support the fourth point rest on correlations between infrastructure development and inequality. Drawing inferences from these correlations neglects important considerations. First, even if the quantity and quality of infrastructure are correlated with reductions in income inequality (and therefore presumably positive effects on poverty alleviation), the measures tell us about the outcomes of *successful* infrastructure development rather than the magnitude of infrastructure investment. The nations that have invested heavily but poorly in physical infrastructure (because of incompetence, corruption, emerging political opposition, or politically motivated priorities to place infrastructure in inappropriate areas) may have little to show for the investment. It is all too obvious that investments in huge dam projects that become stalled for decades, or expensive roads that quickly deteriorate for lack of maintenance, may lead to a nation's low score in infrastructure quantity or quality, even if the investment was high. Such cases would mask the fact that investment may not provide positive benefits for either growth or distribution.

Second, the correlational analyses cannot even guarantee that infrastructure quantity and quality themselves have a causal impact of reducing income inequality. For example, Calderon and Serven (2004: 26), using time series data on over one hundred countries, conclude that "infrastructure quantity and quality have a robust negative impact on income inequality," making the astonishing claim that their econometric methodology *proves* that the direction of causation is from the quality and quantity of physical infrastructure to the reduction in inequality. This claim neglects the possibility that one or more other causal factors are operating on both the development of infrastructure and the income distribution. We would expect highly competent, developmentally oriented governments to often pursue infrastructure expansion *and* policies of human-resource development and modern-sector job creation, resulting in the patterns that Calderon and Serven find, even if there is no direct impact of infrastructure expansion on reducing poverty or income inequality.

Third, a correlation between infrastructure development and declining income inequality does not demonstrate that the infrastructure investments are the most effective means of reducing inequality. The pitch for infrastructure development neglects the possibility that other investments, for example, in greater social services, could have a more robust impact on alleviating poverty and reducing inequality.

A related equity issue concerns the location decisions of new infrastructure investment. Should the government focus on attracting investment in more densely populated urban areas, or should more remote, underserved regions be prioritized? Which might contribute to faster economic growth? As explained in Estache and Fay (2006), the idea encased in the "new economic geography" literature is that infrastructure expansion and improvement can be used to motivate investors to invest in underdeveloped regions, thereby helping to improve wealth distribution and economic opportunity, especially in disadvantaged rural areas. Improved transportation infrastructure improves access and connectivity of isolated regions, allowing them to "connect" with the rest of the world.

On the flip side, increased connectivity also means that the local firms face new competition, which may lead to lower prices, lower profits, and bankruptcy, especially if the quality of their products is below that of the new entrants. If there are significant differences in wages across regions, increased connectivity can help reduce the gap, bringing more jobs and opportunities to the lower-wage, disadvantaged regions (as long as the productivity of local factors is justified by the wages.) There is also a concern that in addressing inequality by focusing infrastructure *expenditures* on disadvantaged areas, overall economic growth may be slowed for the entire country (de la Fuente 2002). Thus, the equity-efficiency tradeoffs in making infrastructure location decisions are quite complex and context-specific, and there may be unanticipated dynamic effects over time of prioritizing rural vs. urban infrastructure investments, especially given different assumptions about factor mobility.

Fourth, and perhaps most important, the central tendencies of a multicountry ("cross-national") statistical analysis gloss over the fact that some countries with greater improvements in physical infrastructure quality and quantity have lower-than-average progress in poverty alleviation and reductions in inequality. Serven and Calderon find that variations in the quality and quantity of physical infrastructure each account for less than 30 percent of the variation in income inequality, and the measures of quantity and quality are themselves highly correlated.

In short, although infrastructure development *may* be a good avenue for poverty alleviation and reduction of income inequality, no aggregate, multicountry study can demonstrate that infrastructure development will be effective for a given country, let alone that it would be the *most* effective means of addressing poverty and income inequality. Cross-national correlations cannot tell us whether the fate of any particular country would follow the general pattern. More importantly, they cannot tell us whether investment in infrastructure is the best way to address distributional and poverty-alleviation challenges. If other targets for the investments that are going into physical infrastructure could do more to alleviate poverty and reduce income inequality, then the infrastructure investments would be counterproductive in both respects.

In this chapter, we present an analysis of the distribution effects of various types of infrastructure financing options as it is our belief that such an analysis is necessary given that previous studies fail to explore the burdens of funding infrastructure expansion. Here are the various dimensions of our analysis:

Distributive Dimensions. The distributive implications of physical infrastructure financing have to be assessed along several dimensions. To begin with, there is the obvious distinction between the distribution of cost burdens and the distribution of benefits. On the one hand, a road or port has financing that must be raised; on the other hand, the road or port will be used differentially by different people or firms.

A second distinction is between intragenerational distribution and intergenerational distribution. The intragenerational distribution of either burdens or benefits most prominently involves regional differences or income-level differences, but can also involve differences among ways of life within a given region or among people of similar income levels. For example, pastoralists may not benefit from a road that benefits farmers by easing the transport of their crops to market.

The intergenerational distribution question asks whether the burdens and benefits fall largely on today's generations or on future generations. Some financing modes defer payments far into the future, thereby increasing the burdens on future generations. However, this needs to be balanced against the possibility that a lower current burden for financing infrastructure may imply greater disposable income to invest in the health, education, and job opportunities for future generations.

Risk Dimensions. Finally, there is an important but less obvious distinction between the distribution of burdens and benefits if the infrastructure initiative goes according to plan or if it experiences serious setbacks. Therefore, the burden of risk is a consideration that has to be integrated into the analysis. The three most important risk categories are as follows:

1. *Planning risk:* Faulty aspects of design (magnitude, location, materials, etc.) and scheduling can undermine the completion and value of the project. A particularly common design problem is the exaggeration of use and therefore the calculated rate of return, such that the use of the infrastructure would fail to materialize as planned, yielding insufficient revenues compared to the revenues required for profitability, loan pay-backs, or funding for maintenance.[1]

2. *Construction risk:* The project will suffer delays, diversion of funds through corruption, cost overruns, subpar construction, or other construction problems that would reduce its profitability and socioeconomic worth.

3. *Financing risk:* Either public or private sources would fail to meet their financial commitments (e.g., government bonds or loans would be defaulted; private operators would go bankrupt or otherwise fail to put in the agreed-upon investment).

In exploring the distributional implications of alternative financing instruments, we must keep in mind that the broad implications may be different for developing when compared with developed countries. The fragility of government finances, capital markets, and institutions that is generally more common among developing countries can pose different risk burdens.

Another related issue that the literature on the growth-enhancing effects of physical infrastructure investment fails to adequately address is that of opportunity costs. As every trained economist recognizes, every choice brings with it a set of alternative choices that were foregone. The highest valued alternative choice is the opportunity cost of the investment. Thus, if the government chooses to finance the building of a new road, it necessarily chooses *not* to fund something else with those funds, such as building a new healthcare clinic, a school, or repairing a deteriorated sewer system. We cannot ignore opportunity costs when we consider the costs and benefits of choosing to finance different infrastructure projects since they have significant efficiency implications. There are many examples of well-intended public works projects that ultimately led to crumbling roads that washed out soon after they were completed, bridges that fell down, and school buildings equipped with computers that were unusable because of the lack of electricity.

We are not suggesting that physical infrastructure investments are bad for poverty alleviation, but rather, that different investments will have differential effects on the poor. To the extent that the government seeks to substantially reduce poverty, its choice of investment projects should be influenced by the opportunity cost of the project and its costs and benefits to the poor. One of the key issues to consider is the accessibility of the infrastructure services to the poor, and we will show how various modes of financing will have different implications for accessibility. Another issue is the nature of the infrastructure investment chosen: to what extent is it "pro-poor?" Building superhighways around an urban center may be growth-promoting for those who commute from the suburbs to the city for work, but it is unlikely to benefit the urban poor directly. Balancing the choice of projects by examining and being aware of their impact on the poor is a useful exercise for policy-makers who are committed to poverty alleviation as well as pro-moting economic growth.

The opportunity cost question illuminates the issue of the nature and type of infrastructure investments in some developing countries and whether they "make sense" from both a development and a poverty alleviation perspective. Consider the case of Shanghai, China: this city has grown tremendously since 1991 (Lim 2006c), and it has become a very modern-looking city with lots of skyscrapers and neon lights. Traffic, however, is very congested, and the huge influx of migrant workers arriving from rural western China in the early years (1980s) have burdened the water, sewer, trash, and electricity systems, and there is a chronic lack of decent affordable housing. (There are also restrictions on access to long-term housing by migrant workers, which exacerbates the problem.) Would the expenditures that were made on gleaming skyscrapers have been better devoted to building more afford-able housing? Beefing up the water, sewerage, and electricity networks? Investing in better public transportation systems? There are also claims that residents living in older sections of the city (especially close to the river and port) are being evicted from their homes and apartments without adequate compensation, to make way for "urban renewal" projects. The compensation they receive is too small to find similar housing within 25 miles of the city-center, according to an interview with a local resident in 2006 (Lim 2006b). Certainly, the real-estate developers to whom their land is ultimately sold can vastly increase their incomes by developing the land, but the disenfranchised former owners are impoverished by the decision.

Shanghai's population is approaching 19 million people (Lim 2006a). Massive relocation and building of satellite towns outside of Shanghai has been ongoing since 2000, each with the architecture and design of a different European city or town. One, known as Thames Town, has replicas of Middle Age churches, pubs, and inns, bricked streets, and Tudor-style homes. Unfortunately, only the wealthiest Chinese people can afford to live there. According to a National Public Radio report titled "China gets its own slice of the English countryside," the town has "...empty streets and un-rented shops...and homes priced out of the market for many..." (Lim 2006a). This is hardly a solution for urban overcrowding in Shanghai.

We discuss six different modes of infrastructure financing, and examine the distribution of burdens and benefits of each, as well as the risk dimensions. The opportunity cost issue is very context-specific, but we endeavor to include it in our discussions in order to keep our focus on how different modes of infrastructure financing may impact the poor.

Modes of Infrastructure Financing. Six modes of financing infrastructure investment have been prominent:

1. General obligation bonds (the government borrows with the promise to its constituents to undertake the investment with "full faith and credit" to repay when the bonds are due).
2. Revenue bonds (i.e., the issuer's obligation is to collect revenues), issued by the government or by state entities created by the government, either from
   a. the use of the infrastructure, such as highway tolls or port-facility fees,
   b. more general revenue sources, such as general sales taxes or fuel taxes.
3. Direct expenditures from the nation's central budget that do not entail borrowing; an increase in such financing can be funded either by
   a. raising taxes,
   b. diverting funds from other purposes,
   c. using grants from donors.
4. Loans from domestic and/or international sources.
5. Public-Private Partnership arrangements.
6. Infrastructure development trusts funded through fees or taxes (e.g., fuel taxes).

Assumptions. Several assumptions are necessary to assess the distributional implications of these instruments:

1. An increase in taxes will reduce family expenditures, but discretionary household spending will be reduced more than spending on food, education, and healthcare.
2. The personal tax structure is mildly progressive or neutral.
3. A general obligation bond or loan, in adding to the government's debt burden, is more likely to contribute to a debt crisis that will require austerity in the future.
4. Higher perceptions of risk on the part of private operators or investors will increase the returns they will demand, and thus, will increase the costs to users or borrowers.

Categorizing Benefits and Costs of Infrastructure

During the construction of and after provision of new infrastructure, there are both direct and indirect benefits to local citizens, as well as costs. The following are lists of possible benefits and costs, depending on the nature of the infrastructure project.

The primary benefits from the infrastructure (e.g., roads, bridges, ports, sewerage systems, etc.) can be divided into two categories:

- Direct benefits: Lower transport or usage costs, time savings, less depreciation of complementary goods (e.g., transport vehicles), higher employment and wages directly associated with constructing and maintaining the infrastructure.
- Indirect benefits: Increased access to markets (higher prices for suppliers, more varieties and lower prices of goods to buyers), increased access to social services (health clinics, schools, etc.), improved employment opportunities and wages, increased land values with improved accessibility, reduced disease incidence (in case of health infrastructure, water, and sewerage projects).

The primary costs associated with the infrastructure that local citizens may face include the following:

1. Higher taxes collected to pay for the funding of the infrastructure project and its maintenance (e.g., consumption taxes, income taxes, fuel taxes, vehicle registration fees, VAT, etc.).
2. User fees associated with the new infrastructure (e.g., bridge toll, highway toll, basic water and sewerage charges, etc.).
3. Loss of land and housing if relocated to make way for the infrastructure project.
4. Reduction in government social services if budget allocation is diverted to infrastructure projects.

To what extent can these costs and benefits accrue disproportionately to the poor? This will depend on the location of and access to the infrastructure relative to the areas where poor families tend to live, the extent to which poor families are displaced by the project, the opportunities that arise once the infrastructure has been provided, and the impact of the way the infrastructure project is financed. The focus of several of the chapters in this book is on the larger issues of infrastructure provision and the poor, including displacement and access to social services and income-generating activities. Our focus is on the financing implications and their effects on the poor.

In essence, the more infrastructure tends to be "pro-poor" the greater the access to employment, new goods and services, and social services attributed to the infrastructure for poor families, and the more progressive the financing mode. Access issues, including the cost of using the new infrastructure, will be important in assessing whether the new infrastructure can contribute directly to poverty alleviation.

Implications of Alternative Financing Mechanisms

We discuss each of the six different modes of infrastructure financing introduced earlier, and assess their impact on the poor and nonpoor current generations, as well as the likely impact on future generations. In addition, we will consider who bears the risk (the risk burden) of each financing approach and how this may affect the cost of financing the project. In general, to the extent that an infrastructure project yields relatively higher direct benefits to the poor, and if the financing scheme is progressive, then income distribution can be improved.

Long-term Debt Financing: Government Borrowing

Let us begin by contrasting the modes of infrastructure financing that involve long-term debt obligations for the government or its state entities: loans, general obligation bonds, and revenue bonds. In having the common characteristic of involving long-term payback periods (e.g., 25- to 30-year periods are not uncommon), these instruments obligate future taxpayers to service the interest and principal payments over this lengthy period. Therefore, they involve less current sacrifice than does financing infrastructure development out of today's budget.

One analytic complication is that the infrastructure investment may be formally financed from the central budget rather than through loans, but in order to fund these investments as well as all of its other expenditures, the government may borrow the equivalent amount. If the length of the loan period is the same, the practical difference is much less. However, in many instances, it is likely that loans directly tied to infrastructure development are longer term than are the general loans that governments secure to cover their overall deficit spending. This is based on the fact that many capital improvement bonds are in the 10–30-year range, while several types of short-term government bonds are used to cover deficit spending. Of course, it is hard to specifically identify that bonds are used to pay for which types of expenditures, but we know that infrastructure financing tends to require longer-term investments.

In terms of intragenerational distribution of *burden*, loans and general obligation bonds are similar in that they call for repayment from the central treasury. All taxpayers bear the burden of paying the interest and repaying the principal. Thus, the burden will be as progressive or regressive as the tax system itself, unless the loan obligations provoke a new tax of distinctive burden. Most typically, this would be a tax on fuels, which would tend to be progressive insofar as higher-income people consume more fuel for personal transportation.

In terms of the intragenerational distribution of *benefits* coming from the objectives and design of the infrastructure per se, it is useful to compare financing infrastructure through loans and general obligation bonds with the implications of straightforward funding from the central budget. Financing through loans or general obligation bonds shapes the nature of the projects (and therefore the distribution of the benefits) insofar as the proposals have to be designed to be attractive enough to be approved and to find lenders or bondholders. If the loans come from private banking sources, there will probably be pressure to design projects that can be justified in terms of their financial rate of return. This is often the case even when the loan or bond is backed by a government guarantee, which, in theory, would ensure timely servicing and repayment even if the project itself were unprofitable or simply a failure. Therefore, financing through loans or general obligation bonds is more likely to require revenues from the project itself, often in the form of tolls or fees. Insofar as these tolls or fees exclude lower-income people from directly accessing the infrastructure, this funding mechanism would decrease the relative benefit to the poor.

Burden of Risks. If the government overborrows (in terms of the total of loans, not just for physical infrastructure development, but also for other investment or consumption purposes), then the ensuing debt crisis will often require adopting austerity measures. Historically, austerity programs have been borne heavily by low-income families who typically have fewer options to adjust to economic contraction. The poorest segments of the population of developing countries may not be touched by restrictions on imported goods, which, in any case, they are unlikely to be able to afford. Yet their chances to obtain better employment, or to maintain incomes from informal-sector work, are likely to be diminished under austerity conditions.

General Obligation Bonds

The general obligation bond commits the government to secure repayment of the bond, but the funds for repayment are not contractually tied to specific revenue streams. The government may have to resort to higher taxation or borrowing from other sources, yet these actions do not necessarily impinge upon the infrastructure project itself. If financing is provided through general obligation government bonds, infrastructure users may not have to pay any direct user fees to access the direct benefits from it; rather, the bonds are paid through the government treasury. However, the government does have the option of ensuring its capacity to service the bond through user fees (e.g., tolls or fuel taxes in the case of payment for roads). Therefore the burden implied by general obligation bonds depends on how the government approaches the challenge of securing resources to meet its obligation. Nevertheless, compared with other debt instruments, the general obligation bond can be far less connected to any burdens borne by the users of the infrastructure. If the government is hard-pressed to pay general obligation bonds through its tax revenues, the result may be a decrease in public services, as central-treasury funds are redirected to pay off the government debt. If the tax is levied under a progressive tax system, wealth inequality should be reduced. The intragenerational impact would also depend on the type of social programs affected by the government's diversion of funds to pay for the bonds issued. Although some social-program funding is distributively regressive (e.g., subsidizing university education and expensive curative medical services), it is reasonable to assume that reductions in social programs are generally more likely to negatively impact the poor than the wealthy.

Thus, with general obligation bond financing, the government's intertemporal budget constraint becomes:

$B_t(1+i_t) = T_{t+1} - T_t$ (Pay the principal and interest (i_t) on the bond (B_t) from a future tax increase, where $T_{t+1} > T_t$)

$B_t(1+i_t) = G_t - G_{t+1}$ (Pay the principal and interest on the bond by reducing other government spending, where $G_{t+1} < G_t$)

$B_t(1+i_t) = \Delta T - \Delta G$ (Pay the principal and interest by a combination of higher taxes and lower government spending)

Intergenerational Distribution. The use of bond revenue to finance infrastructure expansion reduces the annual costs that the initial generations must pay, compared to up-front financing through central-treasury appropriations. Thus, a highway financed through bonds may entail principal and interest payments for 15 years, 20 years, or other lengthy periods. Many bond payments are structured such that the government pays the same sum of principal and interest each year, but the payment schedule can vary considerably in terms of debt servicing from year to year, ranging from heavier early payments that then decline over the period of the bond, to lower early- and late-period payments, with the heaviest payments made in the middle years, to graduated ("back-loaded") higher payments in later years. The payment schedule therefore can be very revealing of the government's disposition to delay imposing the financial burden on the current generation.

The greater the delay in paying to cover the obligation of the bond, the greater the likelihood that the interest rate that the government will have to pay for further borrowing will be greater. This is another pathway by which bonds can put a greater burden onto future generations.

Risk. Bond-financed infrastructure development is more likely to be subject to political considerations than would privately financed development, and therefore, both poorly designed and overly ambitious projects are more likely to emerge from general obligation bond financing initiatives. The risks of poor design and scheduling will be borne by the intended recipients of the benefits of the project. However, the risk of exaggerated estimates of returns is indirectly borne by those who are not benefiting directly from the project, because the financial waste diverts resources from spending that could have benefited them. When the overly ambitious projects are the highly publicized urban or intercity transport projects that would benefit commercial operations and urban residents, the marginal populations bear the costs of the waste.

The construction risks entailed in infrastructure initiatives financed through general obligation bonds are also magnified by the lack of private sector contractors' exposure to losses if the construction goes poorly. The separation of bondholders from the contractors carrying out the construction does not force the contractors to internalize the risk of poor construction. Therefore, the people who would have benefited more from a well-constructed project bear the risk.

General obligation bonds place some of the *financial risk* on the government itself, which stands to lose credibility and future borrowing potential. Some financial risk is also borne by the bondholders, who may lose their entire investment if the bonds become worthless, or may have to sell the bonds at a discount. Among the public, the consequence of failures to meet bond repayment obligations will depend on what other aspects of government spending would be squeezed out if the government's borrowing capacity is compromised by default. Again, this would often impinge more heavily on the poor, insofar as they are more dependent on government social programs.

Revenue Bonds

Revenue bonds are backed by a particular income stream that is guaranteed as part of the commitment of the bond issuer. The revenue stream could be a sales tax, a fee specific to the use of the infrastructure, or other source. However, it is very common for the income stream to be based on the project being financed. Therefore, arranging financing through revenue bonds will focus attention explicitly on the nature—and burdens—of the revenue stream.

Let the bond principal (Bt) plus interest (it) be the value of the revenue bond that must be repaid, and adequate financing requires equality with the sum of the user fees per use (j) and over t time periods:

$$B_t(1+i_t) = \sum_j \sum_t F_{jt}$$

Generational. Revenue bonds, insofar as they are based on revenue streams from the infrastructure project itself, will mean higher costs for users, and will be located in relatively wealthy areas where the revenues are more certain. In many instances, then, lower-income people will lack access.

However, special cases arise when the structure of the revenue stream entails some sort of cross-subsidy. When the revenue stream comes from direct user fees, such as tolls in the case of transport systems or tariffs in the case of energy or water consumption, the distributional impact will vary according to whether low-consumption or high-consumption users are subsidized. Even in the case of certain indirect revenue streams, such as fuel taxes, some cross-subsidization is possible, by imposing different tax levels on different products (e.g., low-octane gasoline, high-octane gasoline, diesel, etc.). Block pricing for electricity and water is common, where *lower* rates on larger-volume users ("declining marginal rates") are offered in some cases, and in other cases, *higher* rates are imposed on larger-volume users ("rising marginal rates"). The rate structure usually depends on how marginal and average costs behave with higher volume usage, although it can certainly be designed specifically to improve equity outcomes. Insofar as those designing the revenue stream are worried about sufficient demand to provide the expected revenue, there will be a temptation to stimulate demand through declining marginal rates, which would disadvantage low-income (and hence, generally low-consumption) users. The evidence on the distributional impacts of rising marginal rates in block pricing are mixed, because in some instances, such as charging higher water charges for greater consumption, low-income residents who share the water connections with other families may end up having to pay the higher rates (Boland and Whittington 2000, Hellegers, Schoengold, and Zilberman 2008).

Risk. In theory, general obligation bonds provide greater assurance than revenue bonds that repayments will be on schedule. Mathur (1997: 168) points out that at least in the case of India "[g]eneral obligation bonds pledge the full faith and credit of the issuing government. The issuing government makes an unconditional pledge of its powers of taxation to honour its liability for interest and principal repayment. Revenue bonds pledge only the earnings from revenue-producing activities, often the earnings from the facilities being financed with the revenue bonds." However, this does not take into account the possibility of government default, or simply the perception that a default may occur. In such cases, the value of the loan instrument or bond may decline because it is not backed by a dedicated income stream. In short, revenue bonds that rely on project-associated revenues, in contrast with other government-backed loans, face a different sort of risk, namely, the business risk associated with the project. Therefore, floating such bonds dictates high fees and will tend to exclude low-income people from direct use. Revenue bonds that rely on revenues from broader levies do not face this same pressure.

When a revenue bond is used to pay the construction costs of a new road, most of the risk inherent in the project will be borne by private actors, since their bond repayment depends on the actual road use during its lifetime. The risk that demand was incorrectly calculated in these situations is great, and this risk will fall on the private bondholders. The government will be responsible for the risk of construction cost overruns, but, ultimately, the funding is coming from these private sources, and they will serve as the final risk bearers. In practice, however, governments have been known to cover extra costs incurred through general treasury funds because they are unwilling or unable to sell more revenue bonds. If this is the case, the government has essentially taken over a great deal of risk, by guaranteeing the revenue bonds irrespective of the revenue produced by the infrastructure use. This is not the way revenue bonds are supposed to be handled, but it cannot be ignored as a possible outcome. If this were to happen, the risk distribution would be similar to that of the general obligation government bond.

Public Sector Procurement: Direct Government Expenditures

1. Financed by Current Taxes
2. Financed by Budget Reallocation from Other Sources
Here, the government funds the infrastructure investment through current tax revenues, or by diverting funds from other sources in the budget. Both of these methods result in all of the financial responsibility falling on the current generation. If the tax system is mildly progressive, then the poor will not be harmed from higher taxes, but with the budget diversion method, they will be harmed if the diverted funds come from social programs primarily benefiting the poor. The government, in a design-bid-build arrangement, specifies the design of the infrastructure, solicits bids from private contractors for the construction, and then, after hiring and financing the construction, maintains and operates the infrastructure. All ownership and responsibility for the infrastructure stays with the government in this scenario.

Government Funding (Tax Increase)[2]

If the government decides to fund the road construction and maintenance through a tax increase, users of the road will not have to pay a user fee. Rather, users will pay for the road indirectly through some sort of taxation system. If the revenue for the road comes from an increase in general taxes (e.g., sales taxes), all people will be taxed alike, whether or not they use the road. If the people using the road are predominantly nonpoor, then the poor suffer an added burden, as they will be paying for a road they do not use. We assume that all community members receive indirect benefits from the road; therefore, any difference in wealth distribution must be from the difference in access to the direct benefits of the road.

If, however, the tax increase is linked to road use, wealth distribution effects will change.[3] There are a number of ways that a government could fund a road from a tax linked to road use, for example, through a fuel cess or an automobile tax. In this case, those using the road would, by-and-large, be the ones paying for it. If the tax system is a progressive one, this financing option would decrease the wealth inequality between the community's poor and nonpoor by charging the poor less and providing them greater benefits (direct or indirect). However, if the tax system is regressive, allowing loopholes to the nonpoor or giving them a greater proportion of the benefits provided by the road, wealth equality in the community will only increase as a result of the road being built.

It is important to note the possibility that the funds raised through taxes might not be enough to cover the cost of the infrastructure investment, or there might not be the political support necessary for an adequate tax to cover the full cost. In this case, the government would have to look for other types of financing. One way of doing this is by diverting funds from other parts of the budget to finish paying for the infrastructure investment. This is discussed below.

Generational. Early users of the infrastructure will pay fees until the tax revenue accumulated is enough to cover the costs of the construction and operation. At this point, the tax will decrease to cover only the necessary upkeep and maintenance, which we have assumed remains constant and will not affect the generational distribution of costs or benefits. Therefore, in the case of a new road investment, the road users in the early days of the road will pay for its creation, while the later users will not have to face these costs. If the tax is well-directed (i.e., through a tax that actually depends on road use, such as a fuel cess), there should not be any additional intergenerational inequalities between those generations who are paying the tax, however, this financing method does put a greater financial burden on the current generation during the road-building phase.

Risk. In this case, the risk of the operation is placed on the government who will have to handle the changes in cost or any issues with construction and maintenance. This risk can be lessened, depending on the contracts negotiated with local builders, but in the case that costs grow or there are unanticipated problems with the construction, it is the local communities who will bear the ultimate costs. They are the actors who will have to pay higher taxes for longer while the government continues its construction.

Government Funding (Diversion of Funds from Other Programs)

When governments are unable, for whatever reason, to obtain funding for the project through taxes, their other choice is to divert funds in the general budget to the project construction and maintenance. It is very difficult to pinpoint the exact effects such a funding decision would have on wealth distribution, since the programs from which the funds are diverted will vary from country to country, depending on the political situation. If the funding decrease is aimed at programs that primarily benefit the nonpoor, this will decrease wealth distribution inequalities. On the other hand, if the programs targeted to increase infrastructure funding primarily benefit the poor members of the community, the infrastructure investment will probably increase wealth inequality.

The benefits will also have an effect on wealth distribution, and it is important to look at these to determine the final effects the infrastructure project will have. The direct benefits of a public nonrival infrastructure project will be available to all members of the community, and they will be charged regardless of their usage. All the members of society will gain as well from the indirect benefits provided. As before, the wealth distribution effects of the project depend on who receives the greatest amount of these benefits. The benefits must be taken into account when determining the final distribution effects the project will have on the community.

One important thing to note is that by decreasing funding to some social programs in order to finance the project construction, this could decrease access to the social programs in question, despite the building of the infrastructure. In this case, the effect such a change in access would have on the wealth distribution in the community must be taken into account.

Generational. Theoretically, only early users will face a decrease in social programs as a result of the construction until the costs are paid from the diversion of funds from other government programs. If postconstruction program funds are directed back toward their original functions, later generations of users might not face any costs relating to the construction of the infrastructure. However, it is possible that there could be a transitional period, after funds are returned to their original purposes, when the original funds are not actually enough to bring the social programs back to their former quality. During this period, the local community will face low-quality social programs until the funds are adequate to restore the quality to its former levels. Fund diversions will also cause stagnation in the improvement of or innovations in social programs. Although programs might be able to keep the quality levels steady, they will likely lack funds to incorporate new technologies or otherwise enhance the services they provide. In this way, generations during this transitional period will also be paying for the infrastructure, just in a different way than did the generations during the time of the actual fund diversions. Finally, at some point in the future, a third generation in the community will not face any costs resulting from the initial project construction.

Risk. The project risk, in the case of this type of government funding, is placed squarely on the public entities building the project—there is no private investment to take over some of this risk. In the case that costs grow or there are unanticipated problems with the construction, the local communities will bear the ultimate costs. They are the actors who will have to endure fewer social programs as the government continues to finance construction.

Loans from International Sources

If the government borrows in the private capital markets to finance infrastructure investment, either directly from foreign commercial banks or by selling long-term bonds to foreign investors, it will necessarily have to demonstrate the creditworthiness of the investment in order to qualify for decent financing terms. This kind of financing will depend on the country's past borrowing and repayment record, its level of country risk, and the willingness of outside investors to finance capital investment projects. Bonds and loans are very similar in this case, in that they are tied to specific projects and must offer an attractive risk-adjusted return to generate sufficient investor interest. We have already discussed the distributive implications of bond financing, and the same implications apply to foreign commercial loans.

There are important differences between loans and bonds that must be kept in mind, especially when considering the source of the financing. Aside from commercial borrowing, another option is to borrow from bilateral or multilateral foreign assistance agencies. The World Bank and its private sector financing arm, the International Finance Corporation (IFC), have provided such loans on concessional terms to qualified developing country government borrowers, as have international development banks and other government-funded foreign assistance agencies such as the U.S. Agency for International Development (USAID). Such loans are often disbursed in multiple tranches rather than a lump sum. This means that the borrower can be held accountable and required to demonstrate that the money was used in accordance with the terms of the loan agreement. If there is a dispute, or if the lender believes the borrower is misusing the funds, it can delay or withhold the disbursement of the next tranche of funds and exert pressure on the borrower to address problems that have arisen. It can also impose conditional terms of action ("conditionalities") to explicitly link future tranches to the achievement of specific, measurable outcomes.

There is no similar procedure for bondholders, and so, there is less influence and leverage over the government's subsequent use of the funds. Once the bonds are sold, the government has full use of the funds without additional restrictions or the opportunity for the lenders to impose them. This will have further distributional implications: under loans distributed in tranches, the lenders can make sure that the interests of the poor and displaced people are safeguarded as the infrastructure project proceeds. Under a bond issue, the bondholders lack this leverage, there is less opportunity to hold the government accountable, and little recourse if it fails to spend the bond funds efficiently.

Before the global financial crisis hit in the late summer 2008, there was evidence that interest in such borrowing was waning in many countries. This is allegedly due to both the wider availability of financing from private investors, the desire to avoid restrictive conditionalities imposed on borrowing country governments, and better fiscal health that enables more local financing and a reduction in debt service payments to foreign lenders.[4]

When the government of a developing country borrows from a multilateral institution for an infrastructure project, it often must agree to undertake policy reforms that increase private-sector participation in the economy and to liberalize its investment rules to open the market to more competition. There are also co-financing and credit guarantee arrangements between multilateral organizations and private lenders that constrain the ability of borrowing country governments to renege on contract terms, since it would negatively affect the ability to borrow for other needs in the future. Thus, these "conditionalities" can lead to positive changes in the functioning of the country's markets and an improvement in the business environment, which can certainly help protect the poor and improve the growth potential of the economy.[5]

What are the distribution implications of such financing? As discussed previously in the case of long-term government bonds, the distribution impact of private borrowing will depend on how the funds for debt service and repayment of principal are collected. If general taxes are collected, and there is no link between usage of the infrastructure and payment, then the poor are disproportionately burdened, paying for infrastructure they may not be using. If the tax system is progressive, this effect may be mitigated.

Generational. As in the case with domestic borrowing, to the extent that repayment of the principal is pushed into the future, current generations will effectively pay less for the infrastructure, and future generations will bear more of the burden.

Risk. The foreign lenders bear more of the risk under this type of financing. If the government defaults on the loans (as was the case in many Southeast Asian countries following the Asian financial crisis in 1997), the private lenders are left with little recourse other than to renegotiate the terms of the loan in an attempt to recover at least some of the funds. There will, however, be consequences for a government default: damaged credibility, much less liquidity, and far higher risk ratings, making future private borrowing unaffordable.

There are some additional risk considerations in the case of borrowed private-sector funds for government infrastructure investments. There are project-specific risks associated with design or construction flaws, and these are increased if the project designers are not accountable to the local stakeholders. There are also generic risks of borrowing internationally (loans or bonds). An unexpected rise in global real interest rates may increase the debt service burden dramatically, as was the case in Latin America in the 1980s. In addition, there is less accountability to domestic stakeholders if the government borrows foreign funds since it is primarily answerable to the lenders' terms. Exchange rate risk exists if the loan is denominated in foreign currency terms. The Asian financial crisis was exacerbated by the massive amount of foreign currency-denominated debts incurred by private firms and governments that became nonpayable once the home currencies suffered massive devaluations.

These two types of risk, the generic risks of borrowing internationally (loans or bonds) and project-specific risks raise the potential costs of the projects and thus have distributional implications. Private bondholders are more likely to insist on charging enough to ensure full cost recovery (this raises the likelihood that they'll recover their investment, and it raises the bar for them to buy the bonds). For private lenders, adequate collateral or provision of guarantees is necessary, and if the government has a shaky repayment history, these costs will rise. In both cases, this may mean higher revenues for the bondholders and lenders, and higher borrowing costs for the government. To avoid unfairly burdening the poor, some of these higher costs can be offset by price discrimination (block pricing), particularly for the low-income users and citizens. Setting a single uniform price to everyone can result in more harm to poorer users, so price discrimination may be useful.

There are many forms of infrastructure financing arrangements involving multilateral and bilateral players. For example, the multilateral organization can act as a catalyst to attract more private capital to infrastructure investment projects; it can invest as a partner (equity shares), offer full and partial credit guarantees, and participate in risk-sharing and shared ownership agreements such as Build-Own-Operate and Build-Operate-Transfer arrangements. Multilateral and bilateral organizations can also help with project appraisal, design, and selection of contractors through a competitive bidding process, including the conduct of feasibility studies, and social and environmental impact studies for potential projects. The distribution implications of such financing arrangements are discussed in more detail in the next section, when we discuss public-private partnerships.

Public-Private Partnerships (P3)

There are many types of public-private partnership arrangements for financing and operating new infrastructure investments, with varying degrees of private and public ownership. In many cases, the private sector undertakes the construction of the infrastructure according to contractual terms agreed to with the public authority. Thereafter, the private contractor can either charge user fees to recover the cost of construction, or the public authority can pay these fees ("shadow tolls" or infrastructure service fees) over a specified period of time to cover the cost of construction. Here is a short list describing the primary types of P3s in use:

BOO: Build-Own-Operate (ownership of infrastructure remains with private investors)
BOT: Build-Operate-Transfer (purchaser of infrastructure services [e.g., power, water] is a public authority, and at the end of the contract, ownership would pass from the private investors to the public sector)
BTO: Build-Transfer-Operate and DBFO: Design-Build-Finance-Operate (ownership is transferred to the public authority upon completion of the facility, and it remains with the public authority throughout the contract. The private-sector interest is based solely on the contractual rights to operate the facility and receive revenues from doing so, rather than owning the physical assets.)

In developing countries, BTO, BOT, and DBFO contracts are relatively common in the power sector since they enable cash-strapped state authorities to fund investment in more efficient plants without relinquishing control over generation or distribution (including the prices charged to consumers). Thus, the private sector delivers services on behalf of the public authority, but the public sector retains owner-ship and control.[6]

In major infrastructure investments, long-term debt financing is often required (payments spread over a long period into the future) given the huge capital costs involved, and P3s have evolved as a way for state authorities to undertake these kinds of projects without having to pay up-front for the full cost of construction. Under one scenario, private investors own the project company selected to build the infrastructure, and they finance the capital costs through shareholder equity as well as issuing debt. This firm subcontracts the engineering, procurement, and construction services to firms based on a fixed-fee contract. This means that the contractor agrees to deliver a completed and fully equipped turnkey facility (e.g., power station) according to specifications and by a specific date. Thus, the private investors must cover any cost overruns. There may be a separate operations and maintenance contract with the contractor or another provider once the facility is constructed, or the government can assume this responsibility.

Build-Operate-Transfer (BOT)

If the financing and construction of the infrastructure is arranged through a Build-Operate-Transfer program, private companies will be responsible for the construction and operation of the road for a cer-tain period of time (as opposed to certain amount of revenue). For the purposes of illustration, we will consider a particular case (building a new road), and we will assume this is a 30-year BOT agreement.[7] Road users must pay a user fee to travel on the new road, but after the BOT arrangement is finished, the road reverts to the government and is free of charge to the users. We will assume that until the end of the 30-year period, the government plays no role in the operation of the road, mean-ing that there will be no change in the availability of social programs for the local area or taxation related to the provision of the road.

If the road fee is set at a low level, which allows most members of the local community, both poor and nonpoor, to take advantage of the road, these members will benefit directly (lower transportation costs of taking goods to market and of bringing inputs into the town) from the construction of the road. All segments of the local society will also receive indirect benefits from the road being built, including changes in access to social programs, access to greater variety of consumer goods, higher land values, and higher wages.[8] If all the benefits of the road are spread evenly between the poor and nonpoor, then the road will have no significant effect on the existing wealth inequality. On the other hand, if the benefits accrue more to one segment of the local population than the other, wealth inequalities will be increased. Inequalities will rise if the benefits are greater for the nonpoor, or they will be decreased if the benefits are greater for the poor. These will all vary from case to case and depend on what effects, both direct and indirect, the road has, as well as the size of these effects. One study suggests that direct benefits are higher for nonpoor, whereas indirect benefits tend to be higher for the poor, and benefits overall tend to be higher for the poor when regulation is efficient.[9]

If the road use fee is too high for the poor segments of the local population to use the road on a regular basis, they do not receive as many benefits as the nonpoor segments of the population that can afford to travel on the road and take advantage of the direct benefits it provides. Although direct use of the road would not necessarily require the poor to be driving on the road—they could transport their goods through another party—road use costs may be too high for poor members of the society to pay the costs of transportation by another party, which would keep them from gaining the direct benefits. We will assume, however, that the poor are still able to take advantage of the indirect benefits provided by the road, including better access to consumer goods, social programs, and job opportunities. If the poor and nonpoor receive the same amount of indirect benefits from the road—or the nonpoor receive greater indirect benefits than do the poor—the wealth inequalities are increased, since the nonpoor are also receiving all the direct benefits derived from use of the road. Even if social programs are designed such that the poor benefit more from any indirect benefits than do the nonpoor, there will only be a decrease in wealth inequality if this benefit is also greater than the direct benefits the nonpoor gain from use of the road. This would require a very effective system of progressive wealth redistribution in the local area. It may be possible to affect wealth inequality through a differentiation of the user fee itself, charging poor users a lower fee than nonpoor users.[10] This would have to be done in a way that eliminates the possibility of arbitrage, where the nonpoor find a way to pay the lower fee, a difficult task.

Finally, there is the possibility that the user fee is actually set too low. In this case, any revenue generated from the user fees will not be enough to cover the construction costs already incurred or the routine maintenance necessary for general road upkeep. At this point, the company can do one of two things: raise user fees, or carry out some type of contract renegotiation that would require the government to cover some of the road costs. If the fees are raised, this returns us to either of the situations above, depending on the demand impact of the new fee. The situation described below, government financing, explains the effects of the second possible situation.

Generational. Users will pay fees for the entire 30-year period. Any intergenerational conflict between users during this time will arise when/if fees are changed. Since only users pay the road fees, there will not be any problem with users *in this 30-year period* paying amounts for the road that does not correspond to their levels of road use. The main intergenerational issues arise when we also look at generations that come after the 30-year contract has expired. These later generations will not have to pay for use of the road, and they will be able to gain both the indirect and direct benefits of its use (Hodge and Greve 2007: 549). In essence, the earlier generations will pay for the road use of the later generations.[11]

Risk.[12] In theory, BOT models put the burden of the risk of a construction project on the shoulders of private actors, and the government only steps in if project sponsors fail to meet project requirements for completion (Walker and Smith 1995: 193). In practice, however, this does not always hold. Many times, the increased risk inherent in such projects translates into bids that are very low during the contracting process, essentially charging the government for the risk of project failure.[13] In this case, it would be expected that the private actors take over complete responsibility for the risk, but there have been cases when the private entities still look to renegotiate contracts during the established period because expected demand has not been met, or costs have risen past expected levels to the point where they can no longer be met by user fees.[14] If this happens, then some of the risk is transferred back to the government, despite any preimplementation agreements.[15]

Although in theory this should not happen, it has happened on numerous occasions and must be taken into consideration. That being said, private actors do face a great deal of risk in these projects, and their fears are not misplaced—there are a number of cases of governments taking over private assets before the contracted transfer time without adequately compensating the private operators. The BOT model holds a great deal of promise for distributing risk between government and private actors, but only if contracts are upheld more consistently.[16] After the BOT period is over, the government assumes all risk concerning the infrastructure, although this should be relatively low, concerning only regular maintenance and upkeep issues.

Infrastructure Development Trusts

There are two types of trust funds that have emerged to coordinate and finance infrastructure investment, especially in developing countries. The first involves a regional international financial institution (e.g., European Investment Bank) working with regional government authorities and donors to provide a trust fund to promote cross-border infrastructure development. One prime example of such a trust is the Infrastructure Consortium for Africa (ICA) working with the African Development Bank and the European Investment Bank to raise donor funds and channel them to infrastructure development projects in sub-Saharan Africa.[17]

Another type of financing relies on the sale of securities whose underlying assets are comprised of revenues from infrastructure development projects in emerging-market countries. This new kind of security is currently being offered by Credit Suisse,[18] and it targets those investors who seek to financially gain from the projected increases in infrastructure investment needed in fast growing emerging market countries. The underlying assets are those of private companies in the capital investment business (e.g., construction, design, etc.) whose fortunes depend on the global surge in infrastructure investment, most notably in India, China, and the Middle East.

Generational. Since these assets are sold to foreign investors, there is little inter- or intragenerational impact. The ability of governments to tap funding for infrastructure investment in order to contract with these private firms has already been discussed.

Risk. Donors and investors bear the risk of these investments. To the extent that private investors buy shares of these infrastructure development trusts, more funding will flow to finance the investment, and the rates of return will rise, as long as the projects go according to plan. As in the case of P3s, the private firms have an incentive to manage the projects wisely, in order to increase their returns for themselves and their shareholders, some of whom are holders of these trusts.

The Issue of Cross-Subsidies

Infrastructure provision by the government typically occurs because of the public goods nature of the investment. Once the road or bridge has been provided, it is difficult to exclude users from accessing it, unless use is monitored and controlled through gates and tolls (which are also expensive.) Given the high sunk capital costs to provide the infrastructure, the average total costs fall as more people use it. Thus, the economics of many types of infrastructure are those of a natural monopoly. While the monopolist would prefer to restrict output and charge a higher price (and earn supernormal profits), equity considerations imply marginal-cost, or at least fair-rate-of-return (average-cost) pricing and much higher provision of services. Cross-subsidies arise when the government allows or engages in price discrimination wherein some customers (those who are wealthier) are charged higher prices (above average total cost), thereby subsidizing the below-marginal-cost prices paid by the poor.

An important question to consider is whether some financing mechanisms are more likely to lend themselves to cross-subsidies. What are the costs and benefits (and effects) of cross-subsidies?

Cross-subsidization occurs when the government charges differential tariffs (or user fees) on infrastructure services in order to achieve equity goals (helping make the services more affordable to the poor) while ensuring that the natural monopoly can cover its costs to continue providing the services. In setting differential tariff rates, Irwin (1997) points out four criteria that are important to satisfy:

1. Target accurately (ensure that the subsidies are reaching those whom the government really wants to reach, that is, the poor).
2. Keep the costs clear and measurable.
3. Keep the administrative costs as low as possible.
4. Raise the revenues for cross-subsidies from the least-cost source possible.

Once the infrastructure has been provided, cross-subsidies can be used in cases where usage can be monitored, and where additional marginal costs are incurred with usage. For example, as discussed previously, electricity and water usage entails falling average costs with higher volume usage (as long as total usage remains within the capacity of the local utility), thus enabling discount pricing for blocks of higher usage to be efficient. Another form of cross-subsidies can be used if the government can accurately identify poor users (perhaps linked to a minimum threshold of usage) and charge lower rates, while allowing the monopoly to capture higher profits from higher volume users (this would represent reverse block pricing.) In such cases, the poor would certainly benefit from the lower prices, as long as they had access to these services. In cases where the poor are not connected to the grid or water system, the government could provide aid to help these families afford to buy these services from informal providers.

Identifying the target users can be difficult, and this will raise the administrative costs of cross-subsidies. Problems also arise if the subsidies are tied to a specific provider, thereby reducing competition and service availability. Direct income support rather than tied service subsidies would allow the poor to shop for their preferred combination of quality and types of services. In addition, as Cowen and Tynan (1999) discuss in their paper on private infrastructure provision to the urban poor, regulatory processes must be redesigned to correct land ownership and tenure ambiguities in order to promote more long-term commitments to investing in grid and pipeline extensions (electricity, water, and sewer) on the part of both private providers and poor households. The poor may be unaware of their purchasing options, and may be paying higher rates for daily purchases rather than investing in lower-cost but longer-term attachments to the grid. The private providers may be disinclined to invest in grid extensions to areas where land ownership rights are not assigned. Clearly, this chicken-and-egg problem can be solved by clarifying regulations on property rights.

It isn't clear that choosing a different financing option for infrastructure provision affects the decision to cross-subsidize services ex post. First, it is important to ask whether cross-subsidization is feasible and if equity outcomes can be improved through its use. If so, then the next step is to choose a financing mechanism that allows it to be implemented, given the political context. There is a higher risk for private firms involved in supplying the services if the government sets the prices and determines the cross-subsidy scheme, but doesn't set the prices high enough to allow full cost recovery. A larger and more important issue to address is how to balance the need to adequately finance the investment and operating costs with ensuring access to these needed services by the poor. In some cases, it would be infeasible to charge different tolls to different users based on income, given the difficulty of identifying and verifying income differences, and given the perverse incentives it would set up. For example, one could imagine road users choosing to utilize transportation typically used by the poor in an effort to qualify for lower tolls (e.g., jitneys, hand-pulled carts, etc.), thereby increasing congestion, slowing traffic, and resulting in a much less efficient use of the road.

Increasing competition among service providers and providing vouchers to the poor could improve both access and affordability for everyone. The government can also cross-subsidize a basic threshold level of services for the poor by allowing the providers to charge higher rates to higher volume users.

Conclusion

Although there is abundant evidence that infrastructure investment can promote economic growth and development, the modes of financing infrastructure can have significant distributional impacts that must be taken into account. There are many different intra- and intergenerational implications of various modes of infrastructure financing, as well as risk implications. We have endeavored to illuminate some of these issues in our discussion, but it is clear that there is no single mode of financing that perfectly balances equity and efficiency. Governments often step in to provide infrastructure investment given the difficulty of monitoring and restricting access to users and the nonrival nature of the infrastructure once provided. Obviously, no government has the wherewithal to provide unlimited access to infrastructure goods and services to its citizens, the rhetoric about "rights" to clean water, electricity, and sewerage services notwithstanding. Infrastructure investment and service provision is costly, so governments have the incentive to develop and use modes of financing that prioritize efficient provision and generate the incentives for private-sector participation. Equity goals can be addressed in numerous ways, both in the choice of methods for the initial financing, and in assigning user fees for the stream of services provided.

As part of the infrastructure planning process, policy-makers have to think through their distributional goals, and then ask what locational and design decisions are compatible with those goals. Once those priorities are determined, they need to ask what financing arrangements are compatible with their design and location decisions, taking into account cost recovery requirements and the potential equity benefits of cross-subsidization. While infrastructure investments have the potential to improve life for the poor, careful consideration of these factors is necessary to ensure that they actually do.

Notes

1. Flyvbjerg (2003) emphasizes the problem of exaggerated expectations of major transport project use.
2. For discussion of African road funds (an example of this type of funding scheme), see UN Economic Commission for Africa and the World Bank (1997, 2000).
3. For examples of such taxes (and problems associated with recovery), see UN Economic Commission for Africa and the World Bank (1997).
4. See Conde (2008) and Hall (2007).
5. Of course, there are also those who argue that conditionality terms are too strict, favor private sector profit maximization over social goals, and lead to higher prices for public goods and services, thereby disadvantaging the poor. The debate over the costs and benefits of privatization of water and electricity services is quite contentious. See Anonymous (2005) and Barlow and Clarke (2004) for two examples of this debate.
6. Yescombe (2007: Chapter 1).
7. For discussion of Least Present Value of Revenue, an alternative method of organizing BOT programs, see Engel, Fischer, and Galetovic (1997: 109–112).
8. For discussion of direct/indirect benefits, see Boarnet (1996: 5); Gannon and Liu (2002: 6); Jacoby (2000); and Chisari, Estache, and Romero (1997: 14).
9. See Chisari, Estache, and Romero (1997: 15, 27).
10. For a discussion of benefits of price-differentiated services and subsidies, see Briceño-Garmendia, Estache, and Shafik (2004: 9–10); and Estache (2003: 12).
11. Obviously, the costs will not drop to zero for the future generations, given that ongoing operations and maintenance costs must still be paid. The point is that the total costs paid by earlier generations will necessarily be higher than those paid by the post-30-year generation, at least as long as the road lasts.
12. For discussion of the different types of risks in BOT projects, see Walker and Smith (1995). For discussion of ways of measuring risk in BOT projects, see Walker and Smith (1995: 163–166) and McCowan and Mohamed (2002).
13. For a discussion of government attempts to make projects more attractive to private investors, see Walker and Smith (1995: 24–25, 34).
14. For a discussion of demand realization and effects in BOT projects see Engel, Fischer, and Galetovic (1997: 109–110).
15. For a discussion of contract renegotiation see Estache and de Rus (2000: 14, 21).
16. For the importance of contracts in risk allocation see Estache and de Rus (2000: 5–7); Yescombe (2007: Chapter 1).

17. http://www.eib.org/projects/press/2008/2008–011-infrastructure-consortium-calls-for-more-private-investment-to-support-african-regional-integration-.htm
18. This trust is known as Credit Suisse PL-100 Emerging Markets Infrastructure Development Trust. http://www.credit-suisse.com/upload/news-live/40533_1001.pdf.

References

Anonymous. 2005. Water is a human right, *Reason*, August 17. http://www.reason.com/news/show/34992.html.

Barlow, Maude and Tony Clarke. 2004. Water privatization: The World Bank's latest market fantasy, *Global Policy Forum*, January. http://www.globalpolicy.org/socecon/bwi-wto/wbank/2004/01waterpriv.htm.

Boarnet, Marlon G. 1996. The direct and indirect economic effects of transportation infrastructure. University of California Transportation Center Working Paper No. 340. Berkeley: University of California.

Boland, John and Dale Whittington. 2000. The political economy of water tariff design in developing countries: Increasing block tariffs versus uniform price with rebate. In *The political economy of water pricing reforms.* ed. Ariel Dinar. Oxford: Oxford University Press.

Briceño-Garmendia, Cecilia, Antonio Estache, and Nemat Shafik. 2004. Infrastructure services in developing countries: Access, quality, costs and policy reform. World Bank Policy Research Working Paper No. 3468. Washington, DC: World Bank Institute, December.

Calderon, C. and L. Serven. 2004. *The effects of infrastructure development on growth and income distribution*. Washington, DC: World Bank.

Chisari, Antonio Estache and Carlos Romero. 1997. Winners and losers from utility privatization in Argentina: Lessons from a general equilibrium model. Washington, DC: World Bank.

Cohen, Remy and Marco Percoco. 2004. The fiscal implications of infrastructure development: policy recommendations for Latin America and the Caribbean. In *Recouping infrastructure investment in Latin America and the Caribbean*, ed. Juan Benavides. Washington, DC: Inter-American Development Bank.

Conde, Carlos. 2008. Philippines to stop using foreign loans for infrastructure projects, *International Herald Tribune*, February 20. http://www.iht.com/articles/2008/02/20/business/peso.php.

Coppin, Adrian. 2003. Italian initiatives. London: Serco Institute Resource Centre.http://www.publicservice.co.uk/pdf/pfi/dec2003/PJ43%20Adrian%20Coppin%20ATL.pdf

Cowen, Penelope Brook and Nicola Tynan. 1999. Reaching the urban poor with private infrastructure. *Privatesector* (World Bank Public Policy Note #188), June.

De la Fuente, Angel. 2002. *Fondos estructurales, inversión en infraestructuras y crecimiento regional*, Santiago de Compostela, Spain: Centro de Investigación Económica y Financiera, Fundación Caixa-Galicia.

Engel, Eduardo, Ronald Fischer, and Alexander Galetovic. 1997. A new method for auctioning highways. In *The private sector in infrastructure: Strategy, regulation, and risk*, ed. S. Smith. Washington, DC: World Bank.

Estache, Antonio. 2003. On Latin America's infrastructure privatization and its distributional effects. World Bank and ECARES (Université Libre de Bruxelles), April 30.

Estache, Antonio and Ginés de Rus. 2000. The regulation of transport infrastructure and services: A conceptual overview. In *Privatization and regulation of transport infrastructure: Guidelines for policymakers and regulators*, pp. 5–50, ed. Antonio Estache and Ginés de Rus. Washington, DC: World Bank. http://www.worldbank.org/wbi/regulation/books.htm.

Estache, Antonio and Marianne Fay. 1997. Ensuring regional growth convergence in Argentina and Brazil: How can governments help? Washington, DC: World Bank.

Estache, Antonio and Marianne Fay. 2007. Current debates on infrastructure policy. World Bank Policy Research Working Paper No. 4410. Washington, DC: World Bank Institute.

Flyvbjerg, Bent. 2003. *Megaprojects and risk: An anatomy of ambition*. Cambridge: Cambridge University Press.

Gannon, C. and Z. Liu. 2002. Transport: Infrastructure and services. Poverty Reduction Strategy Paper: A Sourcebook, August 22.

Hall, D.J. 2007. Public sector finance for investment in infrastructure: Some recent developments, Public Services International Research Unit, April. http://www.psiru.org/reports/2007–04-U-pubinv.doc.

Hellegers, Petra, Karina Schoengold, and David Zilberman. 2008. Water resource management and the poor. In *Economics of poverty, environment and natural-resource use*, ed. Rob B. Dellink and Arjan Ruijs. Dordrecht, Netherlands: Springer.

Hodge, G.A. and C. Greve. 2007. Public-private partnerships: An international performance review. *Public Administration Review* 67(3): 545–558.

Inter-American Development Bank. 1995. Fostering infrastructure development in Latin America and the Caribbean: A strategy proposal. Washington, DC: Inter-American Development Bank Infrastructure and Financial Markets Division, August.

Irwin, Timothy. 1997. Price structures, cross-subsidies, and competition in infrastructure, *Privatesector* (World Bank Note #107), February.

Jacoby, Hanan G. 2000. Access to markets and the benefits of rural roads. *The Economic Journal* 110(July): 713–737.

Lim, Louisa. 2006a. China gets its own slice of English countryside, NPR report, 12 December. http://www.npr.org/templates/story/story.php?storyId=6608596

———. 2006b. Evictions reflect dark side of Shanghai growth, NPR Morning Edition, December 13.http://www.npr.org/templates/story/story.php?storyId=6614046

———. 2006c. Shanghai urban development: The future is now, National Public Radio, December 11. http://www.npr.org/templates/story/story.php?storyId=6600367.

Mathur, Om Prakash. 1997. Fiscal innovations and urban governance. In *Governance on the ground: Innovations and discontinuities in cities of the developing world*. ed. Patricia L. McCarney and Richard E. Stren. Washington, DC: Woodrow Wilson Center Press. New Delhi, October. http://publications.ksu.edu.sa/Conferences/Business%20Briefing%20World%20Urban%20Economic%20Development%20in%202000/MATHUR3.PDF.

McCowan, Allison and Sherif Ali Mohtady Mohamed. 2002. Evaluation of build-operate-transfer (BOT) project opportunities in developing countries. Queensland, Australia: Centre for Infrastructure Engineering and Management, Technology, Griffith University

UN Economic Commission for Africa and the World Bank. 1997. A new generation of road funds to the rescue of African roads. Sub-Saharan Africa Transport Policy Program and Rural Travel and Transport Program. Sub-Saharan Africa Transport Policy Program and Rural Travel and Transport Program, *Africa Transport* Technical Note No. 2, Washington, DC: World Bank, May.

_____. 2000. Implementing second-generation road funds: Lessons learned, Sub-Saharan Africa Transport Policy Program and Rural Travel and Transport Program, *Africa Transport* Technical Note No. 31, Washington, DC: World Bank, December.

Walker, C. and A.J. Smith, eds. 1995. *Privatized infrastructure: The build-operate-transfer approach*. London: Thomas Telford Publications.

Yescombe, E.R. 2007. *Public-private partnerships: Principles of policy and finance*. Amsterdam: Elsevier Publishers.

CHAPTER 3

Beyond Privatization: Rethinking Private Sector Involvement in the Provision of Civil Infrastructure

Richard G. Little

Introduction

Between January and April 2000, the streets of Cochabamba, Bolivia, erupted in a series of protests over the privatization of the municipal water supply. In response to pressure from the World Bank to increase efficiency and conservation, Bolivia had entered into an agreement with International Waters Ltd. *Aguas de Tunari*, an international consortium, to provide water service in Cochabamba. Within weeks, water rates were increased by an average of 35 percent to about US$20 per month. In a country where many of the customers earned less than US$100 monthly, such an increase was seen as an intolerable burden for what was considered a public good.

Water can exist in many contexts; for example, commodity, natural resource, or mineral. More importantly, after the air we breathe, the water we drink is humankind's greatest necessity of life. Because of this, access to adequate supplies of pure water is taken as a basic human right. This is reflected as the United Nation's Millennium Development Goal: "Between 1990 and 2015, to reduce by half the proportion of people without sustainable access to safe drinking water" (UN 2000). This has led to many calls for water to be made available as cheaply as possible to the public at large; yet, providing clean, safe water is costly. At the same time, water infrastructure and water as a commodity is seen as an emerging investment opportunity (*Business Week* 2005) because population growth, particularly in the developing world, will increase demand only over time and a larger population will invariably require more water. In an era of reduced regulation, private-sector investors find utilities attractive because of the "natural monopoly" inherent in the delivery of networked services, that is, people have little option but to purchase services delivered through the only set of pipes or wires available.

In light of these forces, it is reasonable to ask whether what became known as the "The Cochabamba Water Wars" have anything to teach us more broadly about the current interest in arrangements between the public and private sectors collectively known as "Public Private Partnerships" (PPPs or P3s)[1] and their role in providing public services. What factors are paramount in designing public-private partnerships that result in both efficient and equitable provision of utility services, including water, electricity, and sewerage? What are the benefits and drawbacks of these partnerships? Before attempting to answer these questions, it will be useful to step back and briefly examine the history of infrastructure service privatization in the developing and developed world, the forces driving it, and the lessons learned. From there, we can begin to develop an understanding of private-sector incentives to invest in public infrastructure projects, and the conditions under which public and private collaboration may lead to better service provision at a lower cost.

The Push to Privatize

At the heart of the push to privatize[2] is the widely held, and mostly accurate, belief that public enterprise is less efficient than its private-sector counterpart (Boycko, Shlezfer, and Vishny 1996). To a large degree, this comes about because of a fundamental difference between public enterprise, which aims to address political and social goals and lacks a profit motive, and the efficiency and financial performance goals of the private sector. Much of the economics literature that addresses this question sees full, or least high, employment as the primary objective of the politically driven public enterprise, and privatization as the cure for the resulting inefficiencies. At the same time, public ownership and operation has been viewed as the last defense protecting consumers from potentially predatory pricing practices in monopoly industries. However, the situation may be more complex than that.

In an exhaustive study of the privatization of many formerly state-owned enterprises (SOEs) from all sectors, Megginson and Netter (2001) concluded that privatization is now a de facto legitimate and often core public policy tool used by many nations, but that it is unlikely that full privatization across all sectors in all nations will ever be achieved. The most recent wave of privatizations grew largely out of a reaction to the activist government role that emerged in many nations following the Great Depression and, particularly, World War II. Until the emergence of the conservative Thatcher government in the United Kingdom in the 1980s, socially motivated government ownership of most of what can be considered civil infrastructure (transportation, water, gas, electric, telecommunications) was the desired norm in most of the developed world.[3] In the developing world, government owner-ship of utilities and infrastructure was used more as a means to pro-mote growth, but it was also viewed as a rejection of foreign influence in the postcolonial era (Rondinelli and Iacono 1996).

Although the efforts of the Thatcher government were not the first, the U.K. privatization program and the related Private Finance Initiative (PFI) have probably had the deepest and most lasting impact.[4] Efforts to increase private participation in the provision of formerly public ser-vices in other Commonwealth nations such as Australia and Canada through PPPs build directly on the PFI, and many nations, including governments in the United States at both the national and state level, are attempting more widespread application of PPP to address the chronic underfunding of public infrastructure.[5]

Summarizing the "Lessons Learned" from their comprehensive review of privatization research, Megginson and Netter (2001) con-cluded that privatization programs initiated over the past quarter century have significantly reduced the role of SOEs in most national economies. Privatization has largely achieved its goals of improved effi-ciency and profitability, and in the presence of significant performance gains, the resulting improvements in financial health generally permit increases in capital investment spending and reductions in employment. In addition, more efficient private provision means less budget pressure for the public sector. However, at the time of their study, they found little empirical evidence of the impact of privatization on consumers, although they noted emerging evidence that large-scale privatization efforts may spur further desirable improvements in corporate gover-nance. More recently, Nellis and Birdsall (2005) have assembled case study evidence from several countries on the distributional impact of privatization on prices, employment, access to services, and the govern-ment budget.[6] In many countries, the authors find positive effects on consumer access to services (especially the urban poor), lower short-term employment (but no lasting effects on structural unemployment), improved fiscal conditions, and a positive impact on overall consumer welfare.

Infrastructure Reform in the Developing World

What tends to spur demand for major public utility infrastructure reforms in developing countries? Factors include a lack of access to services for the poor, limited rural connectivity, poor quality services, and budgetary pressures that result in inadequate maintenance and upkeep. As noted at the outset of this chapter, one of the primary economic benefits of private participation is the availability of funds and the expertise to improve the quality of services offered; yet efforts to increase private-sector participation in the infrastructure of the developing world have not been painless. Market-oriented reforms, while producing long-term economic and operational advantages, may have short-term impacts that are often most keenly felt by those least able to bear them. Foster, Tiongson, and Laderchi (2005) examined the impacts of alternate utility reform measures (i.e., public sector reform, private participation, and regulatory reform) in developing economies in three infrastructure sectors (energy, telecommunications, and water), and came to somewhat obvious conclusions that the directions of price and service-quality changes will vary under different reform regimes. Interestingly, they postulate that regulatory reform,[7] even more so than private participation, should have greater impacts on price, quality, and access. Table 3.1 displays their findings across sectors and reform measures.

In chapter 2 in this volume, Ascher and Krupp discuss the distributional implications of various forms of infrastructure financing options, and they find that carefully structured private-public partnerships not only can enhance the quality and availability of public utility services, but can also enable developing country governments to source the funds needed to embark on large, long-term projects relatively quickly. Of course, the devil is in the details, and there are many stories of privatization ventures that didn't yield the anticipated efficiency benefits or the improvements in access that were promised.[8]

Private participation in infrastructure is a major source of foreign investment in the developing world. Between 1990 and 2006, more than US$1 trillion was invested in almost 3,800 infrastructure projects (energy, telecommunications, transport, and water and sewerage) in developing and transitional economies (World Bank 2007). Although private-sector investment was primarily focused in the energy and

Table 3.1 Impacts of Alternative Public Sector Reforms

	Employment and Wages	Price of Service	Quality of Service	Access to Service	Asset Ownership	Fiscal Flows	Entry Conditions
Public sector reform	Employment *may* fall because of increased pressure for efficiency	Prices *may* adjust upward or downward toward efficient cost-reflective levels	Quality *may* improve because of better management	Access *may* improve because of improved finances	n.a.	Subsidies to the sector *may* be reduced	n.a.
Private sector participation	Employment *should* fall because of increased pressure for efficiency	Prices *should* adjust upward or downward toward efficient cost-reflective levels	Quality *may* improve because of better management	Access *may* improve because of improved finances	Asset sales increase private ownership, concentration depends on design details	Subsidies to the sector *should* be reduced, sale revenues *may* be large, and tax revenues *may* follow thereafter	n.a.
Regulatory reform	Employment *may* fall because of increased pressure for efficiency	Prices *should* adjust upward or downward toward efficient cost-reflective levels	Quality *should* improve because of increased oversight and accountability	Access *should* improve because of increased oversight and accountability	n.a.	Subsidies to the sector *should* be reduced as tariffs converge to cost-effective levels	Regulatory decisions may affect terms of competition between providers

Source: Foster, Tiongson, and Laderchi (2005).

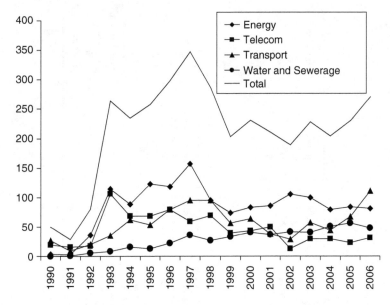

Figure 3.1 Number of Privately Provided Infrastructure Projects by Sector
Source: World Bank 2008

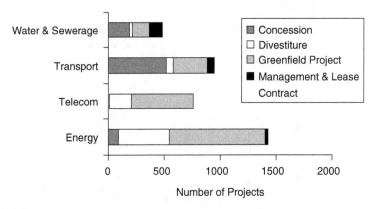

Figure 3.2 Method of Provision by Infrastructure Sector
Source: World Bank 2008

telecommunication sectors (see figure 3.1), there was broad diversity in private investment levels by infrastructure sector, region, and the nature of participation (i.e., divestiture, concession, greenfield project, or management and lease contract) (see figures 3.2, 3.3, and 3.4).

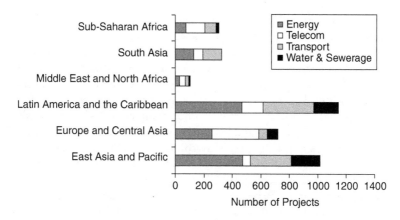

Figure 3.3 Distribution of Projects by Sector and Region
Source: World Bank 2008

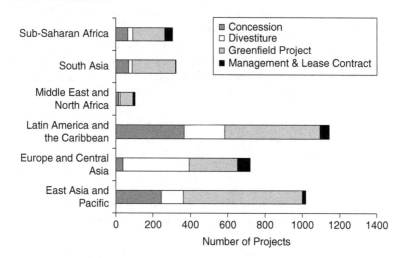

Figure 3.4 Method of Private Provision of Infrastructure by Region (1990–2006)
Source: World Bank 2008

The apparent attractiveness of certain regions and subsectors to foreign capital during this period could offer some insight into future private participation in infrastructure and what form it might take. For example, many problems that arise with infrastructure in developing and transitional economies have been traced to a similar sequence of distinctly nonmarket events. Initially, for political (and/or social) reasons, fees or tariffs are often set below a level sufficient to provide reliable service, perform necessary maintenance and repair, and make capital investments. This results in service inefficiencies and encourages wasteful use that further exacerbates revenue shortfalls, leading to another round of service declines and disinvestment. At some point, government subsidies become the primary revenue source for which support eventually wanes and the system becomes completely dysfunctional and in need of major physical and institutional overhaul. Many state-owned utilities experience a service decay spiral: low tariffs and low collection induce consumers to use water inefficiently; high usage and system losses drive up costs; this results in postponements in investment and maintenance; service deteriorates; customers are therefore less willing to pay; the utility is force to live off of state subsidies; the managers lose autonomy and incentives; efficiency continues to decline; subsidies often do not materialize; the utility cannot pay wages, recurrent costs, or expand the system; the motivation and service deteriorates further; the system's assets erode (Brocklehurst, Evans, and Kariuki 2003).

This is neither a new nor unique issue. A considerable body of empirical research supports some basic and universal principles that should underlie long-term improvement of infrastructure service delivery in the developing world (Kessides 2004). These include the following:

- Designing pricing policies that strike a balance between economic efficiency and social equity.
- Developing rules governing access to bottleneck infrastructure facilities.[9]
- Adapting regulation to address emerging problems, changing circumstances, and new information in regulated infrastructure sectors.
- Finding new ways to increase poor people's access to services.

Although the public model for network utilities has many flaws, no universally optimal private model has yet emerged that appears right for all industries in all nations. The list of "problem" infrastructure projects appearing in the literature is quite long and large projects tend to go awry for a variety of reasons, regardless of where they happen to be located or whether the public or private sector was in charge of the process. Not surprisingly, as the leaders of developing and transitional economies attempted to bring market-based reforms to their utility industries (often under considerable pressure from the international lending community), they have been repeatedly plagued by public discontent with resultant price increases, loss of patronage jobs, and the profitability of firms retained to improve performance (Kessides 2004). At the heart of this issue is the need to strike a fundamental balance between the provision of efficient, reliable, and equitable services and the need for revenues sufficient to sustain the systems. The public and private sectors together need to align profit-seeking with social welfare in the provision of basic services.

The Public-Private Partnership

The role of PPPs in infrastructure projects varies, depending on the nature of the contractual arrangements that dictate the level of private involvement and the way in which risks are assumed by the public and private participants. There are several issues that must be considered in choosing the type of PPP arrangement to use, including the following:

- How are user fees determined? Who sets them? How are increases imposed? (In some cases, given the political ramifications, it might be preferable *not* to have the public sector involved directly in setting user fees.)
- Is there a mechanism for building local capacity to construct, service, and maintain the utility structures and distribution network?
- Is there a clear designation responsibility for upkeep and maintenance? Does that assigned party have the knowledge and skills necessary?
- Were the demand projections for the infrastructure services accurate? (Basing anticipated revenues on overly optimistic demand projections may lead to inadequate funding for maintenance and operations, underutilization of the utility, and inefficient generation.)

The following terms refer to commonly used partnership agreements,[10] and the varying levels of private-sector risk that are implicit in each option.

- *Design-Build (DB):*[11] The private sector designs and builds infrastructure to meet public sector performance specifications, often for a fixed price, so the risk of cost overruns is transferred to the private sector.
- *Operation & Maintenance Contract (O&M):* A private operator, under contract, operates a publicly owned asset for a specified term. Ownership of the asset remains with the public entity.
- *Design-Build-Finance-Operate (DBFO):* The private sector designs, finances, and constructs a new facility under a long-term lease, and operates the facility during the term of the lease. The private

partner transfers the new facility to the public sector at the end of the lease term.

- *Build-Own-Operate (BOO):* The private sector finances, builds, owns, and operates a facility or service in perpetuity. The public constraints are stated in the original agreement and through ongoing regulatory authority.
- *Build-Own-Operate-Transfer (BOOT or, more commonly, BOT):* A private entity receives a franchise to finance, design, build, and operate a facility (and to charge user fees) for a specified period, after which ownership is transferred back to the public sector.
- *Buy-Build-Operate (BBO):* Transfer of a public asset to a private or quasi-public entity usually under contract that the assets are to be upgraded and operated for a specified period of time. Public control is exercised through the contract at the time of transfer.
- *Finance Only:* On behalf of the public entity, a private entity, usually a financial services company, funds a project directly or uses various mechanisms such as a long-term lease or bond issue.
- *Concession Agreement:* An agreement between a government and a private entity that grants the private entity the right to operate, maintain, and collect user fees for an existing publicly owned asset in exchange for an up-front fee and sometimes a share of revenues. Although ownership usually does not transfer, certain rights of ownership may.

Design-Build (DB) and Operations and Maintenance (O&M) contracts and other methods shown at the top of the list above are primarily contracting or financing approaches and do not include the full range of services implied in a PPP. The most common applications for infrastructure PPPs are the Design-Build-Finance-Operate (DBFO) that some consider a variant of the Build-Own-Operate-Transfer (BOOT or BOT) for greenfield projects, and the long-term concession that has proven popular in the United States for existing or brownfield facilities (e.g., the Chicago Skyway and the Indiana Toll Road). The choice of approach will depend in part on the objectives of the public partner, the ability of the government to fund portions of the project from the central budget, and local capacity to manage complex procurements. For example, it might be advantageous for both sides for the public sector to take back ownership of the facility prior to it being placed in service and in which case, a Build-Transfer-Operate (BTO) arrangement might be devised (Levy 1996).

A major issue with PPPs is who actually sets the level of tolls or other user charges and how far and fast they are permitted to rise.

Owing to the natural monopoly characteristics of most infrastructure systems, the public sector must maintain a role in the process lest the problems connected with water service in Cochabamba be repeated continuously. In well-structured PPP agreements, initial fees are usually established jointly and permitted to increase in accordance with predetermined schedules according to inflation or some other economic marker. From a political standpoint, it is actually to the benefit of the public entity *not* to be involved in the direct setting of tolls and the resultant political risk.

In all of these arrangements, the private partner is responsible for operating the facility or system for a period of time, which can be extremely beneficial if the public sector partner does not have access to skilled individuals to perform the necessary technical, administrative, and financial tasks. However, a shortcoming of these methods is that absent a specific requirement to provide training to the local public workforce, these agreements will not build indigenous capacity to operate and maintain the systems once the contract term is fulfilled. Excellent returns on investment to the enterprise for training in the developing world have been well documented (Almeida and Carneiro 2006), and this would appear to be a desirable outcome of a PPP arrangement. Otherwise, once the private contractors leave, the physical plant can quickly fall into disrepair and possibly go out of service.

The Role of Project Finance

The key to most PPP ventures is the use of project finance to structure a highly leveraged arrangement of debt and equity. Typically, the private partner will bring a fraction (often as little as 10 percent) of the total cost of the project to the deal as its equity share and raise the remaining 90 percent through commercial loans and other sources. The private-sector partner usually participates through a "project finance entity" or Special Purpose Vehicle (SPV) especially created to take full advantage of the nonrecourse nature of project finance. That is, the private sector pledges only the revenue to be generated by the project as security for the debt. These revenues may be in the form of tolls or other direct user fees, availability charges where the private partner is compensated for the time the facility is available for service in acceptable condition, or "shadow tolls" paid by the government partner in lieu of direct charges to the user. Shadow tolls are based on actual vehicle counts from sensors and are charged based on a predetermined pricing schedule. They have been used for roads in Finland, Spain, and Portugal and are primarily a way to shift usage risk onto the facility operator. Their effectiveness has been questioned because they decouple the use of a facility from its cost, which can send the wrong signal to the user (Grimsey and Lewis 2004). In either case, these revenues alone are used to retire the debt and create returns to equity. In the event that the project defaults or experiences other difficulties or liabilities, the SPV alone is responsible; the parent organizations have no obligation to honor the debt or otherwise be accountable for the performance of the project. This aspect of PPP arrangements can become problematic if significant cost overruns occur or projected user volumes fail to materialize.

For example, Flyvbjerg, Holm, and Buhl (2005) have shown that these conditions occur in many rail and toll road projects. However, because of the limited liability inherent in the SPV, even if projects experience serious financial difficulties, the potential loss of equity may not be sufficient to compel the private partner to prevent default. This is particularly true if the SPV is comprised of several private parties whose equity share might be quite small compared to the overall cost of the project. For example, the equity investment or "at risk" capital of five equal-equity partners in a $1 billion project could be as little as $20 million. Although this is not a trivial amount, it does represent the upper bound on the financial risk faced by the private partners. Recently, the SPV formed to repair and renovate two lines of the London Underground (Metronet) declared bankruptcy rather that take on the additional risk posed by rapidly escalating project costs (UKHCTC 2008). The public partner here (the U.K. government) can certainly be considered a sophisticated player in these arrangements, but this was still not sufficient to prevent the deal from going bad and the private partner walking away. However, in this case, the members of the SPV can hardly be considered "damaged" considering that

it is most likely that overall the shareholders may not have lost any money on the PPP at all (e.g. 20% of £2 billion is £400 mn.)!! It will be just that they—the shareholders—have made less money on the PPP than they had originally hoped! Blaiklock (2008)

When Should Governments Consider a PPP?

In making the decision about whether or not to use a PPP, governments often use the "value for money" (VFM)[12] analysis. This exercise is intended to determine whether the "best" model for service provision is via public or private delivery, or some combination of the two.

However, a very real limitation of the VFM analysis is that it fails to take into account social and other nonfinancial objectives that public sector policy-makers must address. For example, if cost reductions (and higher VFM scores) are achieved by reducing the benefits paid to workers, eliminating subsidies to low-income customers, or canceling community outreach, then this method would not be the most desirable from a social welfare perspective.

Although there are those who would argue that, subject to a favorable VFM analysis, almost everything within the realm of civil infrastructure should be considered a potential PPP, experience has shown that this is an overly optimistic view of this project delivery vehicle. For example, the assumptions developed early in the life of a project, such as construction cost, projected use, acceptable fee structures, cost of capital, are subject to considerable volatility. A fluctuation of a few basis points in the cost of commercial credit (or its sudden unavailability as during the 2008 credit crisis) can have a measurable and substantive impact on the fees that must be collected through tolls, user charges, or availability payments. If fees must consequently be set so high that use is negatively impacted, the financial viability of the overall project could be affected.

With so many potential caveats, why should private participation in public infrastructure services be considered at all? If capital markets are functioning well, the public sector should be able to raise the necessary capital, build, and operate the desired infrastructure economically and efficiently, and provide reliable service at a fair price. However, developing economies often lack expertise, stability, and access to capital that would make public provision possible. In addition, they may lack the knowledge and expertise to construct and maintain the facilities and distribution network, and fee-setting may become politicized, resulting in too little revenue to cover costs. It may also be more politically acceptable to provide infrastructure on a fee-for-service basis rather than diverting limited funds from the central budget. The following sections discuss some of the factors that influence whether a PPP is appropriate for a project under consideration and some of the issues that influence how these arrangements perform in practice.

Risk Management

Public-private partnerships are subject to a broader range of risks than more routine procurements, and the identification and management of risks is at the core of the design of any PPP (Estache, Juan, and Trujillo

2007) In fact, one of the strongest arguments for the PPP delivery model is that the various project risks are transferred to the party best able to manage them. Some of the more common risks to a PPP project include the following:

- *Political risks*, such as the unanticipated change in government, cancellation of a concession, unanticipated tax increases, arbitrary toll or fee imposition or increases, or new and unilateral regulatory policies;
- *Construction risks*, such as incorrect or inappropriate design, delays in land acquisition or escalation of land costs, project delays, unanticipated site conditions, or poor contractor performance;
- *Operation and maintenance risks*, such as the physical condition of a concession facility, operator's incompetence, poor construction quality;
- *Legal and contractual risks*, such as the concession warranty, or incomplete or inadequate contracts;
- *Income risks*, such as inaccurate estimates of traffic volume or revenue, construction of a competing facility that would reduce use or profitability;
- *Financial risks*, such as inflation, local currency devaluation and difficulties in conversion to hard currency, interest rate fluctuations, changes in monetary policies, highly leveraged positions; and,
- *Force majeure*, such as war, natural disasters, extreme weather conditions, and terrorism.

The assignment of risk would be most efficiently determined by considering the degree of influence and control over policy variables and circumstances held by the parties. For example, the government should bear the risk of future legislation discriminating against the project, while the private partner should be expected to control construction risk. If neither party can assume all of the risk, then risk allocation should be based on the price the private party will charge to take on the risk and whether the government is able and willing to pay that price. Many of the problems ascribed to PPPs can be found rooted in poor risk allocation such as when governments try to shift all of the usage or revenue risk for a new facility to the private party. This can be done, but then the private partner will set fees and returns accordingly that may require user charges that are too high to be sustainable or acceptable. For some risks, private insurance provision may be the best management strategy. The key to risk management lies within the concept of partnership. If risk can be transparently identified, equitably allocated,

Table 3.2 Ranking of Relative Political Risk Factors *within* Selected Asian Countries

	Currency Inconvertibility and Transfer Restrictions	Expropriation	Breach of Contract	Political Violence	Legal, Regulatory and Bureaucratic Risks	Nongovernmental Actions/ Outside Risks
Bangladesh	1	4	3	6	2	5
Cambodia	1	4	3	6	2	5
China	4	3	2	6	1	5
India	5	6	2	4	1	3
Indonesia	4	6	2	3	1	5
Japan	5/6	no risk	2	3	2	1
S. Korea	6	5	3	4	2	1
Malaysia	1	4	3	6	2	5
Philippines	1	5	3	5	4	2
Singapore	6	5	3	4	2	1
Taiwan	6	4	4	3	2	1
Thailand	5	2	6	3	1	2
Vietnam	1	5	3	6	4	5
Asia, excluding Japan, Korea, & Singapore	2		3	6	1	4
Japan, Korea, Singapore	6	5	3	4	2	1

Note: highest risk for that country = 1; lowest risk for that country = 6.

and valued appropriately, successful projects will result. If the objective is just to shift risk away from one party to the other, success will be much less likely.

The importance of political stability to the success of PPP projects cannot be overstated. In a comparative assessment of BOT transportation projects in Asia, Tam (1999) described three tunnel projects constructed in Hong Kong during the 1970s, 1980s, and 1990s. All were completed ahead of schedule and within budget. The Hong Kong government took a major equity position (20 percent) in the Cross Harbor Tunnel that was completed in 1972, but was able to reduce its equity participation to zero by the time the Western-Harbor Crossing was completed in 1997. The success of these projects contrasts sharply with experience in Thailand during the 1990s. Thailand attempted to have two toll roads and an urban rail project delivered using BOT arrangements obtained through public tenders, but all projects experienced difficulties due to government instability and currency fluctuations.[13] Although the projects were all completed eventually, the political risks translated into serious financial impediments to the projects (Tam 1999). Sachs, Tiong, and Wang (2007) have ranked relative risks that various Asian countries face, based on a survey of public and private individuals and institutions.[14] Their results are presented in Table 3.2.

Developing economies are more vulnerable to certain types of risk, such as political, currency, and natural hazards, than they are to other categories of risk, and the results are likely to be more deeply felt than in the more developed world where the systems are generally more insulated from or resilient to various shocks. Currency fluctuations pose significant risk in that project revenues will be in local currencies rather than more readily convertible foreign exchange. Unrelated crises also can serve as focusing moments for those opposed to market-based reforms and counterreform movements have emerged from them (Henisz, Holburn, and Zelner 2005).

Abednego and Ogunlana (2006) note that the inability to control all aspects of risk properly is a key factor in poor project performance and believe that proper risk allocation can be achieved only if decision-makers consider the type of risk (what) to be allocated, which party should accept the risk (who), when to allocate the risk, as well as application of proper strategy to prevent or minimize its consequences (how). Figure 3.5 illustrates their useful concept of risk allocation.

Given the difficulties that many developing country governments have in managing the large and complex risks associated with the financing and construction of major infrastructure projects, isn't the

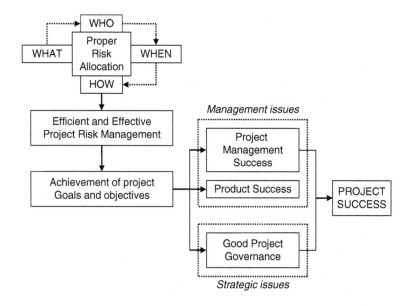

Figure 3.5 Effects of Proper Risk Allocation on Project Success
Source: Abednego and Ogunlana 2006

argument for more private participation and risk-sharing obvious? The real issue isn't whether a PPP leads to some private risk-sharing, but the extent to which risks are actually borne by the participants who have some control over the outcome. Several recent studies suggest that risk transfer to the private sector may be less complete than is often claimed. Bloomfield (2006) reports on a sewer project in Massachusetts where the contract that was ultimately negotiated left the performance risk with the customer rather than the with the contractor, the party who had a much stronger influence on performance. Hodge and Greve (2007: 549) in a literature review note that

> it is one of the surprises of the existing PPP literature to find that for the size of the financial commitments to PPPs being entered into by governments around the globe, the evidence on cost and quality gains for techniques such as PFI[Private Finance Initiatives] seems limited.

Finally, in an assessment of experience with PPP projects in the United States and Canada, Vining, Boardman, and Poschmann (2005) note that in two decidedly successful Canadian projects (the Highway 407 Express

Toll Route and the Confederation Bridge), the government, rather than the project SPV, ultimately assumed the project's financial risks. A more recent analysis of ten Canadian PPPs shows that the private partner is unwilling to take on high levels of cost risk when the revenue risk is also high (Vining and Boardman 2008). This raises a question of the benefits of risk transfer in a PPP if it apparently occurs so infrequently. A definitive answer to this question lies beyond the scope of this chapter, but the effectiveness and value of risk transfer is certainly an issue demanding attention during the negotiation phase of a PPP.

Although risk is ubiquitous to all PPPs and infrastructure projects in general, developing countries face additional risks to project success because they are often less likely to have mature regulatory and adjudication structures that are widely acknowledged to be essential to successful implementation. The relatively high transaction costs of PPP projects, absence of uniform regulatory structures, and the asymmetry of public and private capabilities in the developing world are cited as major factors in the frequent, and often detrimental, renegotiation of infrastructure concessions (Guasch 2004).

Infrastructure privatization has been promoted as part of a suite of neoliberal business practices aimed at promoting entrepreneurship, investment, and long-term growth along with market-based reforms of SOEs. This agenda was also advanced by the World Bank, which made a commitment to market-oriented reform a prerequisite for project lending (Henisz, Zelner, and Guillén 2005). These same authors conclude that unfortunately

> privatization of state-owned utilities coupled with de jure regulatory reform only, and unaccompanied by any true competition, imbues private (and often foreign) investors with unchecked market power and is thus likely to have a deleterious effect on consumers and citizens...the current backlash against neoliberalism in many parts of the world is driven partly by the fact that local and foreign investors have benefited disproportionately and sometimes at the expense of consumers.

The Public Interest

"Protecting the public interest" has become a mantra of those who demand accountability from the PPP process, but this catchphrase means different things to different people. Ortiz, Buxbaum, and Little (2007) examined recent experience with the concession model in the United States and found that most concerns with "the public interest" could be distilled down to whether the presence of the private sector in the transaction would cause system users to pay more than they would have under a public provision model. The general perception, underscored by articles in the popular press, is that revenue-based projects, operated by any entity other than a government agency, will somehow cost more and provide a lower level of service. At the same time, upfront concession payments and the ability to move infrastructure costs off the books remain attractive lures to public officials concerned with dwindling revenue streams and out-of-balance budgets—the same decision-drivers found in the developing world. Those opposed to any private involvement in the delivery of "public" services see price gouging as an inevitable outcome of these arrangements. A legitimate question to ask is whether the public interest is well served by a system where prices are kept artificially so low as to preclude the delivery of safe, reliable services and where sufficient revenue cannot be generated to support routine maintenance, repair, and renovation.[15]

For example, despite arguments that water is too necessary to life to be priced or treated as anything other than a public good, "free" water comes with its own costs. In Dar es Salaam, Tanzania, water was historically subsidized and provided below cost. In addition to the negative impacts of such policies on capital investment in the system, these practices actually hurt the very people they were intended to help. By reducing revenues to a level below which system expansion and improvement can occur, the availability to poor people of even marginally purified water is also reduced, leaving them the undesirable options of using more expensive or unsanitary sources (McKague and Branzei 2007).

Although there are definitely social and moral questions regarding what constitutes equitable charges for the basic building blocks of civil society and necessities of life, these questions do not obviate the fundamental reality that projects and services must be paid for, if not directly, by some or all of the users, than by the larger "public." There is no way to finesse this issue over the long term. Civil infrastructure must be supported by revenue streams, generated either by taxes or by fees that are paid to a service provider, whether public or private (Little 2008). The affordability issue is often raised as an argument against cost recovery in the developing world, but Foster and Yepes (2006) have shown that at least in Latin America there does not appear to be a major affordability problem except for those in the poorest quartile. They partially explain this by the fact that cost recovery in Latin America is influenced more by the lower local prices than by international prices,[16] whereas in other parts of the world, international prices play a bigger role. Although they opine that targeted safety nets for utility services can help to balance the objectives of cost recovery and social protection, the international nature of most PPP consortia (and their need to calculate returns in readily convertible currencies) could exacerbate affordability concerns in some poorer countries.

Whether the provider is in the public or private sector should be primarily based on whether the customers receive good value for their money. Several recent assessments have demonstrated somewhat mixed results in this regard (see Hodge and Greve 2007, Vining, Boardman, and Poschmann 2005, Vining and Boardman 2008). Vining and Boardman (2008) indicate that for a suite of Canadian PPP projects representing several sectors, the total costs (production costs and all contracting costs) did not differ appreciably from what might have been achieved under a more traditional publicly financed design-build approach. The higher transaction costs of PPPs are ascribed to inherent goal conflicts between the public and private partners and the unwillingness of the private partner to take on high levels of cost and revenue risk.

If PPPs are going to serve as a useful model for the developing world (and the developed world, for that matter), there needs to be a robust set of metrics that can capture the essence of the arrangement, and quickly and transparently convey to all interested parties whether the venture has been a "success," however one wishes to define it. Success in a PPP needs to be carefully defined and based on the input of all stakeholders in the process. PPPs developed to date have notably lacked the input of the user community who will actually pay for the services. The details usually are explained after the fact (if at all) which is fertile ground for the skepticism and mistrust that inevitably seems to follow.

How the local community views private participation in infrastructure will also determine whether it believes its interests are being protected. Typically, the equity partner in a PPP will be an international consortium of engineering, construction, utility operations, finance, and legal firms. The debt component will likely be provided by an international lending institution. Both of these entities, but particularly the SPV, will exert considerable influence on the provision of local services. Increasingly, in an era of dedicated global infrastructure investment funds, urban infrastructure is becoming little more than a financial product subject to what Torrance (2008) speaks of as "glocal" governance, where local stakeholder concerns will not be the first priority. Thus, financial decisions made a continent or half a world away will have very real and personal local impacts. To the extent that this strikes the locals as reminiscent colonialism, and this could strongly influence their reaction to the PPP arrangement.

Empirical research suggests that this is not a binary decision process; that is, to turn to a private concession or retain public operations. In countries with a high level of political risk, it may be difficult or impossible to attract private capital to marginal projects. In such cases, it might best pursue a strategy of seeking local private investment or NGO support. This trend toward local and regional, as opposed to international, investment was noted by Kikeri and Kolo (2005). They cite four privatizations of electric utilities where the investors were from Malaysia, Brazil, Hong Kong, and Thailand.

It also is not clear what the long-term impact of the U.S. mortgage-backed security crisis (and its spillovers) will have on the availability of commercial credit to finance infrastructure PPPs. However, given the important role that debt plays in project finance, it is likely that uncertainty will persist at least until the crisis is resolved. This may create further opportunities for local and regional participation in these projects, possibly marrying foreign technical expertise with local and regional investment capital.

The Future of PPPs in the Developing World

For a variety of financial and public policy reasons, it appears that PPPs will be an infrastructure provision option in the developing world for the foreseeable future. However, as governments increasingly rely on private initiative to improve infrastructure provision and increase efficiency to achieve public policy goals, they will need to consider both the possibilities and pitfalls of privatization (World Bank 1996).

A benefit of private participation in infrastructure is that private financial incentives replace more diffuse systems of accountability under government ownership. However, even where operations are technically efficient, monopoly pricing can lead to allocations of a society's resources just as inefficient as public provision. Thus, competition in the marketplace is a highly desirable complement to private incentives, and even if *competition for customers* is not feasible owing to the presence of a single network, it is possible to foster *competition to provide the service* under a concession. Where competition is unable to provide the required market discipline, regulation may be necessary; however regulatory bodies must, above all else, be perceived as fair and not captive to special interest groups seeking to tilt the system to their benefit. Private financial markets should also produce more accountability than that provided through oversight of governmental budgets. However, PPPs usually have some public financing component (even if only the financial risk retained by the government), and the relationship between government and private financing in a project should be transparent and readily accessible.

Overall if PPP arrangements are to prove beneficial to all of the parties involved, at a minimum, some guidelines need to be developed, adopted, and implemented. Guiding principles for a PPP should include the following:

- Participation, by all involved parties, needs to be informed and organized.
- The "Rule of Law" must be in place so that fair and equitable legal frameworks are enforced impartially.
- All decisions and their implementation must be transparent to the public and abide by established rules and regulations. Information must be freely available and directly accessible to those who will be affected by the decisions.
- The process must be consensus oriented, responsive to the needs of all stakeholders, and equitable.
- The project should be effective and efficient, producing results that meet the needs of the local society while making the best and sustainable use of available resources.
- All project participants must be accountable to those who will be affected by their decisions or actions.

Contract law is the vehicle by which the performance requirements and accountability standards for a PPP are defined and enforced. This is a compelling argument for the PPP structure as opposed to the more "flexible" public policy statements and performance goals that normally define the performance of the public sector. However, all contracts are imperfect to some degree (Hart and Moore 1988, Hart 2003), and here again, the asymmetry in skill sets between the public and private sector is glaring. In addition, although contracts are generally binding instruments where the "Rule of Law" is in place, actually achieving performance through contract enforcement can be costly, time-consuming, and politically embarrassing to the public sector organizations that negotiated it. The overall ability or willingness of developing countries in particular to underwrite these high transaction costs is open to some question.

Conclusion

Globally, the world's 20 largest private equity infrastructure funds now have nearly US$130 billion under management, 77 percent of it raised in 2006 and 2007. Taking into account leverage, a billion dollars of equity funding could, in some situations, pay for up to $10 billion in projects (Palter, Walder, and Westlake 2008). The need in the developing world for infrastructure and the capital to build and maintain it will continue to grow with increasing population and rising expectations. Revenue-supported infrastructure projects are attractive to the investment community because, properly structured, they can produce stable, long-term returns to equity that are particularly attractive to pension funds and other income-oriented investment vehicles. These factors would appear to support an optimistic forecast for the future of PPP arrangements in the developing world.

However, as has been described here, there are many challenges to the successful application of the PPP model broadly, and in particular, in the developing world. The ultimate success of PPPs in the nations most in need of private investment will depend on the degree to which the issues discussed in this chapter can be addressed to the benefit of both parties. In particular, the question of equitable, universal access to basic services must be resolved. In addition, promoting competition among providers in the bidding process can help hold down prices and spur efficiency gains. Given their lack of negotiation experience with PPPs, however, leaders in the developing world are probably least able to secure an equal bargaining position with their potential partners from the private sector. Thus, the acquisition of knowledge and capacity building in negotiation skills, either indigenous to the countries involved or through trusted NGO representation, is a critical step to placing both parties on an equal footing in negotiating service contracts or concession agreements.

For its part, the developing world must seek to provide stability to the international financial community if the investment capital so needed is to be provided. Although the private sector is viewed overall as risk-taking, considerations of prudence, regulation, and shareholder oversight all dictate that risk be minimized to the extent possible. Both public and private participants must share these risks in a transparent manner. Ultimately, the question for both sides in PPP negotiation to answer is whether the public or private sectors (or some combination) are best positioned to deliver reliable, equitably priced, and universally accessible services to the public at large. In cases where the private sector

can do so at lower overall cost and make a profit at the same time, a PPP
should be the preferred method of provision.

Notes

1. PPPs are a policy option available to governments for the provision of basic
   services (e.g., health, transportation) that seeks to involve the private sector. As such, they are an alternative to traditional full public provision of
   those services, particularly where the services are private in their nature
   and government resources are limited (UNESCAP 2008).
2. Estache, Perelman, and Trujillo (2005) believe that "privatization" is an
   excessive word when it comes to public services. The actual sale of public
   assets to private operators has been relatively common only in some dimensions of the electricity generation, telecoms, and the service component of
   the transport sector. In most other segments of the business, concession
   contracts, licenses, or leases have ensured the continuation of public property of the assets in the long run.
3. The U.S. experience was mixed. Regulation of privately owned enterprise
   was favored in the electricity, natural gas, and telecommunication sectors
   while highways and water and sewerage were mostly in public ownership
   (Jacobson and Tarr 1996).
4. Interestingly, privatization has continued apace and probably accelerated
   under the Labour governments of both Tony Blair and Gordon Brown.
5. For example, the recently completed report of U.S. National Surface
   Transportation and Revenue Study Commission (2007) in noting the
   inability of the U.S. Highway Trust Fund to generate sufficient revenues to
   meet projected demand identified PPP as a potentially significant funding
   source.
6. See Nellis and Birdsall (2005).
7. Regulatory reform refers to actions to improve entry, market-based price
   setting, and establish an independent regulator, separate from a ministry
   and from the operator.
8. Some of these incidents are described in Nellis and Birdsall (2005).
9. Bottleneck facilities are essential infrastructure components to which all
   potential private competitors must have equal access if they are to compete
   fairly.
10. See Canadian Council for Public Private Partnerships (2007).
11. Design-Build is a contracting method that is at the heart of private pro-
    vision of infrastructure, but many do not consider DB a formal PPP
    strategy.
12. "Value for money" (VFM) is a term used to assess whether an organization
    has obtained the maximum benefit from the goods and services it both
    acquires and provides, within the resources available to it. Achieving VFM
    can be described in terms of economy (careful use of resources to save

expense, time, or effort), efficiency (delivering the same level of service for less cost, time, or effort), and effectiveness (delivering a better service or getting a better return for the same amount of expense, time, or effort).

13. During this period, the average longevity of a government in Thailand was about one year. Following execution of the contract for the rail systems, the government changed by means of a coup, two controversial elections, and the ousting of a military junta.

14. Table 3.2 indicates which risks are judged to be more important for that country, compared to other risks; it is not comparing the riskiness of one country with the others.

15. The previously cited report of the U.S. National Surface Transportation and Revenue Study Commission (2007) found that the chronic revenue shortfalls besetting the U.S. Interstate Highway System are partially the result of not indexing fuel excise taxes (the major source of revenue to the Highway Trust Fund) to inflation and the rapidly rising costs of construction.

16. This is apparently due to purchasing power parity across economies in Latin America where there are larger middle-income countries than in other regions of the developing world.

References

Abednego, M.P. and S.O. Ogunlana. 2006. Good project governance for proper risk allocation in public-private partnerships in Indonesia. *International Journal of Project Management.* 24: 622–634.

Almeida, R. and P. Carneiro. 2006. The return to firm investment in human capital. Policy Research Working Paper No. 3851. Washington, DC: World Bank.

Blaiklock, T.M. 2008. Memorandum from T. Martin Blaiklock (PPP 02) Written evidence in the London underground and the public-private partnership agreements: Second report of session 2007–2008, House of Commons, Transport Committee, London: The Stationary Office Ltd.

Bloomfield, P. 2006. The challenging business of long-term public-private partnerships: Reflections on local experience. *Public Administration Review* 66(3): 400–411.

Boycko, M., A. Shlezfer, and R.W. Vishny. 1996. A theory of privatisation. *The Economic Journal* 106: 309–319.

Brocklehurst, Clarissa, C.B. Evans, and R. Mukami Kariuki. 2003. New designs for water and sanitation transactions: Making private sector participation work. water and sanitation program and public-private infrastructure advisory facility. Washington, DC: World Bank.

Business Week. 2005. Now that's a liquid investment, April 18.

Canadian Council for Public Private Partnerships. http://www.pppcouncil.ca/aboutPPP_definition.asp. Accessed November 16, 2007.

Estache, A., E. Juan, and L. Trujillo. 2007. Public-private partnerships in transport. Policy Research Working Paper No. 4436. Washington, DC: World Bank.

Estache, A., S. Perelman, and L. Trujillo. 2005. Infrastructure performance and reform in developing and transition economies: Evidence from a survey of productivity measures. Policy Research Working Paper No. 3514. Washington, DC: World Bank.

Flyvbjerg, B., M. Holm, and S. Buhl. 2005. How inaccurate are demand forecasts in public works projects? The case of transportation. *Journal of the American Planning Association* 71(2): 131–144.

Foster, V. and T. Yepes. 2006. Is cost recovery a feasible objective for water and electricity? The Latin American experience. Policy Research Working Paper No. 3943. Washington, DC: World Bank.

Foster, V., E.R. Tiongson, and C.R. Laderchi. 2005. Utility reforms. In *Analyzing the distributional impact of reforms*, Vol.1, ed. A. Coudouel and S. Paternostro. Washington, DC: The World Bank.

Grimsey, D. and M.K. Lewis. 2004. *Public private partnerships: The worldwide revolution in infrastructure provision and private finance*. Cheltenham, UK: Edward Elgar Publishing.

Guasch, J.L. 2004. *Granting and renegotiating infrastructure concessions: Doing it right*. Washington, DC: World Bank.

Hart, O. 2003. Incomplete contracts and public ownership: Remarks, and an application to public-private partnerships. *The Economic Journal* 113(March): C69–C76.

Hart, O. and J. Moore. 1988. Incomplete contracts and renegotiation. *Econometrica* 56(4): 755–785.

Henisz, W.J., G.L.F. Holburn, and B.A. Zelner. 2005. Deinstitutionalization and institutional replacement: State-centered and neo-liberal models in the global electricity supply industry. World Bank Policy Research Working Paper No. 3690, August. Available at SSRN. http://ssrn.com/abstract=801446.

Henisz, W.J., B.A. Zelner, and M.F. Guillén. 2005. The worldwide diffusion of market-oriented infrastructure reform, 1977–1999. *American Sociological Review* 70(6): 871–897.

Hodge, G.A. and C. Greve. 2007. Public-private partnerships: An international performance review. *Public Administration Review* 67(3): 545–558.

Jacobson, C.D. and J.A. Tarr. 1996. No single path: Ownership and financing of infrastructure in the 19th and 20th centuries. In *Infrastructure delivery: Private initiative and the public good*, ed. Ashoka Mody. Washington, DC: World Bank.

Kessides, I.N. 2004. *Reforming infrastructure: Privatization, regulation, and competition*. Washington, DC: World Bank.

Kikeri, S. and A.F. Kolo. 2005. Privatization: Trends and recent developments. World Bank Policy Research Working Paper No. 3765. Washington, DC: World Bank, November.

Levy, Sidney M. 1996. *Build, operate, transfer: Paving the way for tomorrow's infrastructure*. New York: John Wiley & Sons.

Little, Richard G. 2008. Time to ask the infrastructure funding question. *San Francisco Chronicle,* March 5.

McKague, K. and O. Branzei. 2007. City water Tanzania(A): Water partnerships for Dar es Salaam. Richard Ivey School of Business. Case Study 907M25. London, Ontario, Canada: Ivey Publishing.

Megginson, W.L. and J.M. Netter. 2001. From state to market: A survey of empirical studies on privatization. *Journal of Economic Literature* 39: 321–389.

Nellis, John and Nancy Birdsall, eds. 2005. *Reality check: The distributional impact of privatization in developing countries.* Washington, DC: Center for Global Development.

Ortiz, I.N., J.N. Buxbaum, and R. Little. 2008. Protecting the public interest: The role of long-term concession agreements for providing transportation infrastructure. Proceedings of the 84th Annual Meeting of the Transportation Research Board. Washington, DC: National Academies Press.

Palter, R.N., J. Walder, and S. Westlake. 2008. How investors can get more out of infrastructure. *The McKinsey Quarterly,* February.

Rondinelli, Dennis and Max Iacono. 1996. *Policies and institutions for managing privatization.* International Training Centre, International Labor Organization, Turin, Italy.

Sachs, T., R. Tiong, and S.Q. Wang. 2007. Analysis of political risks and opportunities in public private partnerships (PPP) in China and selected Asian countries: Survey results. *Chinese Management Studies* 1(2): 126–148.

Tam, C.M. 1999. Build-operate-transfer model for infrastructure developments in Asia: Reasons for successes and failures. *International Journal of Project Management.* 19(6): 377–382.

Torrance, M.I. 2008. Forging glocal governance? Urban infrastructure as networked financial products. *International Journal of Urban and Regional Research* 32(1): 1–21.

United Kingdom House of Commons, Transport Committee (UKHCTC). 2008. The London underground and the public-private partnership agreements: Second report of session 2007–2008. London: The Stationary Office Ltd.

United Nations. 2000. Millennium development goals, Goal 7, Ensure environmental sustainability. http://www.un.org/millenniumgoals/. Accessed February 12, 2008.

United Nations Economic and Social Commission for Asia and the Pacific (UNESCAP). 2007. Public-private partnerships in infrastructure development: An introduction to issues from different perspectives. Prepared for the High-level Expert Group Meeting Jointly organized by UNESCAP and the Ministry of Planning and Budget, Republic of Korea, October 2–4, 2007, Seoul. http://www.unescap.org/ttdw/common/TPT/PPP/text/ppps_infrastructure_development.pdf. Accessed March 23, 2008.

U.S. National Surface Transportation and Revenue Study Commission. 2007. *Transportation for tomorrow.* http://www.transportationfortomorrow.org/final_report/. Accessed March 15, 2008.

Vining, A.A. and A.E. Boardman. 2008. Public-private partnerships in Canada: Theory and evidence. *Canadian Public Administration* 51(1): 9–44.

Vining, A.A., A.E. Boardman, and F. Poschmann. 2006. Public-private partnerships in the U.S. and Canada: There are no "free lunches." *Journal of Comparative Policy Analysis* 7(3): 1–22.

World Bank. 1996. *Infrastructure delivery: Private initiative and the public good*, ed. Ashoka Mody. Washington, DC: World Bank.

———. 2007. Private activity in infrastructure continued its recovery in 2006, *Private Participation in Infrastructure Database*. http://ppi.worldbank.org/features/Nov2007/2006GlobalDataLaunch.pdf. Accessed March 29, 2008.

CHAPTER 4

Infrastructure Development in India and China: A Comparative Analysis

M. Julie Kim and Rita Nangia

Introduction

Global interest in India and China, the two Asian giants, is more than mere curiosity. Never before have such large economies with combined population of 2.3 billion grown so fast for so long (World Bank 2007a). For the last two decades, both India and China have grown at twice the global rate. If this trend continues for next few decades, with their vast labor supply, favorable demographics, and aspirations for reaching the developed world per capita income and consumption standards, these economies can be expected to have a significant impact on the world economy. A large number of studies on China and India focus on comparing sources of economic growth, poverty reduction and inequality issues, political structures, policy and institutional reform processes, trade, or foreign direct investment policies in these two economies. Infrastructure, with its critical input in this spectacular performance, remains in the background. This chapter aims to contribute to the ongoing comparative analyses of these two economies in infrastructure development.

Asian Infrastructure Model—Building Ahead of Demand

Asia has always recognized the role of infrastructure in creating wealth. Archeological evidence points to the exchange of goods between Mesopotamia and the Indian and the Chinese territories between 7500 and 4000 BC. The Silk Road created prosperous clusters of towns and trading posts while connecting Asia and Europe through the Middle East (Kuroda et al. 2007). In more recent history, Asian nations were openly trading with each other long before Europeans arrived in the region. After World War II, the four Asian tigers (Korea, Taiwan, Singapore, and Hong Kong) reported strong growth driven by trade, investments, and infrastructure. The Asian tigers—followed closely by Malaysia, China, and, the most recent entrant to this group, Vietnam—adopted a development model in which manufacturing and exports were key drivers of their economic performance. These governments recognized that export competitiveness and manufacturing require connectivity to the global economy and, as a result, infrastructure development was propelled by a substantial and sustained drive supported by the government. Top leaders and senior policy-makers in these countries were intimately involved in developing comprehensive sector strategies, and they guided (and, in some sense, controlled) how the strategies were implemented and resources allocated (Mody 1997). Not all countries followed a uniform path. In each country, different sectors developed approaches suited for the particular tasks at hand. The most remarkable common factor behind the success of infrastructure in these countries was the single-minded goal of sustaining economic growth and recognition of the importance of infrastructure development in achieving this goal. China has followed the path of these fast growing economies, building impressive infrastructure at lightning speed. China's unparalleled growth and poverty reduction in the past two decades has gone hand in hand with the development of infrastructure stemming from its export-led strategy. India, the other "giant" in Asia, did not follow suit with the successful Asian infrastructure model in building ahead of demand. Its development strategy from time to time focused on redistribution of wealth rather than on growth.

Though China and India began economic liberalization almost at the same time in the late 1970s and early 1980s, China today with its $2.2 trillion dollar economy stands much taller than India. Since 1990, China has posted an average rate of growth of 10 percent, one of the highest in modern history (see table 4.1). China is also remarkably open—exports and imports together account for almost three-fourths of China's economy, a share that significantly exceeds that of other newly industrialized economies.[1] Although India has made significant progress in recent years, its share of global trade has been relatively small compared to that of China, partly because of its average tariff rates that remain relatively high.

Table 4.1 Economic Growth and Poverty Reduction—India and China

	India			China		
	1980	1990	2005	1980	1990	2005
Population (in million)	687	849	1095	981	1,135	1,305
Gross National Income ($ current billion)	182	313	800	188	356	2,244
Average Annual Growth Rate (%)[a]	3.3	6.5	6.4	6.9	10.4	10.9
GDP Per Capita (2000 Constant $)	223	317	588	186	392	1,449
Population Less Than $1 day (million)[b]	382	357	*327*	634	375	*173*
Poverty at Less Than $1 day (%)[b]	54.4	42.1	*30.7*	63.8	33.0	*13.4*
Merchandise Trade as % of GDP	n.a.	13.1	28.5	n.a.	32.5	63.6
Average Openness[c]	0.16	0.17	*0.22*	0.27	0.30	*0.34*
Average Tariff Rate (%)[c]	99.4	61.9	38.3	38.8	39.9	20.9

Note: n.a. = not available.
[a]Reflect growth rates during 1965–80, 1980–90, and 1990–2005. Numbers in italics indicate 2003 figures for poverty and 1995 for trade and openness. [b]ADB (2005). [c]Dollar, et al. (2001).
Source: World Bank Indicators (2007b in CD ROM), except where given separately.

In the early 1980s, China was among the poorest nations in the world, with more than 60 percent of its population, or over 634 million people, living on less than $1 a day. By 1990, China reduced poverty to less than 33 percent and, by 2003, to 13.4 percent. This was possible because of very high growth rates fueled by trade openness (Dollar et al. 2001). India's achievements on growth and poverty during the same period have been steady but relatively modest—the overall population living on less than $1 day declined from 54.4 percent in 1980 to 42.1 percent and 30.7 percent, respectively, in 1990 and 2003. The total number of poor, however, remains high at over 325 million. To some extent, India's overall performance was negatively influenced by the initial development model that emphasized import substitution and self-reliance, which was one of the contributing factors to its lack of trade openness for most of the period since independence.

Both countries adopted planning as an important tool for policy-making, albeit with very different development models. And in no other area have the approaches of these two countries been farther apart than in infrastructure development and the role it has played in economic growth and poverty reduction. A case in point is road infrastructure.

With almost 30,000 km of expressways, China is fast catching up with the United States, which has the world's largest road network to date.[2] Despite significant improvements since the establishment of the National Highway Administration of India (NHAI), in contrast, India's existing national highway network is characterized by slow speeds, heavy congestion, and low service levels. It is not only the Indian road network that has remained underfunded; almost all other infrastructure services remain, at present, far below the level required to sustain the economic growth needed to address pervasive poverty.

This chapter aims to document and analyze the different approaches in overall infrastructure sector performance for these two very different countries from the policy and institutional dimensions. It identifies factors that have worked in China and India. It also identifies some important lessons that are relevant for both economies in future infrastructure development. The chapter addresses three key topics. First, it provides an overview of the overall infrastructure experience in China and India across several sectors, in terms of physical growth and its impacts on the overall agenda of "inclusive" development. The infrastructure story here includes the way planning and coordination were undertaken in both of these countries, how the risks were handled, and what type of incentives and institutional accountability structures were in place to deliver infrastructure. Second, special attention is given to road sector comparisons between China and India, which arguably exert the greatest influence on economic growth and poverty reduction. Finally, the chapter concludes with a summary of findings and recommendations on the way forward.

Infrastructure in China and India—An Overview

Given the different level of importance accorded infrastructure development in China and India, overall outcomes are very different today even though in the early 1950s and 1960s both countries had fairly similar levels of infrastructure assets and services. For example, China's electricity output at 7.3 billion kWh in 1952 compares well with India's power output of 6.3 billion kWh in 1950–1951. The Indian road network in 1950s was extensive at 400,000 km compared to about one-third that in China. In both countries, about 40 percent of roads were paved then. India's railway network at 53,000 km was more than double that of China at 23,000 km. India and China had similar numbers of telephone subscribers. Table 4.2 presents annual compound growth rates for basic infrastructure access for three periods, 1950–1980, 1980–1990, and

Table 4.2 Infrastructure Development in China and India (in Annual Compounded Growth Rate, %)

	India			China		
	1950–1980	1980–1990	1990–2005	1950–1980[a]	1980–1990	1990–2005
Electricity Generation	10.8	9.4	6.5	14.2	8.4	9.5
Road Network Length	4.6	3.4	3.8	7.2	1.7	3.4
Railway Network	0.5	0.2	0.1	2.8	0.8	1.1
Telephone Subscribers	10.2	8.9	28.7	6.6	13.8	40.9
Annual GDP Growth	3.7	5.7	6.4	5.2	9.8	10.2

Note: [a]Data for China refers to 1952–80.

Source: China Data Online and National Accounts for India Various Issues.

1990–2005, indicating the significant growth achieved by China in the past 25 years. India was not able to continue higher levels of growth achieved in earlier years of planning.

Infrastructure Investment Environment

Though most Indian planning documents have continued to emphasize the importance of infrastructure, until very recently, they did not embrace the Chinese single-minded goal of infrastructure development, anticipating future demand and building ahead of time. India's development model, which began with a balance between growth and distribution in the early 1950s, was changed in mid-course with a greater emphasis on redistribution during the critical period of growth.[3] A number of pro-poor programs were introduced that reduced overall fiscal space for infrastructure development.

Even within infrastructure priorities, political interests drove the overall resource allocation: for example, in the 1970s and 1980s, government emphasized development of minor irrigation and rural roads as part of antipoverty programs. Employment generation through construction of rural roads and through ground water and minor irrigation to support food security received much higher priority compared to the need to enhance logistics to support industrial growth and improving overall economic efficiency. In the Fifth Five-Year Plan, a major goal was to connect all villages (with population of more than 1,500 inhabitants) with the rural road network; however, this was done through a "minimum needs program" supporting employment creation and leading to waste and inefficiency. Most of the roads thus laid did not meet quality standards because fiscal space was not adequate to accommodate both the demand for resources for rural roads and also the national highway network that was getting congested. Despite the significant investments on roads in India, only a small percentage of these were paved due to the need to spread limited resources over longer length. Most of these roads were washed away.

Even in the case of power sector, village electrification was a priority so as to provide power for the farms, but not necessarily to households.[4] Emphasis on connectivity without improvements in overall economic efficiency meant unsustainable financial burden on the government budgets. In the time of slower economic growth or external shocks such as wars and high oil prices, infrastructure investments were a major casualty. As the evidence from table 4.2 indicates, India found it difficult to sustain this redistribution model without the robust and sustained growth that could potentially have been fueled through additional infrastructure development. Overall availability of resources for infrastructure sectors was also influenced by the macroeconomic environment in these countries (see table 4.3). China, with its high economic growth rates and higher savings rates was able to allocate much larger resources for investments in general. In the 1980, China saved 35 percent of the GDP whereas India's savings rate was less than half at 15.5 percent. This, combined with higher fiscal deficits in India, meant that it was not always possible to invest in infrastructure. It is very hard to get consistent time series data on infrastructure investments across Asian countries. According to the World Development Report on Infrastructure, developing countries, on average, invested 4 percent of GDP on infrastructure (World Bank 1994). East Asia steadily increased its level of investments,

Table 4.3 Macroeconomic Environment of India and China (% of GDP)

	India			China		
	1980	1990	2005	1980	1990	2005
Gross Domestic Savings	15.5	22.6	29.7	35.0	39.9	49.0
Gross Fixed Capital Formation	18.5	22.9	28.1	29.3	26.0	42.3
Gross Capital Formation	18.7	24.1	33.4	35.4	36.4	43.5
Foreign Direct Investments	0.04	0.07	0.82	0.03	1.0	3.54
Government Deficits	−5.1	−7.8	−3.7	−13.7	−2.8	−0.7

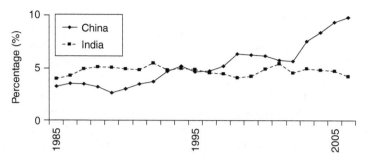

Figure 4.1 Infrastructure Investments in China and India (1985–2006)
Source: Government of India . *Economic Survey*, Various Issues, New Delhi .

both in absolute and relative terms, from 3.6 percent in the 1970s to 4.6 percent in 1980s, and to 5.3 percent in 1993. After the Asian financial crisis in the late 1990s, infrastructure investments collapsed in many of the affected countries. Infrastructure investments in India slowed down after reaching a peak level of 5.5 percent of GDP in the early 1990s (see figure 4.1). The gap between infrastructure investments between China and India is widening not only as share of GDP, but also in absolute levels given that India's GDP is only one-third that of China.

Following the 1991 fiscal crisis in India, the Government of India adopted several reform measures to make the economy globally competitive. It recognized that the success of these policies would crucially depend on the expansion and improvement of physical infrastructure. In 1994, the government set up an Expert Group to recommend a policy and reform program to guide the future course of infrastructure development.[5] The Expert Group found that for India to maintain its target growth of 7–9 percent per annum, its infrastructure investments would need to increase from the 4–5 percent of GDP experienced in the 1980s and 1990s to 8 percent in 2005, requiring a three-fold increase in absolute levels. The group recommended several strategies to encourage this investment, including privatization. However, compared to what was needed, actual levels of investments have remained well below the suggested levels, given the competing demands for fiscal resources by other sectors.

Planning Framework—Institutions, Processes, Incentives, and Accountability

Development planning in any country can follow two broad models—it can either be an integral part of the political decision-making process or be divorced from politics where technocrats keep a firm hold on the planning process as a matter of rational and efficient management. In China, planning followed the first model. The State Planning Committee (SPC), and its subsequent variants, have been and remain at the center of China's political and economic affairs. The SPC sets the national policy agenda, makes important policy decisions, and even guides the law-making process to ensure that these decisions are implemented. Through a dual-track implementation system, its policy-making role also extends to closely monitoring and guiding policy implementation (Liu 2005).

Thus the Chinese planning institutions fully integrate political economy considerations in the process of designing and implementing development plans. In China, strong accountability for delivery of plans was embedded through the powerful party structure and this has so far led to better economic outcomes in terms of growth and infrastructure development. In India, there was disconnect between targets and performance, planning and implementation, and demand for resources and actual availability of funds. As a result, in most years until recently, infrastructure projects were actually built on a piecemeal approach.

For India, the decade of the 1970s was tumultuous. On the political front, this included a war with Pakistan, the birth of a new nation on its border with a million refugees, an oil crisis, the public announcement of nuclear ambitions with an explosion at Pokhara, and a brief experiment with the cessation of civil liberty. The economy was hindered by this political turmoil as indicated by its slow rate of growth. In the 1970s, the underlying economic trend did not differ much from that observed since the early 1950s. The rate of growth of national income, for example, was 3.5 percent, including a 2.7 percent growth rate in agricultural production and a 6.1 percent growth rate in industrial production. Per capita income grew by 1.3 percent per year, while per capita consumption grew by 1.2 percent (Patel 2002). In the late 1970s, a non-Congress government took power at the center for the first time since independence. The new government had to change the old ways of running the government and economy, and thus began the phase of slow liberalization in the 1980s.

The Indian planning process historically tended to be more technical than political. Although the Planning Commission, with the Prime Minister as the Chairman, had some institutional ties to the political decision-making process, the process has tended to be more technical in reality, captured at times by technocrats who wanted to ensure rational and managerial efficiency.[6] The planning institutions in India at the national and state levels adopted a consultative process for the formulation of plans. Plan formulations for important sectors were undertaken by working groups with broad mandates and high levels of technical expertise. These working groups included representatives not only of the line ministries, but also from the financial sector, private sector, and academic institutions. This process of participation, however, worked well only in the initial phase of the preparation of formal plan documents. Unlike the dual-track system in China, overall implementation in India has more often been divorced from the planning process. Similarly, policy-making, too, was fragmented where, for example, a number of policy reforms have been often decided by committees and working groups, without the Planning Commission always being in charge of the process of reform designs or action plans for implementation.

Being a pluralistic democracy, Indian development plans in the past have indicated directions but not specific goals. As a result, plans often did not articulate an appropriate policy framework based on a set of priorities. Rather, most of the earlier plans were essentially statements of intentions for public expenditures, implemented by the annual budget process. In addition, the targets set for private-sector participation soon provided a rationale for the public sector to effect an industrial licensing policy with its inherently large transaction costs. Unlike the East Asian economies, incentives were rarely used as instruments of economic policy in India until much later, partly because of the belief in the wisdom and supreme ability of the government (Patel 2002). In some sense, the Prime Minister's statement in the *Foreword to the Sixth Plan* that *"the measure of a plan is not intention but achievement, not allocation but benefit"* (emphasis added) needed to be heeded via the use of incentive structures and monitoring to bring results that were essential in India's planning process.

In China, the party's organizational structure is set in parallel to the administrative organizational structure at every level of the government. Under this system, every government agency is led by an official who serves both as the party secretary and the administrator (commonly seen at the central level), or jointly by two officials, one as party secretary and the other as an administrator (more commonly seen at the provincial and local levels). In the second case, the party secretary does not engage in the day-to-day administrative functions, but closely monitors the policy implementation process and always has the final say on major policy and personnel decisions. He or she is accountable to the higher level party secretary. The administrators need not be party members, but many of them are. The career of a government official with party membership, moreover, is not limited to just the party or administration track, but it could be both (Liu 2005).

Unlike the Chinese system of administrative accountability emanating from the all-embracing party, Indian planning institutions or processes have limited interaction with the government personnel management. In short, India's planning ability, widely regarded as world class, was not backed by underlying incentives and accountability systems that in China delivered better outcomes.

Infrastructure Sector Reforms

The planning framework for infrastructure was very different in China than in India. Similar to their efforts in rural transformation and agricultural modernization, China was able to adopt a dual-benefit infrastructure development policy—to build infrastructure that will promote economic growth and to build systems that directly target poverty reduction. The vast program of building expressways was complemented with several programs that would directly benefit the poor. This was possible because of China's very pragmatic approach to reforms and modernization, as suggested by Deng Xiaoping's statement, *"black cat, white cat, it does not matter so long as it catches mice"* (emphasis in original). Having a centralized political system with complete state control made it possible to take risks that would have been more difficult under alternate political paradigms. The political costs of direct dissent were relatively small, if not entirely absent in China.

Until 1994, the Indian government did not have a comprehensive framework for infrastructure. Most of the government interventions were through a large number of sector ministries and departments—Ministry of Finance, Planning Commission, pricing bureaus, state-owned enterprises (SOEs), and so on. Since there were so many actors, the entire spectrum of infrastructure functions, namely, planning and policy-making, regulation, production, and supply tended to be dominated by public sector SOEs. The SOEs in these sectors had the skills and capabilities to influence important decisions; however, accountability structures were being weakened by excessive interference by political "bosses" (Virmani 2005).

With the exception of pricing reforms, most infrastructure reforms in India did not begin until the late 1980s and early 1990s. Telecommunications was selected as a technology mission where connectivity was considered a priority.[7] Indigenous entrepreneurship was unleashed and the Village Public Telephone system spread to every village under the public-call office, providing telephone access and thus breaking the long time monopoly of post offices. In the early 1990s, the telecom sector was the first one to allow entry of private-sector firms in both basic and cellular telephone systems. Even though the telecom reforms had many ups and downs, the government was committed to allow growth of access of service and connectivity through entry of the private sector and the creation of markets (see table 4.4 for a comparison of basic performance indicators between India and China for telecom and other infrastructure sectors).

In contrast to the telecom sector, reforms in the Indian electricity sector have not been very successful, despite the fact that these were pursued more systematically with amendment of the Electricity Act in 1991, which allowed private-sector participation and even 100 percent foreign ownership. This alone did not lead to real improvements on the ground until recently. Part of the problem lay in the lack of a credible regulator, partly owing to a political setting that remained uncoordinated. The electricity sector in the Indian federal system remains on the "concurrent list," implying responsibility for the sector by both the central government and the state governments. One of the most important factors that remained uncoordinated was the funding issue. A large number of states had followed the practice of subsidizing power for agriculture and, as a result, there was ambiguity regarding who was going to pay for the power. The financial status of most of the State Electricity Boards (SEBs) was grim, with most experiencing large and unsustainable deficits. In the early 1990s, the rate of return on all SEBs combined was highly negative (−13.5 percent of capital employed). A large number of private projects were also approved with guarantees by the state governments to private project sponsors, representing a significant share of the cumulative state GDP.

Until 1998–1999, private investments were allowed only in power generation in India. Private-sector participation in power transmission was allowed but private-sector participation in power distribution did not occur until 2003 (Virmani 2005). Although many states have set up independent regulators that have been fairly effective, the fundamental issue of who pays for the subsidized power has remained an important challenge. Unless there is a viable system of paying for the needed capacity for power generation and investments in transmission and distribution, financing of the power sector will remain a major challenge in years to come.

Unlike India, however, China's power sector reforms have been relatively more successful in terms of the level of foreign and private sector

Table 4.4 Basic Infrastructure Sector Performance Indicators of India and China

	Units	India			China		
		1980	1990	2005	1980	1990	2005
Communications[a]							
Telephone Connections	per 1,000 person	2.3	5.07	185	4.3	11.1	626
Mobile Phones	per 1,000 person	n.a.	0	148	n.a.	.02	348
Energy[b]							
Power Capacity	1,000 mwh	33.3	71.8	137.6	65.9	126.6	442.4
Power Generation	billion kwh	119.3	275.5	661.6	285.5	590.3	2371.8
Primary Energy Production	10^{15} BTU	3.1	6.8	11.7	18.1	29.4	63.2
Per Capita Energy Consumption	10^{6} BTU	5.9	9.4	14.8	17.8	23.5	51.4
Energy Intensity	$ GDP/kg	3.4	4.0	5.5	1.3	2.1	4.4
Transport[c]							
Roads	1,000 km	644	2,000	2,526	883	1,181	1,931
Paved Roads	%	n.a.	47	57	n.a.	n.a.	82.5
Road Freight	million tons	195.9	318.4	557.4	3,820	7,240	11,600
Rail Lines Route Length	km	61,240	62,367	63,465	49,940	53,378	62,200
Rail Freight	billion ton-km	158	236	407	571	1,060	1,934
Water and Sanitation Access[c]							
Safe Drinking Water	% population	42	70	86	n.a.	70	77
Sanitation	% population	7	14	33	n.a.	23	44

Note: n.a. = not available.
Source: World Bank. 2007b. *World Development Indicators* (CD-ROM).

participation in reducing the funding gap. The foreign private sector was welcomed into China, not only because of the need to augment financial resources, but also for the needed manufacturing capacity to produce the power generating equipment for an ambitious capacity expansion program. Foreign direct investments (FDI) in China took various institutional forms such as joint ventures, Build-Operate-Transfer (BOT) types of arrangements, equity joint ventures, loans, and equity in the existing energy enterprises. In 1996, the sector was further reformed under the new Electricity Law that created the State Power Corporation of China as an entity separate from the Ministry of Electric Power, thus signifying a first step to separating regulation from actual production and supply. Given the dual pricing system of "new plant, new price," China's power sector funding gap has not been as large as that of India.[8]

The transport sector of India is one of the largest in the world. Serving over a billion people, Indian roads carry about 85 percent of passenger traffic and about 70 percent of freight traffic in the country (International Road Federation [IRF] 2003). Accelerated economic growth in the 1990s has meant a surge in demand for both freight and passenger transport by 12 percent and 8 percent per year, respectively. India had a large network of roads at the time of independence; however, the overall quality of roads reflected the underlying weak and inefficient institutional structures responsible for planning, designing, and maintaining the highway network.

When it was decided in the 1990s to strengthen the road network, it was recognized that allocating more money to the Central and State Public Works Departments would not lead to better outcomes. It was believed the resources would be wasted and siphoned off in the end because these institutions had become inefficient and obsolete. One of the institutional innovations introduced in 1995 was to set up a new organization. The National Highways Authority of India (NHAI) was given a very clear mandate to upgrade the road network. A fuel "cess" (tax) was introduced to pay for the transport network upgrade, and private sector participation was also allowed through collection of user tolls to partly pay for the new roads. An ambitious transport upgrade plan was launched with very clear targets even though overall accountability structures continued to remain low.

Visible differences have been seen in a very short period of time. The fuel cess is being leveraged for raising debt in the domestic market. There has also been a rapid rise in toll revenues. Capital expenditure by NHAI has risen rapidly from $175 million in 1999–2000 to $2.2 billion in 2003–2004. At the same time, the Indian government has also initiated a program of rural connectivity so as to connect all habitations with a population of 500 or more. It is funded from a central road fund supported from the multilateral development banks and domestic borrowing.

Road Sector—"To Get Rich, Build Roads First; To Get Rich Fast, Build Fast Roads"

A majority of farmers in China believe in this saying. Although arguments have been made to the contrary, numerous recent studies have demonstrated that the greatest effect on poverty reduction can come from investments in the transport sector, particularly roads. It has been shown that an efficient road network increases access to services and economic opportunities, facilitates domestic market integration, lowers the cost of production and transportation, and allows healthy competition both domestically and internationally. In addition to accessibility, the quality of the roads also plays an important role in economic development.

A 1999 study in India, for example, used a general equilibrium model to evaluate the effects of government expenditures in a number of sectors—agricultural research and development, irrigation, roads, education, rural and community development, power, health, and soil/water conservation—and found that the greatest effect on poverty reduction came from roads (Fan et al. 1999). Recent research in the Philippines that covered 73 rural provinces also suggested that road infrastructure endowment proved to be, by far, the strongest predictor of successful poverty reduction (Balisacan 2001). A study in Indonesia that covered 25 provinces from 1976 and 1996 found that poverty was most sensitive to road investments, followed by education, agriculture, and irrigation (Kwon 2000). In a recent study of 17 Indian states from 1970 to 1994, it was found that a 10 percent increase in the road network (measured by km of road per square km of land) would lead to a 3.4 percent increase in income per capita (Nagaraj et al. 2000). Another study in Mexico showed that a 10 percent increase in market access (as defined by the density and quality of the road network within the region) would increase labor productivity by 6 percent (Deichmann 2000). In former Zaire, the road quality was found to be the key factor in determining the significant differences in food prices across regions (Minten and Kyle 1999). These are but a few examples that indicate the importance of the road sector in economic development and poverty reduction.

An overview of road sector development in China and India is provided in this section, followed by a more detailed comparative look at the two countries from the viewpoint of the road sector development scope, institutional setting, and investment and funding climate.

Road Sector Comparative Overview

The development of the road infrastructure remained relatively unimportant in China's national development strategy during the pre-reform period. When the reforms began in 1978, China, consequently, was poorly endowed with road infrastructure and the road density was well below that of India; it remained 20–30 percent below India throughout the 1980s. Despite the priorities given to develop the road infrastructure, relatively low levels of investment in the transport sector in the early years of the reform period—compared to investment levels in the industrial sector—combined with significant growth in inter-regional trade following the reforms created serious road shortages and urban congestion. Since 1985, however, the government has geared up its investments in roads, particularly for high-quality roads such as highways connecting major industrial centers in the coastal areas. In the 1990s, as the infrastructure investments became a national priority, China started to invest massively in road construction. Road projects are now an important part of China's strategy to develop the western region and to reduce the disparities between the well-developed coastal regions and inner provinces, and between the urban and rural areas.

As mentioned earlier, India, home to more people living on less than US$1 per day than any other nation, faces significant hurdles in its efforts to combat poverty and stimulate economic growth. Even so, progress over the past decade and a half has been notable. Beginning in 1991, the government launched a series of economic reforms aimed at market liberalization that stimulated annual GDP growth on the order of 6 to 6.5 percent in the ensuing years. The first wave of reforms deregulated and expanded foreign trade, deregulated and privatized domestic industries, and cut many government subsidies; the second wave, now underway, is focused on eliminating redundant public sector employees, as well as attracting increased private and foreign investment (Bansal 2002a).

Not surprisingly, sustained growth in the Indian economy has led to a corresponding increase in the demand for transportation services within the country. Regrettably, considerably less attention has been devoted to improving the transportation infrastructure over the same period, and the country's transportation systems remain in a rather dismal state. Within the road sector, for instance, India has only 3,000 km of highways with more than two lanes, and major economic centers are not yet linked by access-controlled expressways. Congestion along the existing network is both rampant and chronic, leading to significant economic losses associated with wasted time and fuel. Safety is another major concern, as indicated by a crash-related death rate per vehicle that is about ten times higher than that within the European Union. Finally, because of scarce funding and lack of investment in the road program, about 40 percent of India's 661,000 rural villages do not have all-weather access to markets and social services. Many of the 70 million urban residents living below the national poverty line lack access to basic infrastructure services such as affordable transport (Bansal 2002a). Given such circumstances, poor transportation is now viewed as a major threat to the continued growth of the Indian economy (Akanda 2003).

To put India's relative lack of progress in the road infrastructure sector into perspective, it is useful to contrast the country's experience with that of China over the past 15 years. As mentioned previously, at the beginning of the 1990s, India's road structure was actually more advanced than that of China, but that advantage reversed dramatically in the intervening years. Between 1991 and 2002, China's annual investment in its road network increased from about US$1 billion to around $38 billion; meanwhile, India's annual investment, starting at a similar level in 1991, increased to just US$3 billion over the same 12-year period. China also adopted a different investment allocation philosophy, focusing first on arterial networks to connect its 100 largest cities. Projects included the 35,000 km national trunk highway system, along with an additional 25,000 km of low-grade four-lane highways without access control. In total, China devoted 60 percent of its investment to new arterial networks, 25 percent to upgrading existing networks, and 15 percent to rural roads. India, in contrast, focused mainly on rural roads, adopting the basic goal of stretching a limited budget as far as possible (Harral and Sondhi 2005). India's choices have had severe consequences; whereas China currently boasts an impressive road network infrastructure capable of supporting its continued economic growth into the future, India must now find a way to deal with an undersized and overcrowded road system that threatens to choke further economic progress. Indian officials are well aware of this dilemma and have taken initial steps to reverse this trajectory. Initial results appear promising, but much remains to be done.

Road Sector Development Scope

China. Although China had a late start, its achievement in building an extensive national road network in the past two decades has been unprecedented. As shown in table 4.5, the total length of roads increased more than two-fold to 1.9 million km by 2005 from 0.9 million km in 1980 at the start of the economic reforms. During the same period, the length of the high-quality roads (expressways, Class I and II roads combined) increased from 13,000 km (barely 1 percent of the total length) to over 325,000 km (over 15 percent of the total).[9] The extent of the road network in rural areas also increased greatly. In the short seven-year period from 1997 to 2004, the length of roads in rural villages increased more than two-fold, from 400,000 km to almost 950,000 km. Other relevant performance metrics include the road density, which increased from 95 km per 1,000 sq. km. in 1980 to 190 km per 1,000 sq. km. in 2002, and the road carrying capacity,

Table 4.5 China Road Characteristics (1980–2005) (in 1,000 km)

Length of Roads	1980	1990	2000	2005
Classification[a]				
Expressway	0	0.5	16.3	41.0
Class I	0.2	2.6	25.2	38.4
Class II	12.6	43.4	177.8	246.4
Class III	108.3	169.8	305.4	344.7
Class IV	400.1	524.8	791.2	921.3
Substandard	367.1	287.2	363.9	338.8
Total	888.25	1,028.4	1,679.8	1,930.5
Jurisdiction				
National	n.a.	107.5	119.0	132.7
Provincial	n.a.	166.1	212.5	233.8
County	n.a.	340.8	461.9	494.3
Village/Township	n.a.	370.2	800.7	981.4
Special Purpose	n.a.	43.8	85.9	88.4
Total		1,028.4	1,679.8	1,930.5

Note: n.a.=not available
[a]Expressway and Class 1 roads represent access-controlled divided highways with more than 2 lanes; Class 2 roads represent all 2-lane highways, divided or undivided, without access control. Expressways and Class 1 and 2 roads are considered "high quality" roads. All other roads, i.e., Class 3 or below, are considered rural roads.

Source: China's National Bureau of Statistics, *Statistical Yearbook of China (various issues)*.

which increased from 2.2 billion people and 3.8 billion tons of freight to almost 15 billion people and 11 billion tons of freight in the same period.

Great progress has also been made in raising both the quantity and quality of rural highways to reduce the disparities between the coastal regions and inner provinces in the western regions. Between 1994 and 2000, the government spent over US$800 million to build 300,000 km of new rural highways for 529 poor counties in 21 provinces. By 2002, the extent of rural highways (county and village highways combined) reached a total of 1.1 million km, an increase of 244,000 km from the 1995 level. Despite such remarkable progress, however, large regional variations exist in the density and quality of roads; the western regions' standards still fall short of the national average (see table 4.6).

In early 2003, the government launched a nation-wide, 78,000-km inter-county and rural highway construction program, which was subsequently expanded to 162,000 km with more than 15,500 projects and US$14 billion in new investments. In addition in 2004, the government decided to expand the original 35,000-km National Trunk Highway System (NTHS)[10] to an 80,000-km program to be completed in 2020. By 2020, the government's overall goal is to reach 3 million km in total length, of which, 650,000 km will be high-quality road, a two-fold increase from the 2004 level.

Table 4.6 China Road Characteristics by Region (2002)

	Length of Roads (km)	Road Density (km/1,000 sq.m.)	Share in Total Length of Roads (%)	
			High Quality Roads [a]	Below Class 4
North	146,745	392.2	19.7	8.5
Northeast	152,192	193.3	17.7	5.3
East	368,500	463.3	20.5	15.5
Central	372,061	478.4	16.6	24.3
Southwest	391,790	166.2	5.6	38.1
Northwest	277,637	65.7	10.5	18.2
National Total	1,765,222	184.7	14.1	21.7

Note [a] Represents expressways and Class I and II roads combined.

In terms of the level of investments, the cumulative expenditure in road construction during the 13-year period from 1990 to 2003 was about US$250 billion.[11] The rate of the investments also increased dramatically in recent years. In the four-year period between 1998 and 2001, the investment in road infrastructure was US$115 billion, which was almost twice as much as the cumulative investments made during the prior 48-year period from 1949 to 1997.

India. Before discussing the current state of the Indian road network, it is useful to touch upon three important trends that have significantly influenced the way in which road infrastructure has been developed and utilized in recent decades. First, there has been a gradual but persistent mode shift in India from rail to roads. In 1960, rail carried 85 percent of goods traffic and 51 percent of passenger traffic; by 2001, those percentages had declined to 23 percent and 13 percent, respectively (Akanda 2003). The vast majority of this demand appears to have shifted to the road system, which currently accounts for 70 percent of freight transport and 85 percent of passenger transport (IRF 2003).[12]

Second, with rising GDP, demand for automotive and freight travel has grown rapidly and consistently. Between 1951 and 1998, the overall size of the vehicle fleet in India expanded from 300,000 to 12.5 million, a 42-fold increase. From 1951 to 2000, meanwhile, the size of the truck fleet grew from 82,000 to 2.64 million, a 32-fold gain. Throughout the 1990s, the annual growth in road freight was around 12 percent, while the annual growth in passenger freight was about 8 percent (Bansal et al. 2002b).

Third, despite the stunning growth in road transport demand, investment in new highway capacity has been anemic. Between 1951 and 1995, the total length of national and state roads increased by a factor of just 3.4. Over this same period, the percentage of India's annual budget plans devoted to the transport sector as a whole, as well as specifically to roads, has consistently declined. This relationship is illustrated in table 4.7.

These three trends, taken together, help explain the current state of India's road infrastructure, which is now both woefully underdeveloped and overutilized. The network, which serves a land area of 3.3 million square km and a population of 1 billion, comprises approximately 2.3 million kilometers, yielding an overall geographic density of 0.66 km of roadway per square km of land (this is actually about the same density as that found in the United States, at 0.65, and much higher than that in China, at 0.16) (Bansal 2002a).

The network can be broken down into about 58,000 km of national highways, 137,000 km of state highways, 470,000 km of major district roads, and 1.65 million km of rural roads, which collectively must handle 870 billion ton-km of freight and 2.45 trillion passenger-km per year (IRF 2003, Bansal et al. 2002a). It is difficult to compare the networks across these two countries using national data. However, these can be seen as approximate.[13] Even though the Indian road network as a whole is denser than that of China, its highway component is comparatively underdeveloped. One significant problem is that many of the highway links have only one or two lanes, as indicated in figure 4.2.

Another major issue is the low grade of engineering. Just one-quarter of the road network is surfaced with bituminous blacktop or concrete,

Table 4.7 Capital Expenditures in India—Transport and Road Sectors (in % of total plan outlay)

	Years	Transport Sector	Road Sector
First Plan	1951–1956	22.1	6.9
Second Plan	1956–1961	23.5	4.8
Third Plan	1961–1966	23.1	5.1
Annual Plan	1966–1969	15.6	4.7
Fourth Plan	1969–1974	16.0	5.5
Fifth Plan	1974–1979	14.1	4.3
Sixth Plan	1980–1985	13.0	3.5
Seventh Plan	1985–1990	13.5	2.9
Annual Plan	1990–1992	14.1	3.1
Eighth Plan	1992–1997	12.9	3.0

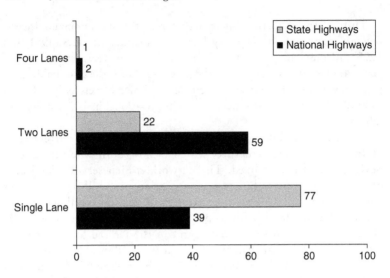

Figure 4.2 Indian Highway Characteristics

while another fifth has been constructed with water-bound macadam; the remainder is unpaved (Bansal et al. 2002a). Finally, and not surprisingly, given its surface composition, much of the road network is in ragged shape, a problem that is compounded by the high number of older, rigid two-axle freight trucks on the road network, which can cause significant damage to the roadbed. More than a quarter of the national highways are categorized as being in poor surface condition, while more than half of the state highways are listed as being in poor or very poor shape. The specific breakdown is listed in table 4.8.

Despite the fact that India's highway system is relatively sparse, underengineered, and in fairly poor condition, it still serves the vast majority of transport demand within the country. At 58,000 km, the national highways represent just 1.7 percent of the road network, yet they carry about 40 percent of all traffic. Taken together, national and state highways account for about 6 percent of the network, but collectively carry close to 80 percent of all traffic. Not surprisingly, many of these roads are heavily and chronically congested (IRF 2003).

In contrast, congestion is not particularly problematic for the 2.7 million km of rural roads in India. Rather, connectivity is the pressing issue. Approximately 70 percent, or around 700 million, of India's inhabitants live in rural areas, comprised of 661,000 villages. Unfortunately, about 40 percent of these villages are not yet connected by all-weather roads to market centers and main road networks; this problem is particularly pronounced in the peripheral states in the north and northeast of the country, which are poorly connected with major economic centers (Bansal et al. 2002a).

In reviewing the current state of the system, it is clear that many of the problems may be attributed to insufficient capacity along various critical links within the road network. However, it also appears that much of the existing capacity is poorly managed and used inefficiently. For instance, capacity shortages along many links are exacerbated by mixed traffic, encroachment, crowded and unsafe urban crossings, and frequent stops at state and municipal checkpoints. In addition, widespread overloading by outdated, rigid two-axle trucks plays a major factor in the damage imposed on road pavement. Finally, in rural roads, there is almost a total lack of critical maintenance categories such as grading and drainage, leading to an extremely rapid deterioration of road surface condition (Bansal et al. 2002a).

Clearly, then, significant steps must be taken to shore up India's road network in order to facilitate continued economic growth and poverty alleviation. Akanda (2003) has summarized the important goals for future development of India's road infrastructure as follows:

- Upgrading the capacity and efficiency of existing infrastructure
- Establishing total connectivity for an all-weather rural road network
- Developing a modally balanced transport system, particularly in urban areas
- Contributing to a reduction in regional disparities
- Contributing to subregional economic cooperation
- Putting a much greater emphasis on safety

More recently, officials at various levels of government within India, along with concerned multilateral funding organizations and

Table 4.8 India Highway Condition Breakdown (in % of total)

Internal Rate on Investment	National Highways	State Highways		
		Single Lane	Intermediate lane	Two Lanes
< 4 (Good)	50.7	11.0	10.8	11.2
4–6 (Fair)	23.6	23.4	31.8	48.4
6–8 (Poor)	25.7	35.3	34.6	35.5
>8 (Very Poor)	0.0	30.4	22.7	4.9

representatives of private development, have initiated steps that should contribute to the achievement of these aggressive and noble goals. These steps include efforts to reform the institutional and legal framework within which development decisions are made and implemented, as well as efforts to broaden and strengthen the base of financial resources available to support the road network.

Institutional Setting

China. Prior to the reform period, the central government in China was accountable for the development of national roads, while provincial and local governments were responsible for the provincial and local road network. Following the economic reforms and until the early 1990s, China's road sector administration continued to remain relatively straightforward as outlined in table 4.9. This institutional arrangement is still in effect for most of the inland provinces. As explained in the next section, private capital played an important role in infrastructure development in China. With the availability of private capital, complicated organizational structures for highway administration began to emerge for the fast-developing coastal regions—for example, holding companies, toll road operating companies—to meet the legal, technical, and marketing requirements involved in using such capital. The administration of the road sector also became increasingly decentralized. Provincial Communications Departments (PCDs) continued to develop the provincial network plan for approval by the provincial government but with increased power and authority (Weingast 1994, Li et al. 1999).

The present legal and institutional framework of the road sector in China reflects the transition from a system of state-owned enterprises (SOEs) to a mixed system with increased privatization as a means to seek outside investment by providing listing on a stock exchange (J.P. Morgan 1997). In the past several years, a number of important pieces of legislation have been enacted, providing a general framework for that process of change.[14] The PCDs have established separate but 100 percent owned provincial expressway companies to carry out specific highway projects and to have control over these highways.

In the past, a sweetheart arrangement with the PCD allowed provincially controlled expressway companies to benefit from preferential treatment. Often the management and board of directors of these companies were former PCD employees who still had close ties to the

Table 4.9 Institutional Structure for China Road Sector (1980–early 1990s)

Level	Agency	Responsibilities
Central	MOC	• Sets policies and guidelines • Plans and allocates Vehicle Purchase Fee revenues for NTHS • Provides technical and financial support to counties on a limited basis
	MOF	• Administers multilateral and bilateral bank loans
	SPC (now NDRC)	• Deals with major policy issues related to highway development and land use, intermodal planning and coordination, highway financing strategies • Reviews national highway plans and project proposals • Helps develop financing at program and project levels
	State Council	• Same as SPC
Provincial	PCD	• Develops provincial network plan for first 4 road classes (expressways and Classes 1 through 3) for approval by provincial governments • Plans, designs, constructs, and manages approved road network plans in the province under consideration, including national roads • Provides technical and financial support to counties
County	Various	• Responsible for Class 4 and substandard roads

Notes: MOC=Ministry of Communications; MOF=Ministry of Finance; SPC=State Planning Commission; (now National Development & Reform Commission or NDRC); PCD=Provincial Communications Department

PCDs. However, under World Trade Organization (WTO) rules—such preferential treatment will need to change to an arm's length relationship with open and competitive bidding for concession or operating rights. If the private sector—particularly the international private sector—is to be attracted to invest in these companies, transparency and proper accountability in the companies' internal operations and decision-making process must be assured (CPCS 2001).

India. The current woes of India's road transport sector can be at least partially attributed to a deep-rooted philosophical attitude—one that has permeated many of the country's governmental institutions—that transport should be viewed as an area in which economic efficiency should not necessarily take precedence over social equity. This belief is reflected in the low priority given to road infrastructure during most of the 1970s and 1980s, when many road tax revenues were earmarked for other forms of government spending (IRF 2003a). Paradoxically, the lack of reinvestment on roads reduced the much-needed connectivity of the rural road network, often penalizing the most remote and poorest areas of the country.

Most of the social equity objectives set for the transport sector have not been achieved, and economic efficiency, and in the meantime, has been seriously compromised (Bansal et al. 2002a).

Vestiges of this philosophy are still apparent within the current institutional and legal structure within India. Although there is some mixture of public and private activity within the transport arena, it remains divided along fairly strict lines. The public sector dominates in the area of transport infrastructure, while the private sector is heavily engaged in road transport services (providing, for example, all freight trucking along with about 70 percent of intercity bus services), consultant services, and civil works (Bansal et al. 2002a).

Within the public arena, the Indian constitution assigns responsibility for the national highway network to the central government, while state governments are charged with developing and maintaining state highways and rural roads. At the state level, highways are typically provided and maintained by state public works departments (PWDs), while rural roads may be taken care of either by PWDs or by local government engineering departments. At the central level, responsibility for the national highway system is split between the Ministry of Road Transport and Highways (MORTH) and the recently created National Highways Authority of India (NHAI), although the maintenance of national highways under MORTH is increasingly delegated to state PWDs (Bansal et al. 2002a).

In order to perform their tasks more effectively, these national, state, and local agencies must collectively overcome a number of structural challenges, many of which can be solved only through policy or institutional reform. At the broadest level, the most pressing issues fall under the categories of poorly defined bureaucratic structure/mission, insufficient accountability, poor asset/system management, and inadequate resource mobilization.[15] These categories can be broken down into greater detail as follows:

Poorly defined bureaucratic structure/mission
- Unclear or overlapping responsibilities, often with no agency in charge
- Multiple mandates including roads, buildings, and irrigation
- Absence of clear strategic goals, mission statements, performance indicators, or investment plans

Insufficient accountability
- Failure to separate policy and operational roles for clear accountability

- Not enough consultation with road users
- Failure to report all relevant information
- Failure to impose sanctions on poor performance
- Absence of independent bodies to verify information and assess performance
- Inappropriate evaluation techniques that are merely input-based, focusing solely on accounting for expenditures against the budget and not taking into consideration the physical or operational conditions of the actual road network

Poor asset/system management
- Inadequate attention to data collection and analysis in decision-making
- Excessive focus on new investment vs. maintenance
- Uneconomical investments made under political influence
- Lack of competition in procurement
- Need for leaner staffing with greater skill-set diversification
- Declining investments in transport relative to GDP
- Limited inputs from private finance
- Need to make better use of user charges in the form of gas taxes or tolling

Though these problems are daunting, agencies at various levels within the government have taken initial steps to address them in recent years. Within the central government, notable examples include the following:

- Increasing the level of public funding for transportation within the Ninth Five-Year Plan
- Creating the Central Road Fund (CRF) to finance road development and maintenance through an earmarked "cess" (tax) on diesel and gasoline
- Operationalizing the NHAI to act as an infrastructure procurer rather than a provider
- Establishing the National Highways Development Project (NHDP) to upgrade the national major highway routes
- Amending the National Highway Act to expedite land acquisition, permit private participation in road financing, and allow for the tolling of public roads

At the national level, India's road sector received a significant boost in 1995 when the NHAI was set up with the express purpose of modernizing the subcontinent's system of national highways (IRF 2003). The NHAI is a semiautonomous agency that operates only as a client for planning and procuring road construction, and its staff has greater delegation of authority than in traditional Indian road agencies to allow for a quicker decision process. To become more responsible to user demands, the NHAI has recently constituted a Road Users' Advisory Committee, members of which include representatives from states, road users, businesses, and the construction industry (IRF 2003).

The momentum for reform at the national level was further bolstered in 1998, when the Indian Prime Minister Shri Vajpayee announced a strategic vision for upgrading the national highway system that could serve as a model for other developing nations. To support this aim, the NHAI devised the master plan for the NHDP, which calls for an investment of approximately US$10 billion (in 1999 dollars) to upgrade more than 14,000 km of national highways to four, six, or eight lanes. Notable elements of the project include a 5,900 km "golden quadrilateral" linking Delhi, Kolkata, Chennai, and Mumbai, as well as approximately 7,300 km for the north-south corridor between Srinagar and Kanyakumari and the east-west corridor between Silchar and Porbandar (IRF 2003).

Over the course of the NHDP effort, it is envisioned that the project will provide direct employment to nearly 2.5 million workers along with 10,000 supervisors a day. It will also help to jump-start India's cement and steel industries, requiring on the order of 4 million tons of cement and 300 thousand tons of steel on an annual basis. When the work is completed, average speed along the national highways should double to 60 km per hour, resulting in lower fuel bills and significant travel-time savings. The improved arterial network will also help to further integrate India's rural areas and promote their economic development through faster access from the hinterland to main marketing areas (IRF 2003).

In addition to progress at the national level, a handful of states have also undertaken institutional reform efforts with the goal of improving the delivery and maintenance of highway infrastructure (Bansal et al. 2002b). Examples include the following:

- Divesting rural roads to local governments or dedicated central agencies
- Separating responsibility for state roads from building and/or irrigation functions
- Divesting government construction plants and equipment

- Establishing mechanisms for broader road user participation
- Creating Road Development Corporations (RDCs) as implementing agencies with clear mandates and a capacity to raise private finance

Finally, policy initiatives to address the current lack of all-weather connectivity throughout the rural road network are also underway. In 2000, the prime minister introduced the Pradhan Mantri Gram Sadak Yojana (PMGSY), a program designed to improve the rural network in a systematic fashion. Specific goals of PMGSY included connecting road access to all rural communities with a population of greater than 1,000 by 2003, and to all communities with a population of greater than 500 by 2007. As a result, approximately 600,000 km of tracks and trails in total have been refurbished as technically sound and durable roads. PMGSY has been implemented by the newly created National Rural Road Development Agency (NRRDA), which is administered by the Indian government's Ministry of Rural Development. Because the Indian constitution assigns responsibility for developing rural roads to state governments, the NRRDA is working in partnership with the appropriate state agencies to implement the development projects (IRF 2003).

Collectively, then, at the national, state, and rural road levels, recent institutional and policy-related reforms appear to mark the beginning of an important paradigm shift—from treating transport as social service to treating it as an economic development tool that simultaneously combats poverty (Bansal et al. 2002a).

Investment Climate and Funding Sources

China. Under the centrally planned system, provincial and local governments in China typically received funds for infrastructure construction from the central government. Starting in the early 1990s, China recognized that the highway expansion needs would not be met by the traditional revenue sources. To respond to the growing travel demand from the liberalization of the economy and rapid economic growth, other sources would be needed. As a result, the sources of funds for roads became increasingly diversified to include not only funds from central and local governments but also loans and credits from multilateral and bilateral organizations and commercial banks, as well as from foreign and domestic private capital (see table 4.10). These funding sources became critical for China's road infrastructure since 1990, especially for building the high-class highway

Table 4.10 China's Highway Funding by Sources (%)

Sources	1998–2001 Average
Central:	
Ministry Special Funds	7.0
Central Fiscal	1.3
Subtotal	8.3
Provincial:	
Domestic Loans	37.3
Local Fiscal	4.6
Self-Raised	46.1
Subtotal	88
Foreign Capital	3.8
Total	100.0

Source: Fan et al. 2005

network. The use of toll roads also became the primary vehicle for accessing private capital and other new sources of funding. China presently is charging tolls on virtually all high-quality highways. Under various revenue sharing arrangements between the government and private investors, many of these toll facilities now generate significant revenues to provide important funding sources for new construction and for leveraging external financing.

The general transaction of toll roads is centered upon the establishment of provincial toll road companies, which act as the financing vehicles for PCDs. PCDs inject operating assets to these special purpose entities to give them a high level of creditworthiness from the outset to raise new capital for the road development projects. Many of these companies are diversified with comprehensive portfolios. In 1999, for example, the Hong Kong Stock Exchange listed eight stocks that had a substantial part of their assets in Chinese roads, mostly in Guangdong (CPCS 2001). Most of these companies are ultimately controlled by entities associated with the PCDs in provinces where the assets are located. Private funding initiatives for toll roads in China, that is, the creation of private toll road companies with assets securitized on the markets, basically rely on five specific instruments: joint ventures (JV), securitization, loans from multilateral and bilateral agencies, domestic bonds, and commercial rate loans from the Chinese banks. JV arrangements are by far the most popular instrument, followed by securitization.

The multilateral and bilateral institutions historically played a central role in helping to solve the funding shortfalls by enabling the government to experiment with different kinds of road management structures.[16] Multilateral funds were used mainly for purposes of financing national and provincial trunk routes. It is anticipated that these funds will be less attractive in the future because of the conditionality that is usually attached to them. In addition, given that China is no longer eligible for concessional loans, these funds will also become more expensive than domestic rates. They remain, however, an important source for the construction of rural and feeder roads.

Beginning in 1998, another important change was made as the issuance of long-term public bonds to finance road and other infrastructure projects became more prevalent. Between 1998 and 2002, China issued more than US$74 billion in bonds to state-owned banks, such as the Industrial and Commercial Bank of China, for the following types of projects (Fan and Chan-Kang 2005):

- Construction of highways, railways, airfields, ports, and telecommunication projects
- Infrastructure investments in agriculture, forests, water conservancy, and the environment
- Environmental protection
- Upgrading rural and urban electric networks

As local governments gained more autonomy, they became responsible for most of the road projects financed by bonds. For example, local governments applying for expressway construction projects are now required to raise 35 percent of the cost themselves from their own revenue (including tolls) and by selling bonds (Fan and Chan-Kang 2005). The remaining 65 percent of the cost is funded through bank loans. As the investments in roads—especially for high-quality roads such as highways and expressways—has proven to be profitable in recent years, the banks are now more eager to fund road projects, especially in the eastern region.

This is reflected in the breakdown of highway investments by sources of funds averaged over the four-year period between 1998 and 2001. The local governments contributed most of the highway investment (88 percent) in that period, followed by the central government (8.3 percent) and foreign capital (3.8 percent). Two sources of funds make up the lion's share of the investments: domestic loans and self-raised funds by local governments, which together accounted for more than 80 percent of investments in 1998–2001.

The situation is quite different in western China where local governments cannot get enough revenue from tolls to pay for road maintenance and repay principal and interest on the loans. The greater autonomy given to local governments, in fact, contributed to widening regional inequality as the capacity to raise funds to finance road projects depended on local government revenue and their ability to negotiate higher contributions from the central governments. As a result, the central government launched major road construction projects in the central and western regions. From 1998 to 2001, for example, the share of highway investment in central and western China increased from 45 percent to 55 percent.

Between 1998 and 2020, it is estimated that over US$150 billion will be needed to complete the high-quality NTHS roads with only 50 percent of the requirement coming from user fees and other direct charges. The World Bank has estimated the likely shortfall in funding will be approximately 30 percent of this total, or US$50 billion overall.[17] In addition, China's Tenth Five-Year Plan called for a total investment requirement in road infrastructure to be US$120 billion. A major portion of the available funding from this Plan has been directed at the western provinces—mainly in development roads and the high-quality Class 1 and 2 roads,[18] with preference given to expressways linking the western provinces with eastern areas of the country. Under this Plan, it is anticipated that US$20 to $25 billion in private investment will need to be raised to meet the needs of the road infrastructure.[19] As the central government begins to redirect its resources increasingly to the western part of China, the eastern provinces will need to find private capital to supplement their road construction program.

The financial environment in China is in a constant state of flux. On the investment side, due to the increased individual and collective wealth, there is significant interest in investment options in China by both the individual and institutional investors.[20] The domestic capital market represents an important debt and equity finance source for infrastructure projects in China, which has developed extensively in recent years as evidenced by the opening of the Shanghai and Shenzhen Securities Exchanges in the 1990s and the growth in the domestic bond market. China's debt market is currently dominated by government bonds. Under the State Plan, the bond issue quotas are given to ministries and provinces, which, in turn, allocate quotas for highway companies and other domestic enterprises. It is estimated that the bond funds will account for about 20 percent of the needed capital in the roadway sector in the future.

India. Most observers of the Indian transport sector would agree that there has been inadequate financing of roads in the past, with allocations to the road sector consistently declining as a share of the total national budget over successive planning periods. Road financing has also been problematic at the state level, and there has been a consistent bias toward investment in rural access rather than maintenance and rehabilitation of the most economically beneficial roads. Until quite recently, user fees have not been tapped as a major source of revenue, and capital from the private sector has not been widely leveraged.

At the present time, there is, in fact, a wide variety of taxes levied on the road transport sector. These include cesses (taxes) on diesel and petrol, unions customs duties, excise duties, and central sales taxes levied by the central government; motor vehicle taxes, passenger and goods taxes, sales taxes, and entry taxes levied by the states; and octroi (taxes on goods entering a city) and tolls levied by local bodies. Yet even with this wide array of funding mechanisms, road finance in India remains problematic. Major outstanding issues include the following (Akanda 2003, Bansal et al. 2002b):

- Prior to recent diesel and petrol cesses, none of the road-related taxes was specifically earmarked for transportation, and at present, less than 60 percent of road tax revenues are returned to fund transportation.
- Current road user tax burdens are geographically inequitable, varying widely from one area of the country to the next.
- Many forms of taxation (such as passenger and goods taxes, sales taxes, and octroi) are both inefficient to administer and time-consuming for users.
- Other than a few direct tolls levied on some bypasses and bridges, there have been no explicit pricing signals for road use, and cost recovery—at least for maintenance—has not been a clearly articulated policy goal.
- Appropriate incentive structures and institutional frameworks to attract private capital have not been sufficiently developed.

More recently, the Indian government has initiated steps to counteract these long-standing problems. Some of the most notable areas of financial reform include the following:

- Establishing a Central Road Fund (CRF) earmarked for transportation improvements and backed by user fee taxes on petrol and diesel
- Experimenting with rational road pricing and direct road tolling
- Seeking expanded funding from multilateral development institutions
- Bolstering the prospects and incentives for private sector finance

As mentioned above, India first introduced cesses on diesel and petrol in 1998. In 2000, with the passage of the Central Road Fund Act, the cesses were made permanent, and the funds were channeled into the newly created CRF. From a policy perspective, this represents a major step forward, and the financial implications are far from trivial. Annual revenues from the cesses amount to between US$1.0 and 1.3 billion, and are divided according to the following formula: 33 percent for the construction and maintenance of national highways, 17 percent for the construction and maintenance of state highways, 43 percent for the development of rural roads, and 7 percent for the development of rail overbridges to improve safety outcomes (Bansal et al. 2002b, IRF 2003).

Several state and national road projects are beginning to incorporate the notion of direct tolling as well. The major attraction of this approach is that the fees are directly related to benefits received, and they send a price signal that imposes market discipline on both suppliers and users. They are also clearly separable from general taxes and, with new technology, can be reasonably simple to collect. To date, only a few hundred kilometers of India's roads are directly tolled (compared to around 4,700 km in China). Even so, it is expected that direct road tolling will continue to increase in importance as road agencies are granted increasing autonomy in raising funds, as the desire to manage demand grows, and as the impact of debt related to current and recent borrowing within the road sector becomes more severe in future years (Bansal et al. 2002b).

The Indian governments at various levels have also sought to expand the available pool of funding from the multilateral financial institutions. Major partners on this front included the World Bank (e.g., approximately US$1.6 billion in loans approved between 1992 and 2002), the Japan Bank for International Cooperation (JBIC) (approximately US$320 million through 2002), and the Asian Development Bank

(ADB) (contributing an additional US$870 million through 2002) (Bansal et al. 2002b).

Finally, the government has also taken steps to ramp up the application of private-sector finance in highway development and maintenance projects. In addition to standard techniques, such as the issuance of state- and federally backed bonds, more innovative public-private partnership arrangements have also been developed. Examples include BOTs (Build-Operate-Transfer contracts, in which a private partnership builds and operates a facility for a fixed number of years, recouping its expenses plus a reasonable profit through tolling, before transferring the facility back to the state) and other forms of maintenance and operations concessions (Bansal et al. 2002b).

Different combinations of these new finance trends are being employed within the various divisions of the Indian road sector. For national highway projects, of course, the CRF as well as multilateral funding agencies are playing a strong role, but the efforts to lure private involvement are particularly pronounced. In order to enhance the attractiveness of BOTs and other forms of concessions, the government has introduced a variety of strategies to lower the risk and increase the reward to private capital. For instance:

- The government will carry out all preparatory work, including land acquisition and utility removal, such that right-of-way can be made available to concessionaires free of encumbrances.
- The government will streamline environmental clearances for large projects.
- Customs duty exemptions have been offered for a number of types of foreign-manufactured road-building equipment that are not manufactured in India.
- The domestic price preference (which tilts the competitive advantage toward Indian firms) has been removed for a few select projects.
- Bonuses are offered for early completion of projects.
- Procedures for the repatriation of profits have been streamlined.
- The government will provide capital grants of up to 40 percent for BOT projects.
- Earnings on NHDP projects are 100 percent tax exempt for five years and 30 percent tax exempt for ten years; associated housing and real-estate development projects are entitled to the same tax benefits.
- Up to 100 percent foreign equity is allowable for roads and bridges.

• New methods of payment, such as annuities and shadow tolls, are being used to reduce the risk to concessionaires.

The sources of funding for state highways are somewhat similar, including allocations from state budgets, money from the CRF, loan assistance from multilateral agencies, and private capital (IRF 2003). To attract more of the latter, states have begun to experiment with various forms of franchise arrangements, including BOTs as well as maintenance contracts for existing highway links. Contractors are allowed to set up tolls during the concession period in order to generate revenues to cover their costs and profit margins, and in certain cases they are also granted development rights as an added incentive (Bansal et al. 2002b).

The rural road development effort also draws funds from the CRF, from national and state budgets, and from multilateral institutions such as the World Bank and the ADB (IRF 2003). Unlike highways, however, rural roads do not present much opportunity in terms of developing revenue streams based on user fees (after all, their primary role is to help alleviate poverty and promote rural economic development); as such, there has been less effort to attract the private sector into this arena for anything beyond simple construction contracts. The private capital injection and revenues derived from user fees for the national and state highways may provide opportunity to reallocate or free up public funds to invest in rural roads.

Summary and Lessons Learned

The basic aim of this chapter is to record and analyze the overall infrastructure experience and different approaches in infrastructure sector development for China and India. The comparative analysis presented in this chapter provides important lessons learned for other developing countries in addressing the critical infrastructure policy issues and questions described in the following.

What Role Should Infrastructure Play in Developing Economies?

There is a large body of literature that analyzes the impact of infrastructure on both economic growth and on poverty reduction (Klitgaard 2004).[21] Though there is an overwhelming recognition of the contribution of infrastructure in modern economies, the links between infrastructure and economic growth and poverty reduction is neither certain nor automatic. Infrastructure development results in improvements in productivity and in overall quality of life but the impact is still contextual. A study prepared jointly by three major development institutions—the Asian Development Bank (ADB), Japan Bank for International Cooperation (JBIC), and the World Bank—advocated that it is not enough to examine impacts of infrastructure without broadening and deepening the definition of poverty and economic growth (ADB et al. 2005a,b). In the study, the impacts of infrastructure are seen to occur at three levels—first, through facilitating economic growth; second, through improving quality of life; and, finally, through enhancing broader social and economic capabilities.

Nevertheless, manufacturing and exports have proven to be key drivers of economic performance of less developed and developing countries. Infrastructure provides connections to the global economy that are crucial for export competitiveness and manufacturing. As demonstrated by the recent experiences in India and China described in this chapter, infrastructure played an important role for these two Asian giants in their development process. Experiences have shown that it is important for top leaders and senior policy-makers to take an active posture in developing comprehensive infrastructure sectoral strategies that strike an appropriate balance between economic growth and redistribution of wealth.

China adopted the same model as other fast growing economies in Asia, building infrastructure ahead of demand that helped to promote exports and economic growth. China used infrastructure as a policy instrument and active political tool to reduce poverty and trigger growth. The central government had a strategic vision that was combined with a sustained drive toward economic growth, which resulted in unprecedented growth, poverty reduction, and gains in efficiency, but at a cost of increased inequality and great regional disparity. India started with a very rational approach of maintaining a balance between growth and distribution, but changed mid-course to a greater emphasis on redistribution. India learned the hard way that a greater emphasis on redistribution was not viable without robust and sustained growth. The resulting consequences were limited improvements in growth and poverty reduction with relatively little impact on income distribution.

What Are the Critical Policy and Institutional Dimensions to Infrastructure Development?

Infrastructure development has several important institutional and policy dimensions. The infrastructure story, to be complete, must include the way planning and implementation is undertaken, how the risks are handled, and what type of incentives and accountability structures are in place to deliver the infrastructure system. Proper integration between policy-making and implementation and how the market-based systems are phased and merged with the preexisting, centrally controlled and planned economy are all part of the story. In recent years, this story has become further complicated by the tremendous global shortage in short- and long-term funding needs for infrastructure. Multilateral and official lending institutions, the traditional funding sources for infrastructure, can fulfill only a small part of the total funding needs.[22] Deficit funding will no longer be a viable option in the long term and the role of the private sector will become increasingly important. At the forefront of infrastructure development challenges in the future will be the ability to establish a clear financing and pricing policy and, to the extent possible, in proper alignment between the bearers of infrastructure investments and the beneficiaries from the built facilities.

In terms of institutional and policy dimensions, both India and China used planning as an important tool. China viewed infrastructure development in its totality and encouraged strong integration and coordination between planning and implementation. China also allowed a market-based system to emerge on the margin rather than totally restructuring the existing system. The dual-track system between policy-making and implementation coexisted with market-based nonstate arrangements on one hand, and old-style centrally planned command economy on the other. This approach worked because ultimate decision-making authority remained within the central government.

In the period 1966–1977, India also exercised an incremental move toward state controls. India's approach was arguably more participatory and democratic in nature with much more technical and managerial focus in the planning stage; implementation and resource allocation, however, remained fragmented. India's approach to decentralization was to duplicate the central government structure at the state and local levels without coordinated roles and responsibilities and integration between different government levels. This resulted in duplication of responsibilities and weakened accountability, where there were too many political bosses. Unlike China, political interventions had a negative influence on the overall infrastructure outcomes.

Infrastructure reforms in China were easier because of strong central control. Central control also provided the ability to take risks and to go against the market economy when necessary. In the power sector, for example, what they called "new plant-new price" policy was possible where the consumers had to pay a higher price for the electricity generated by the new plants compared to the same service they received from old plants. The Chinese were also pragmatic in their approach and did not shy away from experimenting and using a trial-and-error approach. India's reforms started only in the early 1990s with the telecommunications sector, which resulted in an unleashing of private entrepreneurship. The reforms also focused on attracting increased private and foreign investment. Although the private sector provided a critical funding source, its participation had mixed results for both countries.

Depending on who pays, be they consumers or taxpayers, there will be different challenges for both countries in financing infrastructure projects. For consumers, the challenges will be the pricing and subsidy issues. For taxpayers, the challenges will be transparency and the balance between maintenance of existing facilities versus new construction. For the private sector, the challenges will be to work alongside the public sector to encourage policy improvements and better risk allocation models to continue to provide an attractive environment for private, foreign direct investment. For official lenders and donors, including multilaterals, the challenges will be changing their role with a focus on experimentation, innovation, and sharing risks; helping to build an institutional foundation in host countries to nurture the ability to implement major infrastructure projects; and ensuring sustainability in the long run.

How Should the Road Sector Be Integrated with an Overall Infrastructure Development Strategy?

By providing domestic connectivity and linkages to global connectivity, the road sector represents an important component to overall infrastructure development strategy and is one of the key contributors in triggering economic growth and poverty reduction. As demonstrated by the experiences in India and China, a balanced development between the arterial and rural roads addresses an important concern associated with a balance between growth and redistribution. Studies in developing countries also indicate that road quality and conditions are as important as the length and overall coverage of the roads.

India's road structure was actually more advanced than that of China at the beginning of the 1990s. That advantage, however, reversed dramatically in subsequent years due to a significant limitation in investment compared to China. In the decade following the early 1990s, China's annual investment in its road network increased 38 fold from about US$1 billion to around US$38 billion by 2002. During the same period, though India started out at a similar level, their investment increased by only threefold to just US$3 billion.

The investment allocation philosophy adopted by China was also very different from that of India. China focused first on arterial networks in connecting its 100 largest cities, devoting 60 percent of its investment to new arterial networks and only 15 percent to rural roads. The remaining 25 percent was devoted to upgrading existing arterial networks. India's philosophy, in contrast, emphasized "equity" focusing mainly on rural roads and adopting the basic goal of stretching a limited budget as widely as possible to create short-term employment for rural masses. The quality of roads is also a different story in India. Although the total length of roads is higher, only 57 percent roads are paved in India compared to 91 percent in China. In addition, only 2 percent of Indian roads have four lanes, while the rest are comprised of single-lane (39 percent) and two-lane (59 percent) roads.

Some of India's choices have had serious consequences; whereas China currently supports an impressive road network infrastructure providing a stable foundation for its continued economic growth into the future, India is continuing to deal with an inadequate road system that is not commensurate with the growth they have enjoyed in recent years and that threatens to choke further economic progress. India must address the needs and challenges facing their road sector to ensure continued economic growth in the future. Among others, these challenges include major capacity and safety enhancements, simpler road finance structures with more emphasis on user fees, greater accountability for road agencies in terms of outputs, development of closer ties between road agencies and stakeholder groups, and opportunities to leverage private finance to a much greater extent. Indian officials are well aware of these challenges and have taken initial steps to address them. Initial results appear promising, but much remains to be done.

Notes

1. For example, this share was a mere 38 percent for Japan at its peak.
2. China is adding 5,000 km of expressway every year, expecting to reach a level of 55,000 km in 2010 and over 80,000 km by 2020.
3. One important indicator for this philosophy is the network of rural roads in India versus China. India used the construction of rural roads to support

employment for poor people. At the end of 2005, India's rural road network encompassed over 3.3 million km. The rural road networks in China, in comparison, are of somewhat recent origin.

4. Besides, unmetered power supplies to agriculture users led to serious financial problems of the state electricity boards affecting future investment flows to the sector.

5. In October 1994, the Government of India (GOI) set up an Expert Group made up of both public and private sector infrastructure industry specialists to consider issues relating to the commercialization of infrastructure projects. The Expert Group's findings were presented to the GOI in June 1996 in a report titled "The India Infrastructure Report: Policy Imperatives for Growth and Welfare" (Government of India 1996).

6. Given the federal structure, the political leaders of the states also participate in preparation of the national plans. States have similar structures as the federal structure with the state planning commissions.

7. The five missions started by the Rajiv Gandhi government (1984–1989) did have elements of the Chinese strategic approaches, combined with the technical skills, capabilities, and adequate resources. Adequate implementation and monitoring apparatus were also built in for this particular mission with support from the highest level of the government, the Prime Minister himself. However, this worked as long as the attention and support of the Prime Minister was present. Its success, though very large in terms of access of service and cost reduction, was not backed by a systematic program of reforms necessary to sustain such a large-scale expansion of a service network. When the people who drove these programs moved from the scene, the success began to wear off until the onset of the mobile phone network many years later.

8. China's "new plant, new price" system allows a different tariff structure for new plants when compared to old plants for the same power generated and consumed. The new plants had higher costs compared to old depreciated ones.

9. Expressway and Class I roads represent access-controlled divided highways with more than two lanes; Class II roads represent all two-lane highways, divided or undivided, without access control. Expressways and Class I and II roads are considered "high-quality" roads. All other roads, that is, Class III or below, are considered rural roads.

10. NTHS is often called "high-class roads" and is part of the national highway system connecting the coastal regions and inner provinces in both east-westerly and south-northerly directions.

11. Data obtained from website: www.people.com.cn.

12. As was observed elsewhere in the world, this shift from rail to road may have been due to significantly higher cost of building and maintaining rail facilities, limited flexibility and accessibility inherent in fixed guideways, and other land entitlement and environmental challenges associated with right-of-way acquisitions. The overall financial condition of Indian

Railways was weak because of a number of factors such as subsidies and poor operating performance, and this led to only limited investments in rail modernization. The railway sector was thus unable to improve its capacity to meet the growing demand for passenger and freight transportation.

13. The International Road Federation provides comparable data across countries; however there are long time lags for some countries. See International Road Federation (2003).

14. These include the Highway Law (1997), Company Law (1993), and the Securities Law (1998);other new legislation, such as Contracts Law (1999), the Bidding Law (1999), the Arbitration Law (1995), the Environmental protection Law (1989), and the Land Administration Law (1989), as revised in 1998, are also important in constructing this mixed system.

15. See Akanda (2003); Bansal et al. (2002a, 2002b).

16. The World Bank, for example, has been supporting China's transport sector since 1983. By 1998, China obtained 18 road loans from the World Bank totaling about US$3.3 billion, which helped to support 1,300 km of high-class roads and 4,000 km of other roads. China currently has the biggest road portfolio among all the World Bank's client countries.

17. "Private Public Partnership in Toll Roads in China," *Ushering a New Era of International Cooperation between Engineering Consulting Industry in Asia and the Pacific Region*, Three Gorges, China, October 20–26, 2001.

18. Specific road classifications are defined in table 4.5.

19. By comparison, the total of all private sector contributions to the end of 1999 was about US$1.5 billion.

20. Household savings, estimated at about US$800 billion, now account for the largest share of domestic bank savings in China. Corporate investors have historically been an important source for most domestic enterprises in raising initial private equity prior to their listing on the domestic or foreign exchange.

21. Cited references are provided at the end.

22. In the power sector, for example, it is estimated that the multilaterals can only satisfy 5 to 10 percent of the funding needed.

References

Akanda, A. 2003. *ADB transport sector strategy for India—The roads subsector*, presented at SUMINFRA 2003 Summit on Integrated Infrastructure Development in Southern Region, Chennai, March 20.

Ashoka, Mody. 1997. Infrastructure delivery through central guidance. *Infrastructure strategies in East Asia: The untold story.*

Asian Development Bank. 2005a. *Key indicators 2005.* Manila.

Asian Development Bank, Japan Bank for International Cooperation, and the World Bank. 2005b. *Connecting East Asia: A new framework for infrastructure.* Washington, DC: World Bank.

Balisacan, Arsenio M. 2001. Pathways of poverty reduction: Rural development and transmission mechanisms in the Philippines. Paper prepared for the Asia-Pacific Forum on Poverty. Manila: Asian Development Bank, February 5–9.

Bansal, A., A. Bhandari, Z. Liu, L. Thompson, and P. Vickers. 2002a. Executive summary. In *India's transport sector: The challenges ahead*. Washington, DC: World Bank, May 10.

———. 2002b. Chapter 1: Highway. In *India's transport sector: The challenges ahead*. Washington, DC: World Bank, May 10.

CPCS Transcom Ltd. 2001. Private public partnerships in toll roads in China. Paper prepared for the International Workshop on Ushering in a New Era of International Cooperation between Engineering Consulting Industry in Asia and the Pacific Region. Three Gorges, China, October 20–26.

Deichmann, U., M. Fay, J. Koo and S.V. Lall. 2000. *Economic structure, productivity, and infrastructure quality in southern Mexico*. World Bank Policy Research Working Paper Series No. 2900. Washington, DC: World Bank.

Dollar, David and Aart Kraay. 2001. Trade, growth and poverty. Paper presented at The Asia-Pacific Forum on Poverty. Manila: Asian Development Bank.

Easterly, William and Sergio Rebelo. 1993. Fiscal policy and economic growth: An empirical investigation. *Journal of Monetary Economics* 32: 417–458.

Fan, Shenggen and C. Chan-Kang. 2005. Road development, economic growth and poverty reduction in China. International Food Policy Research Institute Research Report No.138, Washington, DC.

Fan, Shenggen, Peter Hazell, and Sukhadeo Throat. 1999. Linkages between government spending, growth and poverty in rural India, International Food Policy Research Institute Research Report No. 110, Washington, DC.

Government of India 1980. Planning Commission *Sixth Five Year Plan*, New Delhi

———.1996. *The India infrastructure report: Policy imperatives for growth and welfare*. New Delhi.

Harral, C. and J. Sondhi. 2005. Comparative evaluation of highway and railway development in China and India 1992–2002. Presented at the 2005 India Infrastructure Summit, New Delhi, March 28–29.

International Road Federation (IRF). 2003. Road development in India—Realizing a dream, *World highways*, Washington, DC, June.

J.P. Morgan Securities Asia Ltd. 1997. *Industry report: China highway sector*, Hong Kong.

Klitgaard, Robert. 2004. On infrastructure and development. Paper for the Planning Workshop for Infrastructure in East Asia: The Way Forward. Manila, January 15–16.

Kuroda, Haruhiko, Masahiro Kawai, and Rita Nangia. 2007. Infrastructure and regional cooperation. In *Annual World Bank Conference on Development*

Economics 2007, Global: Rethinking Infrastructure for Development, ed. François Bourguignon and Boris Pleskovic. Washington, DC: World Bank.

Kwon, Eunkyung. 2000. A link between infrastructure, growth, and poverty in Indonesia: Stage 1 Report, Economics and Development Resource Center. Manila: Asian Development Bank.

Li, P., Zhang, S., A. Talvitie, and Y. Chen. 1999. New models for financing and managing highways: asset-based road corporations in China, *Transportation* 26: 67–86.

Liu, Zhi. 2005. Planning and policy coordination in China's infrastructure development: A background paper, for *Connecting East Asia: A new framework for infrastructure.* Manila: Asian Development Bank, Japan Bank for International Cooperation, and the World Bank. Washington, DC: World Bank.

Minten, B. and S. Kyle. 1999. The effects of distance and road quality on food collection, marketing margins, and traders' wages: Evidence from former Zaire, *Journal of Development Economics* 60: 467–495.

Mody, Ashoka. 1997. *Infrastructure strategies in East Asia: The untold story.* EDI Development Studies, Washington, DC: World Bank.

Nagaraj, R., A. Varoudakis, and M.A. Veganzones. 2000. Long-run growth trends and convergence across Indian states. *Journal of International Development* 12: 45–70. 2000.

Patel, I.G. 2002. *Glimpses of Indian economic policy: An insider's view.* New Delhi: Oxford University Press.

Pucher, John, Nisha Korattyswaropam, Neha Mittal, and Neenu Ittyerah. 2005. Urban transport crisis in India. *Transport Policy* 12(3): 185–198.

Rondinelli, Dennis A. 1981. Government decentralization in comparative perspective: Theory and practice in developing countries. *International Review of Administrative Sciences* 47(2): 133–145.

_____. 1989. Decentralizing public services in developing countries: Issues and opportunities. *Journal of Social, Political and Economic Studies* 14(1): 77–98.

Shirley, Mary. 1997. Information, incentives, and commitment: An empirical analysis of contracts between government and state enterprises, World Bank Policy Research Working Paper No. 1769. Washington, DC: World Bank.

_____. 1998. Why performance contracts for state-owned enterprises have not worked, Public Policy for the Private Sector Note 150. Washington, DC: World Bank.

Tarschys, Daniel. 2003. Time horizons in budgeting. *OECD Journal on Budgeting* 2(2): 77–103.

Virmani, Arvind. 2005. Economic reforms: Policy and institutions some lessons from Indian reforms. Indian Council for Research on International Economic Relations Working Paper No. 121.

Weingast, B. 1994. The political impediments to economic reform: Political risk and enduring gridlock, Paper. Palo Alto, CA: Hoover Institution and Stanford University.

World Bank. 1994. *World development report 1994: Infrastructure for development*, New York: Oxford University Press.

———.2007a. *Dancing with giants—India, China and global economy*, Washington, DC.

CHAPTER 5

Physical Infrastructure as a Challenge for Farsighted Thinking and Action

William Ascher

Introduction

Developing and maintaining adequate physical infrastructure poses perhaps the greatest challenge for overcoming the widespread problem of shortsighted decisions. Highways, seaports, airports, and other physical infrastructure projects may require a decade or more to construct, and the resources required to maintain these structures often must be secured for many decades. Shortsighted perspectives can lead to the following problems:

- Desperately needed physical infrastructure development may be postponed indefinitely because the benefits seem too far into the future.
- The design and construction of the infrastructure project may be compromised in order to provide earlier benefits. For example, some large-scale highway construction projects employ many hand laborers at the expense of the quality and promptness of completion of the road.
- Poor materials or poor construction techniques may be used in order to reduce short-term costs.
- Maintenance funds may be neglected at the outset of infrastructure use, and fail to be provided thereafter.

How can commitment to improvements in physical infrastructure be promoted despite these long gestation periods? Mobilizing capital for long-term projects is daunting under the best of circumstances, but it is even more challenging when political logic may dictate an emphasis on high-profile if poorly designed projects. The failure to take a long-term view often results in a lack of planning, neglect of long-term maintenance, and failure to make ongoing investments to sustain existing infrastructure. Every country faces a host of immediate needs that can siphon both current and capital expenditures away from infrastructure development and maintenance.

However, applying a comprehensive framework for assessing the causes of shortsighted policies, and identifying strategies for promoting sound farsighted strategies, can provide some guidance for meeting the infrastructure challenges. One such diagnostic and prescriptive framework is presented here, and the strategies suggested by the framework are briefly reviewed.

The Four Roots of Shortsighted Action

Virtually all of the obstacles to sound, farsighted actions can be boiled down to four sources that exist to a greater or lesser degree in every country, whether developing or developed. They are impatience, selfishness, analytic limitations, and vulnerability. The first two are largely, though not exclusively, internal to the people making shortsighted decisions, although the context beyond them can have major impacts on whether they will indulge their impatience or selfishness. The last two are primarily shaped by the external context, although both analytic limitations and vulnerability are also influenced by the perspectives of the individuals who experience and can address them.

Impatience. The pervasive desire to have benefits (and avoid costs) sooner rather than later is an obvious rationale for the diversion of funds away from long-term infrastructure development. Resources devoted to physical infrastructure may reflect shortsighted political agendas. For example, too much of Mexico's dwindling oil wealth is going into the construction of extravagant sports stadiums instead of improvements in roads, ports, and the irrigation system.

Shortsightedness is sometimes also reflected by designs to provide maximum employment opportunities. While there are instances in which labor-intensive construction is desirable, too often the makework nature of these projects results in a poor design and shoddy construction.

Finally, impatience often distracts attention away from the needs for maintenance and rehabilitation, which in developing countries typically have far greater returns than the initial construction.[1] A 2007 assessment by the World Bank's Independent Evaluation Group of the transport projects approved by the World Bank during the 1995–2005 period notes:

> Despite the Bank's emphasis on adequate and timely road maintenance, this objective was seldom satisfactorily accomplished. The limited funds allocated to roads were often wasted through inefficient work methods and too much spending on new construction at the expense of the maintenance budget. As a result, a high proportion of the roads in developing countries remained in poor condition.[2]

The political logic behind the shortsighted favoring of initial construction over maintenance typically rests on the fact that providing a new facility is highly visible, and easily redounds to the credit of the government seen as responsible. Yet maintenance is a generally a low-visibility activity, and if the current government is not the one responsible for the initial facility, maintenance may only remind people of the accomplishments of the past. Scrimping on maintenance when budgets are tight is also tempting because of its low immediate political cost, compared to disappointing people by freezing a road-building project or completing a harbor facility.

Selfishness. The general tendency to put the interests of self, family, and group above those of others cannot be considered an economic evil, inasmuch as it is a foundation of economic efficiency. In light of the difficulty of establishing accountability for long-term consequences, selfishness results in the inappropriate pursuit of short-term rewards at the expense of obligations to pursue long-term objectives for the individual's employer or constituency.[3] The fact that a road may take more than a decade to design, finance, and construct—and even more time to gauge its economic and environmental impacts—means that those involved in the early stages of planning and approval are unlikely to be held accountable if it falls short of expectations, or if the maintenance of budget commitment was not adequately built in. If it is important for political credit or career advancement to have "projects in the pipeline," the temptation to push unwise projects or to give short shrift to assessing long-term consequences may be very great, with little to prevent it from happening. A recent internal survey of World Bank staff involved in the transport sector yielded the following comment: "There is some evidence that economic analysis is manipulated if the economic rate of return is not high enough."[4] However, there is evidence that this problem was far more severe in prior periods, as we shall see further on in this chapter.

Another result of shortsighted infrastructure development arising from selfishness is cheap design and shoddy construction. "Build to last" is expensive up-front. The consequences of cutting corners in infrastructure development are inefficiency and even greater burdens on maintenance and rehabilitation. These impacts are more serious than one might imagine. A 2003 World Bank study estimated that the overall productivity losses in Latin America due to poor infrastructure *quality* are equivalent to 40 percent of real per capita income; matching the effectiveness of the U.S. infrastructure would add so much to Latin American productivity as to reduce the per capita income gap from ten times to seven times.[5]

Finally, corruption[6] is a clear symptom of selfishness, which takes advantage of the fact that accountability diminishes as outcomes stretch farther into the future. Corruption diverts long-term investment to near-term consumption of the bribe-takers, raises infrastructure costs, and allows shady contractors to do shoddy construction. Corruption can also result in highways and bridges that "go nowhere"; that is, they are routed in ways that have no legitimate economic or social justification. Again, the consequences are severe. According to one estimate, if not for the inefficiency and poor design provoked by corruption, the 2005–2010 infrastructure investment needs of US$550–$650 for developing countries would be reduced to US$450 billion. In addition to the money pocketed by corrupt officials, the costs of bribery extend to the shortened lives of infrastructure built with shoddy materials and the inefficiency of infrastructure located and designed for the advantage of those who reward corrupt officials.

Analytic Limitations. The difficulties of anticipating longer-term consequences of infrastructure development—and the realization of these difficulties—can have opposite but equally adverse effects on both the investment levels and the quality of infrastructure. The difficulty of making credible predictions of the success of any given major infrastructure project can undermine "selling" the project, especially to decision-makers representing other areas that would not benefit from the jobs and other benefits that accrue from the construction per se. For smaller scale infrastructure projects that rely on community self-help participation, uncertainty as to whether community effort will be matched by government permissions and support often deters the self-help effort.

On other occasions, policy-makers have rushed headlong into unsound infrastructure development without paying sufficient attention to long-term consequences. If policy-makers know that uncertainty cannot be completely eliminated, they may not bother to undertake intensive analysis. In some countries, the most grandiose infrastructure projects are launched with minimal realistic assessment of demand, construction requirements, and so on.[7] In some developing countries, such as Brazil, roads have been built into environmentally sensitive areas without adequate examination of either the environmental impacts or the sustainability of the farms established by migrants using the roads. In other words, neither the environmental risks nor the economic rationales were adequately analyzed.[8]

Vulnerability. Both policy-makers and citizens are sometimes in such vulnerable economic or political circumstances that they cannot pursue infrastructure development that they know is sound and desirable. Political leaders are often under intense pressure to provide immediate benefits rather than to fund long-term infrastructure; they also typically face political risk if they charge the tolls and fees needed to maintain infrastructure. Thus, one of the most serious problems in the electricity sector is that electricity rates are kept too low for electricity providers to provide reliable electric service, let alone expand the grid. This often creates a vicious circle of dissatisfaction with electricity service, unwillingness to pay electric bills (even if they are actually subsidizing the users), and even less satisfying service. Major public infrastructure projects may encounter strong resistance if they are to be financed through higher taxes; a politically vulnerable government is less likely to enact the needed taxes. If infrastructure development is instead financed through borrowing or related approaches that ultimately require user fees, it may be very tempting for the government to pressure the operators to reduce the fees even if this beggars the maintenance budget and deters others from participating in infrastructure development in that country.

By the same token, low-income individuals may be so close to the economic edge that they simply cannot afford to divert their time and cash to self-help infrastructure development in sanitation, school construction, and so on. The shortsightedness that results from such vulnerability is a strategic impatience rather than a "pure" impatience. Therefore even if people are committed to their (and their children's) long-term future, they will feel constrained to act for the short term. In short, successful appeals to induce decision-makers to bear the short-term costs needed for infrastructure development require both a sufficiently attractive end state and credibility that this state can be achieved.

Overcoming Shortsightedness in Physical Infrastructure Development

The five broad strategic categories emerge from considering how to address these obstacles are

- changing the set of tangible and intangible benefits and costs, and changing their timing, in order to make the long-term outcome more attractive;
- applying self-restraint mechanisms to insulate initial farsighted commitments, in order to resist later temptations, bind successors, and fend off pressures by others to abandon the commitment;
- improving and encouraging the use of stronger analytic routines to focus attention on longer-term consequences, in order to highlight their advantages and to increase the credibility of predictions that the short-term sacrifices will lead to long-term improvements;
- framing the farsighted appeals and communicating them most compellingly; and,
- changing the policy process and institutions in order to empower and insulate farsighted leaders and privilege farsighted over shortsighted considerations.

Obviously the strategies within these may address more than one of the four obstacles.

The ways that these broad strategic categories can be applied to promote long-term infrastructure commitments depend on whether community participation is integral to the particular infrastructure development initiative. For community self-help projects—when community participation in the work per se is important (e.g., in neighborhood sanitation projects or localized road maintenance)—making effective appeals to the local community members is an essential step. When community self-help is not important (e.g., in building major highways or port facilities), the audiences for appeals to make the short-term sacrifices for long-term infrastructure gains are the policy-makers and the general public.

Changing the Set of Benefits and Costs

While some strategies reviewed later in this chapter address the possibility of reducing impatience, the most straightforward way to accommodate existing impatience is to create new benefits and costs, change their magnitudes, or change their timing. Any change in the short-term or long-term benefits or costs of alternative policy options has the potential to change the calculations that people make in choosing among options. Impatience leads people to discount (i.e., give less value to) consequences occurring further into the future. Therefore, the initial design of a sound infrastructure initiative may be insufficiently attractive because its short-term costs seem too high compared to the discounted long-term benefits, but it may be salvageable through modifications. To illustrate some of these modifications involving tangible benefits, we consider three challenges: gaining general public support, encouraging community self-help, and disciplining officials involved in infrastructure planning and execution.

Consider first the challenge of gaining support for a highway project that requires ten years for its completion. The choice of segments to be constructed early on can be sequenced so as to prioritize the segments that will gain the greatest support for the initiative if they are completed earlier. To design such a sequence requires political assessment that goes beyond the engineering considerations.

Another strategy for gaining support for an expensive infrastructure development is to postpone the financial reckoning that policy-makers and the public would have to face. As chapter 2 of this volume elaborates, there are many financing options, some of which spread out the financial burden of the government and the public. Increasingly, highways, subways, tunnels, port facilities, and other major infrastructure projects are financed privately, in whole or in part, through a host of instruments that vary according to the initial and ultimate ownership of the system, whether the financing is shared between the government and the private company, the additional roles of the private company, etc. (these variations on "public-private partnerships" are reviewed in Richard Little's chapter 3 in this volume). For example, with the Build-Operate-Transfer (BOT) approach, the government contracts private sector firms to finance, construct, and operate the infrastructure for a fixed period of time, which is typically two or more decades (Levy 1996).[9] For example, in Thailand much of the financing for Bangkok's transportation expansion has come from Japan, Hong Kong, and Western European sources. Compared to huge budget outlays by the government, the BOT arrangements allow for projects to proceed without the immediate pressure for tax increases or inflation. Yet it should be obvious that because the private firms must recoup their investments and make a profit, they typically earn the proceeds from user charges. Thus, the public does not escape paying, but the payments are spread out over decades. One distributional implication is that the costs are typically borne by infrastructure users, rather than by taxpayers.

These public-private partnerships can reduce the myopic decisions that arise when contractors build infrastructure projects but have little stake in whether the construction is well-designed and soundly built. When private firms finance, construct, and collect user fees, their profits will be greater if the project is completed on time and functions well. If the period during which they collect fees is long enough, the firm will be motivated to build to last and provide long-term maintenance. The soundness of infrastructure initiatives financed through these arrangements is also reinforced by the fact that their economic viability is "market tested" by the need to secure private funding (Flyvbjerg, Bruzelius and Rothengatter 2003: 125–128).

Private financing arrangements are subject to their own pitfalls. Because governments are frequently under pressure to keep infrastructure access fees low, the firms engaged in public-private arrangements have to be concerned about the possibility that the government will insist on cutting the user fees. Or the government may simply appropriate the structures, invoking any number of possible complaints against the firm. For example, the Thai government seized the assets of the Bangkok ring road expressway (the so-called Second Expressway System) just before it was to open in 1993, resulting from a dispute over whether the consortium, led by the Japanese firm Kumagai Gumi, could charge the previously agreed toll (Levy 1996: 372). In order to ensure a profit, the firms may try to offset these risks by requiring a higher fee structure. Ultimately, then, users pay more.

Public-private arrangements also reduce the contribution of today's citizens to the ultimate aim of sustainable development to make future generations better off. In essence, private financing leaves it to future users to pay for what might have been paid for much earlier. The key question is whether the means of avoiding the short-term sacrifices undermines the farsightedness of the infrastructure initiatives.

Long-term bonds or loans provide alternatives to direct private financing and operation, still providing a way to reduce near-term costs in comparison with immediate budget obligations that would either raise tax burdens or divert funds from other programs. Revenue bonds specify the source of income to service payments to the bondholders, usually user fees of indefinite duration or earmarked taxes such as fuel taxes. In general, projects financed through government loans or bonds do not have the reality check on the feasibility of the project that the private sector involvement would provide, with the exception of loans secured through development agencies such as the World Bank, to the degree that these agencies have the will and the bargaining power to impose conditionalities that ensure soundness and sustainability. On the other hand, the question of whether spreading the burden onto future users is sufficiently farsighted holds for these strategies as well.

Next, consider the challenge of inducing community members to devote labor, cash, or both to neighborhood infrastructure improvements, such as sewer upgrading. To increase the more immediate benefits, the government could provide some early benefits, such as improvements in street lighting, as soon as community residents fulfill easily achievable milestones in their own efforts. The government or nongovernmental organizations could commit to further improvements as other community milestones are reached. The prospect and benefits of the externally funded improvements would thus add to the motivation for the self-help efforts even if the external outlay is relatively modest.

A parallel strategy is to reduce the short-term costs of undertaking a long-term initiative. The Orangi Pilot Project (OPP) in Pakistan's largest unauthorized urban settlement, exemplifies this strategy. Following earlier failed efforts to mobilize residents of this million-person slum on the outskirts of Karachi, a nongovernmental organization provided seed money to cover the costs of technical assistance, training, supervision, and tools; the community organizations, organized at the small scale of lanes, collected the money from residents, while also paying for the in-house facilities. By 1994, 97 percent of the lanes in the OPP area had underground sewer lines. OPP expenditures amounted to only 6 percent of the total US$2 million cost (Khan 1997).

Restructuring the criteria for performance evaluation can help to minimize a distinctive temptation that the officials involved in planning, evaluating, and executing infrastructure projects have frequently demonstrated. Many officials could advance their careers by furthering an apparently exciting infrastructure initiative, even if, in fact, the project design or its execution is unwise. Officials may exaggerate the profitability of the project in order to get it into the pipeline (e.g., by exaggerating the expected demand or by neglecting potential problems); they may rush projects in order to show progress, even if the progress is misleading; they may build in high-profile but frivolous features. The result is that government agencies chronically exaggerate the benefits of large infrastructure projects to make them seem more attractive (Flyvbjerg, Bruzelius, and Rothengatter 2003: Chapter 2). The problem for the public is that the project's shortcomings cannot be definitively demonstrated until the project is financed, constructed, and in operation. Therefore, the accountability for sacrificing the common interest for career advancement is typically weak or absent.

One solution is to base the performance evaluation on a parallel assessment of the project design and execution plan, conducted by disinterested, highly respected experts. This is what the World Bank did following its discovery in the early 1990s that many of the projects it had approved for funding ended up with very disappointing outcomes. In reaction, the World Bank created a Quality Assurance Group (QAG) with authority to selectively evaluate the work of Bank officials who, among other things, appraise borrowing countries' project proposals. If the QAG's evaluation faults these appraisals, the staff involved in these appraisals run the risk of diminished career prospects. The QAG's assessments have increased accountability, contributing to a much lower proportion of poorly assessed projects and a better average rate of return on World Bank projects.[10]

While these strategies of modifying *tangible* outcomes erode the farsighted nature of the initiatives that they can help to promote, the modification of *intangible* outcomes can avoid this tradeoff. Because people are motivated not only by material wants but also by pride, loyalty, and the desire for respect and affection, linking these nonmaterial factors to the support of farsighted actions can be a highly efficient approach.

The key is to provide *deference* rewards to enhance respect, self-respect, affection, and power for demonstrated commitment to farsighted goals. For example, at little material expense, people can be honored through awards for community service in infrastructure self-help efforts. The mere recognition of outstanding service can provide sufficient gratification for many people to make the sacrifice of their labor and even some funds for the long-term good of the community. However, the effectiveness of such recognition depends heavily on the perceived fairness of how honorees are selected.

For infrastructure projects of much greater scope, the value of intangible rewards derives primarily from how professional recognition can motivate the officials involved in infrastructure planning and execution. Here, the challenge is to establish professional norms and induce people within that profession to adhere to these norms, through a combination of recognition for professional excellence and opprobrium for violating the norms. In many circumstances, the anchor of professional norms to ensure high-quality physical infrastructure is the code of conduct of civil engineers. These codes vary from country to country, but essentially the professionalism of civil engineers commits them to principles requiring that the design of buildings and other structures will last for the long term, despite pressures to the contrary. For example, *Standard of Conduct for Civil Engineers* of the American Society of Civil Engineers (ASCE) states: "Engineers shall hold paramount the safety, health, and welfare of the public and shall strive to comply with the principles of sustainable development in the performance of their professional duties." Similarly, the *Standard of Conduct*

> prohibits its members to offer or accept bribes, kickbacks, and other similar payoffs and benefits to or from suppliers, regulators, government officials, trade allies, or customers…ASCE members and agents should also be prohibited from giving or receiving, directly or indirectly, anything of a significant value to, or from, an outside source in connection with a transaction entered into by the Employer. To offer or accept bribes or kickbacks is a crime, both morally and legally, and could result in disciplinary action up to and including dismissal. (American Society of Civil Engineers 2000: 11, 5)

The rewards of social interaction per se in solidifying commitment to farsighted action can also be effective. Professional associations provide an alternative identification for professionals who otherwise might find it difficult to fight off pressures from within their employment organizations to support shortsighted designs or execution.

The importance of social interaction can also be seen in successful cases of neighborhood self-improvement. The opportunities for sociability and solidarity are often important incentives for people, especially those who live in newly urbanizing neighborhoods where both physical infrastructure and social capital are initially wanting. Active neighborhood associations can provide the opportunities for sociability, reinforce the norms of community commitment, and strengthen neighborhood identity. A highly prominent success in such efforts can be found in Naga City in the Philippines, where the Kaantabay sa Kauswagan (Partners in Development) Program was a joint local government-NGO initiative that, beginning in 1989, encouraged membership in squatter associations by creating the opportunity for residents to purchase their land and obtain formal titles. The associations provide material incentives, such as savings programs and co-financing of land and neighborhood improvements, and also play a crucial role in surmounting the usual isolation and rootlessness of the squatters. Community activism in self-help efforts has risen impressively as the number of associations increased to 80 by 2005 from only nine when it started. The program is now recognized as one of the world's best examples of collaborative urban policy (UNESCO-Habitat 1996, Prilles 2004, Tumbaga and Sabado 2003).

Applying Self-Restraint Mechanisms: Overcoming Impatience and Political Vulnerability through "Hands-Tying" and Precommitment

One of the key strategies for addressing both impatience and vulnerability is for actors committed to farsighted infrastructure development to restrain the future opportunities to renege on their commitments. This can be accomplished through self-hostaging commitments or through the development of new institutions.

Self-hostaging refers to act of making a commitment that would bring severe costs upon the actor if he or she reneges on the commitment. The costs may be loss of reputation, breach-of-contract penalties to be paid to private partners, the cut-off of loans or grants, or the sacrifice of resources or prerogatives that were put up in some form, analogous to collateral.

For government leaders, loss of reputation can be a very significant cost. If the leaders announce that a particular infrastructure initiative is a cornerstone of their development strategy, reneging can easily be taken as hypocrisy, weakness, or both. For example, in February 2007 India's Prime Minister Manmohan Singh stated, "We have to improve the quality of our infrastructure... It's a priority of our government" (Hamm 2007: 48–58). Various government agencies, from the Ministry of Industry to the Planning Commission, followed up with the target of more than US$500 billion investment in roads, ports, and the like during the Eleventh Five-Year Plan period of 2007–2012. If, in the next few years, the investment (which requires significant buy-in from the private sector and the states, as well as the central government) falls short, the Prime Minister and his National Congress Party will face withering criticism.

The cut-off of loans or grants is a relevant cost when the commitment is part of the "conditionality"[11] of a foreign assistance agreement. Many large-scale infrastructure projects in developing countries rely on partial funding from the World Bank, the regional development banks, or bilateral foreign assistance agencies. The conditionalities may include the amount of investment the government commits itself to provide, requirements to provide adequate compensation for displaced people, and the environmental protections to be observed in planning and construction.

Now, one can ask why any sane political leader would want to be exposed this way. The answer is that if one's hands are credibly tied, those opposing the commitment may back off insofar as they realize that one's costs of reneging (and, in some circumstances, the costs to the country as well), are greater than the costs of maintaining the commitment. Paradoxically, by elevating the stakes, self-hostaging can increase one's power vis-à-vis that of opponents bent on undermining the commitment.

Another mode of hands-tying involves creating institutions that are given some decision-making authority over infrastructure funding. The very existence of an institution creates a momentum that insulates the commitment upon which it is based. To the degree that these institutions cannot be easily dismantled—at least without very great political or economic costs—the commitment is strengthened. The obstacles to dismantling include resistance by the organization's own leadership and staff, the legal and administrative arrangements that are difficult to reverse, and the reputational cost for government leaders if they try to eliminate it.

Infrastructure financing, for both construction and maintenance, can be precommitted through special endowment funds that are protected by regulation or statute from raids by the government itself. Such funds can be established through the initiative of executive or legislative leaders, but in some jurisdictions (such as the State of California), they may also be established through citizen initiative efforts. These funds are often most effective if they have their own secure revenue-raising authority, which is particularly relevant for those aspects of infrastructure that can generate their own revenues. "Transportation authorities" with the prerogative to charge tolls or other fees have, of course, been around for many decades. The Port Authority of New York and New Jersey, as a public corporation, operates the ports, ship-to-rail transfer systems, tunnels, bridges, airports, and some railroad lines for the greater New York City metropolitan area.[12] Although it is formally controlled by both states, its revenues from operating these facilities are largely insulated from the two state governments. On the national level, Japan, New Zealand, and the United States have long-standing, well-developed highway funds (Heggie and Vickers 1998). As Christopher Willoughby (2000: 18) concludes:

> The most promising solution to these problems [of underfunding of transport development and neglect of maintenance], which is attracting an increasing following around the world, is explicitly to recognize the essentially commercial nature of transport infrastructure, to pool the revenues from specifically user charges (for example, the part of the fuel tax representing charge for use of the road, as opposed to general budgetary contribution or compensation for pollution) in a central fund (Road Fund or Transport Fund), and to associate user communities in the management and supervision of the fund and its applications. Such arrangements (most highly developed in New Zealand) have already had a dramatic effect on the quality of maintenance in a number of developing countries, have helped to bring longstanding problems of vehicle overloading under control, and have made acceptable much needed increases of user charges. It does not fully resolve the huge problem of capital funding, but it lays a far more promising base for finding a way out.

Another narrower, but nevertheless important, type of infrastructure institution is the highway *maintenance* fund. While annual maintenance costs of a highway or other major infrastructure facility may be a small fraction of the total construction costs, the failure to maintain expensive structures can dramatically undermine their use. This is why the maintenance and rehabilitation of roads typically have far greater returns than the initial construction.[13] Eleven Latin American countries have been developing road-maintenance trust funds financed by road user charges. The objectives are to create user-controlled funds financed by road user charges, transfer authority from existing road administrations to autonomous road agencies, and establish road management companies to manage entire road networks on a long-term contractual basis, with payments based on "pre-established performance standards of the roads rather than on works executed." (Federal Republic of Germany 2003).

The emphasis on user control and autonomy from the top government executive authority underscores the need to insulate the trust fund from attempts by a shortsighted, fiscally desperate government to raid the fund. The relevance of this concern is demonstrated in the experience with similar funds in sub-Saharan Africa. The success depends straightforwardly on the degree of autonomy the head of the road fund has vis-à-vis the head of government(president or prime minister), and on unhindered access to revenues from tolls or fuel taxes (Benmaamar 2006). Even with earmarking, however, the funds may be subject to government raids, even in developed countries such as the United States.[14]

Strengthening Analytic Routines

Analytic limitations undermine farsighted infrastructure development through a combination of disregard for relevant considerations and a different form of impatience—the "strategic impatience" of taking the shortsighted option because the success of the farsighted option is too uncertain to warrant making the short-term sacrifices.

The disregard for relevant considerations stems from the very complexity of the systems in which major infrastructure projects are situated, ranging from economic and social impacts to environmental consequences. For example, until fairly recently, environmental concerns were underweighted in infrastructure development planning, not only because they typically presented greater costs, but also because they were simply not prominent in the mindsets of transportation engineers. Adding to this basic lack of focus of attention was the difficulty of predicting the environmental consequences of alternative design options. Thus, a combination of inattention and uncertainty minimized the relevance of environmental considerations, and to a certain degree, still does today. The same holds for consideration of the fate of people—especially economically marginal people—impacted by the infrastructure project (see Rosemary Morales Fernholz's chapter 9 in this volume).

Yet the focus of attention can be strengthened and uncertainty reduced by a suite of analytic exercises. These include systematic forecasting and futures-scanning, strategic planning, comprehensive valuation and benefit-cost assessment, and full-cost accounting. A lengthy time horizon for any of these devices will require attention to long-term consequences. All of these analytic devices, if undertaken with serious effort, can discipline the projection of consequences so as to minimize the neglect of important considerations and increase the appropriate degree of confidence in expected long-term effects. The two related keys to the effectiveness of these devices are comprehensiveness and incentives to employ them seriously. Thus, *strategic* planning is a major step beyond the physical planning encountered in any large-scale infrastructure initiative, in that strategic planning links infrastructure development to the explicitly defined goals of economic and social progress.

Valuation, an essential step in determining the benefits and costs of alternative infrastructure options, has to be stretched to its fullest to capture the value of the less obvious, typically less tangible outcomes, such as preserving the environment. The techniques for accomplishing more comprehensive valuation (and hence, more balanced benefit-cost analysis) have undergone impressive methodological advances (Freeman 2003), but they require considerable effort to master and to apply. *Full*-cost accounting covers both direct and indirect costs, including social and environmental costs.

The seriousness with which officials involved in infrastructure development use any of these devices depends on whether their incentives can overcome both the tradeoff of devoting significant efforts and the risk of being explicitly associated with a forecast, plan, or assessment that comes to be regarded as mistaken. Unless the official can gain from taking such risks, the risk-averse official is likely to engage in only superficial analysis, such as simply extrapolating trends rather than undertaking a serious assessment of impacts. The incentives can be professional recognition, as mentioned earlier, but they can also be commitments from higher authorities that the plans, if approved, can be executed with minimal interference. This presumes that regular reviews would be built into the schedule so that needed adjustments could be made.[15]

Framing Farsighted Appeals

Because research in psychology and behavioral economics has discovered that the rate of discounting future consequences is neither constant over time nor the same for consequences that are framed differently, there is considerable scope for strengthening farsighted appeals through careful framing. Five insights are most relevant for this purpose.

First, studies of the rate of discounting have found that far-future consequences are often not discounted very much more than medium-future consequences (Chapman 2003: 402). The essence of declining-rate (or "hyperbolic") discounting is that although earlier outcomes may be weighted more heavily, the salience of delay diminishes as they are extended further into the future.

Second, people may prefer spreading out benefits even if some would come later (Chapman 2003: 403–404), or even prefer that the most favored consequences come later than the less favored ("saving the best for last"), even if this requires sacrificing earlier benefits for later ones. Therefore, framing infrastructure initiatives to emphasize a sense of progress is often not so severely countered by the discounting of later benefits.

Third, important outcomes tend to be less susceptible to steep discounting than less important ones (the "magnitude effect") (Chapman 2003: 402). Therefore, emphasizing the most important results, whether positive or negative (e.g., dramatic improvements in transport, or choking on congestion), can be effective even if these consequences are farther in the future.

Fourth, in a great range of circumstances, distant but important *negative* consequences are discounted less steeply than positive consequences (Rothman and Salovey 1997, Chapman 2003: 402–403). Highlighting threats often can be more effective than highlighting opportunities. Of course, in some situations both can be emphasized, yet if there are serious constraints on how much can be communicated, an emphasis on negative consequences often has greater impact.

Finally, discounting can also be reduced by bringing the psychological pleasures or pains into the present (Elster and Loewenstein 1992). Insofar as future consequences can be vividly brought to people's attention, the current savoring or pain from anticipating future consequences can produce immediate if intangible benefits and costs.

Framing is also important because the receptivity to appeals depends on how the initiative is characterized in the minds of those who need to support it. Because no initiative can be analyzed in all of its detail, and analytic capacity is often quite limited, people use analytical shortcuts, or "heuristics,"[16] to assess current issues. They often assess the prospects of a new initiative in terms of earlier exposure to classes of experiences. The framing can trigger these associations that may bring to mind prior experiences because they are the most vivid, the most emotionally arousing, the most apparently "representative" of the new initiative, and so on. The important point is that if the experiences that are deemed relevant to the current initiative are positive, the receptivity is likely to be more positive than if the experiences evoked by the prevailing heuristic are negative. Therefore, the labeling and explicit linkages conveyed in communications about the new initiative can be crucial, because they can trigger both the application of particular heuristics and the focus of their operation. For example, the so-called availability heuristic prompts people to evaluate the current initiative in terms of the case or cases that most readily come to mind, perhaps because they were highly prominent, recent, highly emotional, and the like. If the most recent or prominent "road rehabilitation" project was a clear failure and if the availability heuristic is likely to be operative, labeling the new initiative differently or linking it to a broader program in a category that has enjoyed a stronger reputation for success can lead to a more successful outcome. Alternatively, before announcing the new initiative, leaders can publicize past successes in the category likely to be invoked as comparable.

The final dimension of framing—the "triple appeal principle"—is based on the insight, derived from psychodynamic theory, that appeals can evoke raw impulse, reason, or conscience (roughly equivalent to the Freudian constructs of id, ego, and superego), or some combination of these (Lasswell 1932). Physical infrastructure development is most typically regarded as an instrumental, pragmatic matter that appeals only to instrumental reason. A deeper appreciation of human motivation would suggest that physical infrastructure projects can benefit from stimulating "negative" impulses such as rivalry and feelings of superiority over those less successful in their efforts, or positive impulses such as affection toward children and grandchildren. The advocates of long-term infrastructure expansion can also try to mobilize support by appealing to aspects of conscience, such as the righteousness of sacrificing for future generations.

Changing the Policy Process

The way infrastructure decisions are made will shape the possibilities for focusing on the long term, deflecting impulsive decisions, insulating farsighted leaders from short-term pressures, and reducing the fears of vulnerability. Four principles should guide the design of institutions and processes that plan and execute infrastructure development.

The first principle is that both political and technical analysis must play a prominent role in determining the design and financing of infrastructure initiatives. The neglect of technical considerations yields poor infrastructure systems; the neglect of political considerations yields failures to address societal wants and needs, and throws up obstacles to successful enactment. "Politics" is not the sordid obstacle to good development that it is often made out to be—it is essentially the process of the "shaping and sharing" of valued outcomes: who should decide on what valued outcomes should be created, and—crucial to the question of farsightedness—when?[17] Although the expression "It was politics rather than a good decision" is commonly heard, this is quite misleading. To be sure, there are many occasions in which special interests, diverging from the pursuit of the public interest, exert political pressure. Yet, the political process as a whole is essential for determining the interests of people and, when it is a healthy process, for securing the public interest. Selfish, shortsighted politics is a problem of selfishness and impatience, not of politics in general.

The second principle is that the decision sequence should involve enough stakeholders, with enough authority, so that no one can impose an impetuous decision, and all relevant considerations have a chance to be taken into account. This "checks and balances" approach may seem obvious, especially for large-scale infrastructure initiatives that take a long time for design and financing, but sometimes key, largely irreversible decisions are made by particular decision-makers along the way that can undermine the soundness and sustainability of the project. Often, broad stakeholder participation is very helpful, although some stakeholders may not be pleased when they do not get their way, at which point they may question the structure and seriousness of the consultation. Stakeholder participation is particularly complicated in the planning of major infrastructure projects that span many communities and have indirect impacts on those not situated in the path of the project. Building in enough time to consider the consequences of design and financing elements is also relevant; many governments build in formal delays and multiple stages so that "due deliberation" is more likely.[18]

The third principle is that it is useful, if not essential, for decision-makers to have some insulation from the risks of being punished for resisting pressures to cater to the short term. This can be accomplished in different ways. One strategy is to give authority to commissions whose members cannot be dismissed during their terms, except of course for illegal actions. A related approach is to provide the head of the financing entity some degree of autonomy from the top government leader, and to explicitly earmark the revenues from particular tolls or fuel taxes. These two forms of insulation have been shown to improve the effectiveness of road-maintenance funds in sub-Saharan Africa (Benmaamar 2006).

The fourth principle is to keep the stakes of "winning" or "losing" within reasonable bounds, so that representatives of communities or interest groups do not have an incentive to take rash measures. Such vulnerability obviously focuses attention on the short-term considerations of economic, social, or even physical survival. The treatment of people displaced by major infrastructure projects is clearly relevant here (see chapter 9 by Rosemary Morales Fernholz in this volume).

Conclusion

The impressive range of strategies with potential for promoting farsighted infrastructure development holds considerable promise. Multiple strategies emerge from the logic of altering the nature and timing of benefits and costs, using self-restraining instruments, strengthening analytic capacity, adopting framing strategies that make farsighted appeals resonate with those who must support them, and restructuring the policy process. We have seen that expanding the focus beyond economic motivations yields a much richer set of considerations—psychological, social, and political—that can serve as the bases for developing strategies.

The specific strategies that should be adopted will, however, depend on the particular context that a farsighted infrastructure initiative will face. Contexts vary drastically in terms of scope, degrees of uncertainty, common identification of stakeholders, receptivity to emotional appeals, and so on. The strategies offered in this chapter are simply intended to stimulate broad thinking about how farsighted infrastructure initiatives can be promoted.

Notes

1. For example, a European Investment Bank estimate of the economic returns on new roads in the Balkan states at 5 percent, but the returns on road maintenance as 20 to 70 percent (Hörhager 2006).
2. World Bank Independent Evaluation Group (2007: 24). A 2006 assessment by the sub-Saharan Africa Transport Policy Program reports that of the 18 sub-Saharan African countries that have established road-maintenance funds and provide enough data to assess the degree to which routine and periodic maintenance is accomplished, only four countries are meeting the full routine maintenance, and none is fully meeting the periodic maintenance needs; the median level of meeting periodic needs is less than 40 percent (Benmaamar 2006: 13).
3. This problem comes under the technical rubric of the "principal-agent problem."
4. World Bank Independent Evaluation Group (2007: 155).
5. Rioja (2003).
6. Best defined as violations of the public trust for personal (defined broadly) gain. Therefore some corruption actions may be legal, such as that of a government official who courts campaign contributions by supporting infrastructure projects that he or she knows are not in the public interest.
7. See Flyvbjerg, Holm, and Buhl (2006) on overbuilt infrastructure. For examples of seemingly willful neglect of examination of the appropriateness of building roads into environmentally vulnerable areas, coupled with

inadequate examination of the sustainability of the initiatives, see Fearnside (1985), Secrett (1986), and Donner (1987).

8. See Mahar (1989) and Lisansky (1990).

9. These are also termed "Build, *Own*, Transfer" arrangements, with the same acronym and apparently the same structure.

10. The Quality Assurance Group case is elaborated in Ascher (2008: Chapter 6).

11. This term simply translates as "condition."

12. Detailed information on the history, structure, financing, and governance of the Port Authority of New York and New Jersey can be found at www.panynj.gov.

13. For Africa, see Benmaamar (2006) and Hook (2006: 3); for the transitional economies of the Balkans, see Hörhager (2006: 10), citing European Investment Bank estimates of the rates of return on road-maintenance projects at 20–70 percent, compared to returns on road construction of only 5 percent.

14. The four federal transportation trust funds have been under both direct and indirect attack for decades. The spending levels of the Harbor Maintenance Trust Fund, the Airport and Airway Trust Fund, and the Inland Waterways Trust Fund have "been artificially held down to mask the size of the operating deficit. In effect, these deficit-proof, pay-as-you-go programs have been cut back to finance other programs, funded out of general revenues, that have been the true cause of deficits. While we believed this to be unacceptable even during the era of budget deficits, it is even more difficult to justify in this new era of budget surpluses." (United States House of Representatives, Committee on Transportation and Infrastructure 2001).

The U.S. Interstate Highway Trust Fund, vigorously defended by road construction interests, has largely escaped this form of raiding, but a significant portion of its resources have been directed to other modes of transportation, especially mass transit.

15. These points are elaborated at greater length in Ascher (2009: Chapter 8).

16. The "heuristics and biases" approach is widely identified with Nobel Prize Laureate Daniel Kahneman and his many collaborators. Collections of their works can be found in Kahneman, Slovic, and Tversky (1982); Kahneman and Tversky (2000); and Gilovich, Griffin, and Kahneman (2002).

17. These two definitions of "politics" within the policy sciences framework converge: Harold D. Lasswell (1936) introduced the definition of politics as "who gets what, when, how," as well as the identification of politics with the "shaping and sharing of values (Lasswell 1962).

18. The multiple readings of legislative proposals before the British House of Commons is a case in point, as is the complicated process of multiple committees considering authorizations and appropriations in the U.S. Congress. See Ascher (2009: Chapter 14).

References

American Society of Civil Engineers. 2000. *Standards of conduct for civil engineers.* Reston, VA. April.

Ascher, William. 2009. *Bringing in the future: Strategies for farsightedness and sustainability in developing countries.* Chicago: Chicago University Press.

Benmaamar, Mustapha. 2006. Financing of road maintenance in Sub-Saharan Africa: Reforms and progress towards second generation road funds. Sub-Saharan Africa Transport Policy Program. RMF Series Discussion Paper No. 6. Washington, DC: Road Management and Financing, September.

Chapman, Gretchen. 2003. Time discounting of health outcomes. In *Time and decision: Economic and psychological perspectives on intertemporal choice,* ed. George Loewenstein, Daniel Read, and Roy Baumeister, pp. 395–417. New York: Russell Sage Foundation.

Donner, Wolf. 1987. *Land use and environment in Indonesia.* Honolulu: University of Hawaii Press.

Elster, Jon and George Loewenstein. 1992. Utility from memory and anticipation. In *Choice over Time,* ed. George Loewenstein and Jon Elster. New York: Russell Sage Foundation.

Fearnside, Philip. 1985. Deforestation and decision-making in the development of Brazilian Amazonia. *Interciencia* 10: 223–247.

Federal Republic of Germany. 2003. Technical assistance program of the Federal Republic of Germany for Latin American and Caribbean Countries in road conservation, October. http://www.zietlow.com/engprog.htm. Accessed January 4, 2006.

Flyvbjerg, Bent, Nils Bruzelius, and Werner Rothengatter 2003. *Megaprojects and risk: An anatomy of ambition.* Cambridge: Cambridge University Press.

Flyvbjerg, Bent, Mette K. Skamris Holm, and Søren L. Buhl. 2006. Inaccuracy in traffic forecasts. *Transport Reviews* 26(1): 1–24

Freeman, A. Myrick, III. 2003. *The measurement of environmental and resource values, 2nd Edition.* Washington, DC: Resources for the Future.

Gilovich, Thomas, Dale Griffin, and Daniel Kahneman, eds. 2002. *Heuristics and biases: The psychology of intuitive judgment.* Cambridge: Cambridge University Press.

Hamm, Steve. 2007. The trouble with India: Crumbling roads, jammed airports, and power blackouts could hobble growth. *Business Week*, March 19.

Heggie, Ian G. and Piers Vickers. 1998. Commercial management and financing of roads. Technical Paper No. 409. Washington, DC: World Bank.

Hook, Walter. 2006. Urban transportation and the millennium development goals. *Global Urban Development* 2(1): 1–9. http://www.globalurban.org/GUDMag06Vol2Iss1/Hook%20PDF.pdf. Accessed November 18, 2007.

Hörhager, Axel. 2006. Financing investment in transport infrastructure: The European Investment Bank [Power Point presentation]. Luxemburg: European Investment Bank. December. http://www.seetoint.org/site/pdf/20-ddf7.pdf. Accessed November 18, 2007.

Kahneman, Daniel and Amos Tversky, eds. 2000. *Choices, values, and frames.* Cambridge: Cambridge University Press.

Kahneman, Daniel, Paul Slovic, and Amos Tversky, eds. 1982. *Judgment under uncertainty: Heuristics and biases.* Cambridge: Cambridge University Press.

Khan, Akhter Hameed. 1997. The Orangi Pilot Project: Uplifting a periurban settlement near Karachi, Pakistan. In *Reasons for hope: Instructive experiences in rural development*, ed. Anirudh Krishna, Norman Uphoff, and Milton J. Esman, pp. 25–40. West Hartford, CT: Kumarian Press.

Lasswell, Harold D. 1932. The triple-appeal principle: A contribution of psychoanalysis to political and social science. *American Journal of Sociology* 37: 523–538.

_____. 1936. *Politics: Who gets what, when, how.* New York: McGraw-Hill.

_____. 1962. The public interest: Proposing principles of content and procedure. In *The public interest*, ed. Carl Friedrich, pp. 54–79. New York: Atherton Press.

Levy, Sidney. 1996. *Build, operate, transfer: Paving the way for tomorrow's infrastructure.* New York: John Wiley & Sons.

Lisansky, Judith. 1990. *Migrants to Amazonia: Spontaneous colonization in the Brazilian frontier.* Boulder, CO: Westview Press.

Mahar, Dennis. 1989. *Government policies and deforestation in Brazil's Amazon region.* Washington, DC: World Bank.

Prilles, Jr., Wilfredo. 2004. Empowering the urban poor: The case of Kaantabay sa Kauswagan Program in Naga City, Philippines. Cambridge: Cambridge University Department of Land Economy. http://www.naerus.net/sat/workshops/2004/papers/Prilles.htm. Accessed March 31, 2007.

Rioja, Felix. 2003. The penalties of inefficient infrastructure. *Review of Development Economics* 7(1): 127–137.

Rothman, Alexander and Peter Salovey. 1997. Shaping perceptions to motivate healthy behavior: The role of message framing. *Psychological Bulletin* 121: 3–19.

Secrett, Charles. 1986. The Environmental impact of transmigration. *The Ecologist* 16(2/3): 77–88.

Tumbaga, L. and M. Sabado. 2003. *Propelling growth, managing costs: A challenge to local governments.* Manila: Ateneo Center for Social Policy and Public Affairs.

UNESCO-Habitat. 1996. Kaantabay sa Kauswagan, An urban poor program in Naga City, Philippines, MOST Best Practices Clearing House, Nairobi, Kenya. http://www.unesco.org/most/asia8.htm, Accessed January 1, 2006.

United States House of Representatives, Committee on Transportation and Infrastructure. 2001. Views and estimates of the committee on transportation and infrastructure. Washington, DC. http://www.house.gov/transportation/views2001.html. Accessed January 4, 2006.

Willoughby, Christopher. 2000. Transport services in the 21st Century: Seamless market or choiceless churning? World Bank Transport, Water and Urban Development Discussion Paper. Washington, DC: World Bank, January.

World Bank Independent Evaluation Group. 2007. A decade of action in transport: An evaluation of World Bank assistance to the transport sector, 1995–2005. Washington, DC: World Bank.

CHAPTER 6

Transit Transformations: Private Financing and Sustainable Urbanism in Hong Kong and Tokyo

Robert Cervero

Transit Value Capture

Few sectors of urban infrastructure have experienced as strong a push to privatize in recent decades as the public transit sector. In the developed world, spiraling operating deficits and falling ridership prompted many public transit agencies to competitively contract out bus- and rail-passenger services to the private sector in the 1980s and 1990s. As protected monopolies, critics charged that public operators failed to rein in escalating costs, innovate in response to changing market preferences, and effectively compete with the increasingly popular private automobile (Estache 1999). In the United States and United Kingdom, privatization of public transit became the centerpiece of urban transportation policy under the Reagan and Thatcher administrations. In less developed countries, international aid agencies openly embraced urban transport privatization, reflected by the following World Bank policy position: "Competition, facilitated by regulatory reform to enable private firms to enter and exit the market more freely, forces transport suppliers to respond to user's needs at lower costs" (World Bank 1996: 33).

Experiences with competitive tendering of bus services in Delhi, Colombo, and Copenhagen generally yielded favorable outcomes: ridership increased, the amount of services increased, and operating costs were held in check (Estache 1999). Such results, however, only appeared under "managed competition"—that is, when a public oversight entity set and enforced service-quality, tariff, and safety standards.

Where private operators openly colluded and the enforcement of operating standards was lax, such as was the case with transit deregulation in Santiago, Chile, service reliability and quality plummeted while
tariffs increased. Absent managed competition and market contestabil-
ity, experiences show that deregulating and privatizing public transit
in large, congested cities can backfire, forcing authorities to reregulate
and reinstall a public operator, as in Santiago.

While neoliberal policies of privatizing bus operations remain popular in much of Latin America and Asia, there has been less progress in
attracting private capital for the construction of public transit infrastructure, particularly urban passenger rail systems. Privatization of
road construction has been far more commonplace. Private concessions for the construction of public-transit systems has had a check-
ered past—due mainly to higher risks and difficulties in coordinating
system designs and services among multiple interests. Private financing
of metros in Manila, Bangkok, and Kuala Lumpur won kudos for expe-
diting project implementation and containing construction costs, but
was faulted for failing to integrate rail transit not only with other modes
but even between metro lines. Ridership suffered as a result, yielding
fewer mobility and environmental benefits than expected. Private takeover of existing public-transit assets has fared even worse, underscored
by the British Railtrack fiasco. While costs fell when British Rail was
broken into almost a hundred pieces and sold in the mid-1990s, service
quality and public safety quickly plummeted (Shaw 2000). In 2002,
British Railtrack was dissolved and its assets sold to Network Rail, a
state-backed, not-for-profit corporation whose profits go mainly to rail
maintenance and expansion. There have been some successes following
private financing of metro systems, notably in Buenos Aires and Rio
de Janeiro where ridership increased and costs fell without a notice-
able decline in service quality (Estache, Carbajo, and Rus 1999, Zegras
2004). These experiences show that privatization of public transit infrastructure works best with the expansion of existing services (versus the
construction of new facilities) and in congested corridors with pent-up
demand, few mobility options, and an emerging middle class (Rodriquez
1999). Also important is the setting and enforcement of service-quality
and safety standards that protect the broader public interest.

The most notable contemporary examples of private railway construction of the majority of urban rail lines, not just extensions (as has
been the case in Latin America), come from two of east Asia's economic juggernauts: Hong Kong and Tokyo. What distinguishes both
cases is private railway companies' reliance on property development to

generate profits. In Hong Kong, a private corporation has assumed the role of building the city's modern urban rail systems, relying mainly on returns from ancillary land development to cover construction and development costs. Metropolitan Tokyo has an even longer history of private railway construction. Over the past half century, private railway corporations have constructed new towns around railway stations throughout the suburbs of Tokyo, exploiting the land-value gains in and around railway stations conferred by improved accessibility. Called *value capture*, this approach to infrastructure finance is fair and efficient. Why, the reasoning goes, let a handful of fortunate landowners, or worse yet, real estate speculators, reap the windfalls created by public investments in transit? Returning the value-added to retire construction bonds can relieve cash-strapped local governments of fiscal burdens while also reducing land speculation and creating a more compact, transit-oriented urban form. Having the transit entity control the land around stations, moreover, increases the chance that major trip generators and transit-oriented land uses—such as retail plazas, offices, and civic uses—occupy strategically important land parcels, thereby increasing ridership and farebox returns. Ironically, transit value capture was first practiced in the United States, the world's most automobile-dependent society today. One hundred-plus years ago, private landholders secured exclusive franchises to build interurban streetcar lines in dozens of U.S. cities, reaping windfalls from land sales to more than cover investment costs (Bernick and Cervero 1997). Never in American history has there been a more intimate connection between rail transit services and urbanization than during this era. Contemporary efforts to build compact, mixed-use, walking-friendly "transit villages" largely seek to recreate a built form that thrived throughout urban America in the early 1900s. The ensuing years of public takeover of transit infrastructure in the United States has been accompanied by a disconnect between rail investments and land development. Most suburban retail development in the United States has turned its back on transit, oriented to freeway interchanges, not transit stations. The dominant land use around most suburban rail stations in even big U.S. cities like Los Angeles and Chicago is surface parking lots.

Today, the historically successful model of bundling urban railway infrastructure and land development is alive and well in both Hong Kong and greater Tokyo, among the few places where transit value capture is still practiced today. These are hardly philanthropic gestures on the part of railway companies. Make no mistake: as private corporations accountable to stockholders, the primary motivation for massing land development around stations in both cities is to secure profits. In traffic-choked cities such as Hong Kong and Tokyo, this can mean pushing density envelopes as high as possible around many stations. Critics warn, however, that profiteering by intensifying land development in and around stations can be at the expense of longer-term public objectives, like provision of public open space and functional pedestrian corridors. In this chapter, I argue that private railway companies in both cities are in the midst of a culture change, increasingly realizing that station-area developments that promote broader public interests can also improve their bottom lines. Ensuring that high-rise structures are architecturally integrated with subway stations, provide efficient and attractive pedestrian corridors, allow for a mix of land uses that appeal to transit customers, and place an accent on public amenities can yield huge land market premiums. Thus, real-estate profiteering and urban place-making can be mutually reinforcing. Private railway companies themselves have institutionally responded by establishing urban planning divisions within their organizations to ensure ancillary real-estate development is of a high quality, promotes local development objectives, and is functionally integrated with transit infrastructure.

The principal lesson to be learned from this chapter—that private profiteering and smart growth of the public realm can be mutually reinforcing—is particularly important to rapidly industrializing countries, such as China, that are building metrorail systems at a staggering pace. Adapting Hong Kong's and Tokyo's models of railway investments and urban development to places like China, I conclude, is among the most promising pathway to achieving sustainable urban futures.

Transit in Hong Kong and Tokyo

Hong Kong and Tokyo are internationally known for successfully integrating rail transit and urbanization. Indeed, their huge populations and exceptionally high urban densities, and the agglomeration benefits that have resulted, could not be sustained without world-class railway services. Greater Tokyo is much larger than Hong Kong (table 6.1). Tokyo's 23rd ward area, however, is more comparable to Hong Kong in population size (8.46 million versus 6.94 million inhabitants) although its densities are one-half of Hong Kong's (13,608 versus 26,473 persons per square km).

Any visitor to Hong Kong instantly recognizes that public transit is the lifeblood of the city. Hong Kong boasts a rich offering of transit services, including a high-capacity railway network, surface-street trams,

Table 6.1 Population, Area, and Density: Hong Kong and Tokyo, 2005

	Hong Kong	*Tokyo*
Population, 2005	6,935,900	34,196,915 (Metropolitan Area)
		8,457,418 (Municipality)
Area (sq km)	1,107 (Total)	13,556
	262 (Urbanized Area)	621
Density (persons per sq km), 2005	6,266 (Total)	2,523
	26,473 (Urbanized Area)	13,608
Population Growth %, 2000–2005	1.02	3.15
		3.97

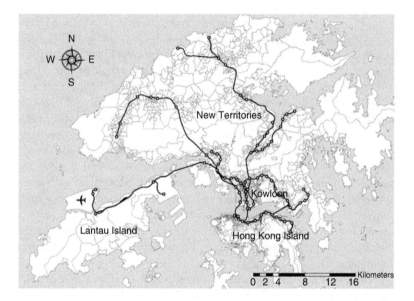

Figure 6.1 Hong Kong's MTR System, 2007

ferries, and an assortment of buses and minibuses. In late-2007, the city's main passenger rail operator, MTR Corporation (MTRC), merged with the former Kowloon-Canton Railway Corporation, forming a 168 km network of high-capacity, grade-separated services in Hong Kong island, the Kowloon peninsula, the Northern Territories (to the Chinese border), and, through a recent extension, to Hong Kong's new international airport (figure 6.1). Today, over 90 percent of all motorized trips in Hong Kong are by public transit, the highest market share in the world (Lam 2003).

The combination of high urban densities and high-quality public transport services has not only produced the highest level of transit usage in the world (570 annual public transport trips per capita) but has also substantially driven down the cost of motorized travel. In 2002, over half of all motorized trips made by Hong Kong residents were a half hour or less (ARUP 2003). Motorized travel consumes, on average, around 5 percent of Hong Kong's Gross Domestic Product (GDP). This contrasts sharply with more automobile-oriented global cities such as Houston and Melbourne, where upwards of one-seventh of GDP goes to transportation (International Association of Public Transport 2002). Hong Kong residents enjoy substantial travel cost savings even in comparison to much larger global cities with extensive railway networks, like London and Paris.

Tokyo's railway network—owned and operated by a mix of public, private and quasi-private entities—is, by far, the world's largest (table 6.2 and figure 6.2). In 2005, 3,216 directional kilometers of track and 1,501 stations served a commutershed that extended more than 100 km from the central Tokyo station. Encircling Tokyo's core area is the Yamanote line, with major intermodal terminals and high-rise office developments found at key stations such as Tokyo-Marunouchi, Shibuya, and Shinjuku. Within the Yamanote loop is a dense network of both the now-privatized Tokyo Metro and publicly owned Eidan subway services. Also crisscrossing central Tokyo are several lines of the privatized Japan Railway (JR) East (formerly the publicly owned Japan National Railway). It is beyond the Yamanote loop where one finds purely privately built, owned, and operated private railways. These lines connect numerous suburban new towns to the major terminuses on the Yamanote loop, allowing passengers to switch to the Tokyo Metro or Eidan subway.

Tokyo's radial railway system supports and reinforces the region's monocentric structure. The geometry of radial rail lines and roadways that converge on the center has given rise to extreme congestion. Due in part to rising car ownership rates and Japan's aging population structure, public transport ridership has been declining over the past 15 years in greater Tokyo, which has exacerbated central-city congestion to some degree.

Rail + Property Development in Hong Kong

Hong Kong is one of the few places in the world where public transport makes a profit, courtesy of MTRC's "rail+property" program, or R+P for short. R+P is one of the best examples anywhere of transit value

Table 6.2 Major Railway Operators in the Tokyo Greater Metropolitan Area, 2005

Company/Agency	Type	Length (km)	# of Stations	Passenger (km million)	Year Opened
Tobu	Private	463.3	202	12,667	1897
Seibu	Private	176.6	92	8,669	1912
Keisei	Private	102.4	64	3,508	1909
Keio	Private	84.7	69	7,186	1910
Odakyu	Private	120.5	70	10,528	1923
Tokyu	Private	100.1	98	9,469	1922
Keikyu	Private	87.0	72	6,220	1898
Sotetsu	Private	35.9	25	2,604	1917
JR East	Former Public	1,698.3	516	76,694	1987 (1870)[a]
Tokyo Metro	Former Public	183.2	168	16,356	2004 (1927)[a]
Toei Subway	Public	106.2	105	5,291	1927
TX	Quasi-Private	58.3	20	NA	2005 (1991)[a]
Total		3,216.5	1,501	159,192	

Note: [a] Years in parentheses denote year of opening as a public operator. Years not in parentheses denote year of transformation from a purely public operator.

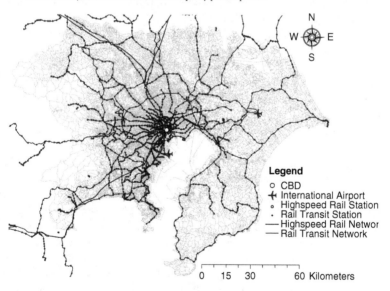

Figure 6.2 Greater Tokyo's Railway Network

capture in action. Given the high premium placed on access to fast, efficient, and reliable public-transport services in a dense, congested city like Hong Kong, the price of land near railway stations is generally higher than elsewhere, sometimes by several orders of magnitude.

MTRC has used its ability to purchase the development rights for land around stations to recoup the cost of investing in rail transit and turn a profit. The railway has also played a vital role in shaping the city. In 2002, around 2.8 million people, or 41 percent of Hong Kong's population, lived within 500 m of an MTR station (Tang et al. 2004). One in five households lived within 200 m of a station.

MTRC and R+P

As a private corporation that sells shares on the Hong Kong stock market, MTRC operates on commercial principles, financing and operating railway services that are not only self-supporting but also that yield a net return on investment. Effectively, the fully loaded costs of public transport investments, operations, and maintenance are covered by supplementing fare and other revenues with income from ancillary real estate development—for example, the sale of development rights, joint venturing with private real-estate developers, and running retail outlets in and around subway stations. Today, Hong Kong MTR is one of the most successful Build-Operate-Maintain transportation systems anywhere, courtesy of R+P. Throughout the 1980s and 1990s, the Hong Kong Special Administrative Region (HKSAR) government was the sole owner of MTRC. In 2000, 23 percent of MTRC's shares were offered to private investors on the stock exchange. The presence of private shareholders exerted a strong market discipline on MTRC, prompting the company managers to become more entrepreneurial and business-minded. However, HKSAR's majority shareholder status ensured that MTRC weighed the broader public interest in its day-to-day decisions, including the promotion of Transit-Oriented Developmemt (TOD).

A good example of R+P at work is Maritime Square, planned and managed by MTRC as part of the development of Tsing Yi station on the new express Airport Extension Line. MTRC was granted 50-year development rights for the site, selling these rights at a substantial premium to underwrite the costs of building the station and portions of the airport line. The resulting mixed-use Maritime Square R+P project boasts a seamless integration between the railway station and shopping center as well as the above-station residential towers. Residents can experience a "temperature-controlled" environment—able to go from their luxury apartments to shopping below and then directly into the MTR station without stepping outdoors. Maritime Square came to fruition because the opportunities for physical integration were assessed at the master planning stage (Tang et al. 2004).

Maritime Square features hierarchically integrated uses. Shopping mall extends from the ground floor to the third level. Station concourse sits on the first floor, with rail lines and platforms above and ancillary/logistical functions (like public transport/bus interchange and parking) at or below. Above the fourth and fifth floor residential parking lies a podium garden and above this, high-rise, luxury residential towers.

R+P: How It Works

The granting of exclusive development rights is what fuels MTRC's R+P program. MTRC does not receive any cash subsidies from the Hong Kong government to build railway infrastructure; instead it receives an in-kind contribution in the form of a land grant that gives the company exclusive development rights for land above and adjacent to its stations. These grants relieve MTRC from purchasing land on the open market.

Timing is crucial in MTRC's recapturing of rail's value-added. MTRC purchases development rights from the Hong Kong government at a "before rail" price and sells these rights to a selected developer (among a list of qualified bidders) at an "after rail" price.[1] The differences between land values with versus without rail services are substantial, easily covering the cost of railway investments.[2] When bargaining with developers, MTRC also negotiates a share of future property-development profits and/or a co-ownership position from the highest bidder. Thus MTRC receives a "front end" payment for land and a "back end" share of revenues and assets in-kind.

Table 6.3 summarizes MTRC's portfolio of R+P projects in 2006. By design, MTRC has pursued a diverse portfolio of projects to shield the company from swings in Hong Kong's business cycle. In addition to R+P, MTRC has diversified its holdings through equity ownership, cash holdings, property management, consulting, advertising, and ownership of other assets (e.g., telecommunication leases, convenience retail shops). Thus, if Hong Kong's real-estate market softens, MTRC is buffered through other asset holdings; if the land market strengthens, the company participates in this upside through both R+P leases and equity ownership. R+P's vital income-producing role is revealed by the fact that during the 2001–2005 period, property development produced 52 percent of MTRC's revenues. By contrast, railway income, made up mostly of farebox receipts, generated 28 percent of total income. Together, MTRC's involvement in property-related activities—that is, development, investment, and management—produced 62 percent of total income, more than twice as much as user fares.

Table 6.3 MTRC's Property Development Overview, 2006

	Type of Land use					
	Residential (# Units)	Commercial GFA (m²)	Office GFA (m²)	Hotel/ Service Apartments GFA (m²)	Government & Institutions GFA (m²)	# of Car parks ($ Spaces)
Urban Lines	31,682	314,923	208,866	0	143,034	6,012
Airport Lines	28,650	306,640	611,963	291,722	24,770	14,360
Tweung Kwan O Lines	8,914	55,814	5,000	58,130	0	1,691
Total	69,246	677,377	825,829	349,852	167,804	22,063

Project phasing is critical to the success of R+P given the cyclical nature of Hong Kong's real-estate market. In recent years, MTRC has relied on property development to generate profits to pay off past debt. This is reflected by figure 6.3, which charts annual profits/ losses from property development and other recurring business over the 1980–2005 period. During the 1980s, MTRC mostly incurred net losses (based on differences between revenues and combined operating and depreciated capital cost as well as debt service). Even during this period of operating in the red, property development moderated losses. Beginning in the late 1990s when MTRC began aggressively pursuing R+P along the Airport Railway Line, the net yields provided crucial income that went to finance the more recent Tseung Kwan O extensions (as part of a massive brownfield redevelopment of former industrial land). It took approximately ten years (1997 to 2007) to fully pay off capital debt for the Airport Line extension. From 2007 onward, earnings from R+P projects on the Airport Line produce funds that are no longer required to be spent paying off this debt, allowing these funds to be used to cover costs of Tseung Kwan O and other planned extensions.

MTRC has hardly been the sole financial beneficiary of R+P. Society at large, reflected by Hong Kong SAR's majority ownership of MTRC, has also reaped substantial rewards. For the 1980 to 2005 period, it is estimated that Hong Kong SAR has received nearly HK$140 billion (in today's Hong Kong dollars) in net financial returns. This is based on the difference between earned income (HK$171.8 billion from land premiums, market capitalization, shareholder cash dividends, and initial public offer proceeds) and the value of injected equity capital (HK$32.2 billion

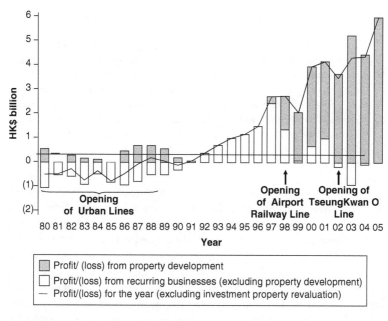

Figure 6.3 Trends in MTRC's Profits and Losses from Property Development and Recurring Businesses for the 1980 to 2005 period

from land grants). Thus the government of Hong Kong has enjoyed tremendous finance returns and seeded the construction of a world-class railway network without having to advance any cash to MTRC. The HK$140 billion figure, of course, is only the direct financial benefit. The indirect benefits—for example, higher ridership through increased densities, reduced sprawl, air pollution, and energy consumption—have increased net societal returns well beyond HK$140 billion.

R+P and Transit-Oriented Development (TOD)

Growing concerns about quality of life and Hong Kong's global competitiveness in an environment of off-shoring manufacturing jobs to mainland China has prompted Hong Kong officials to pursue a policy of integrating high-quality infrastructure investments and land development. Hong Kong has long had tall towers surrounding and above railway stations; however density alone does not make a good transit-oriented development (TOD). Often missing is high-quality urban designs and pleasant yet functional walking environments in and around stations. At its core, TOD is about place-making:

> The centerpiece of the transit village is the transit station itself and
> the civic and public spaces that surround it. The transit station is what
> connects village residents and workers to the rest of the region, provid-
> ing convenient and ready access to downtowns, major activity centers
> like sports stadium, and other popular destinations. The surrounding
> public spaces or open grounds serve the important function of being
> a community gathering spot, a site for special events, and a place for
> celebrations—a modern-day version of the Greek agora. (Bernick and
> Cervero 1997: 5)

The use of the railway station as a focal point for community building is common in Scandinavia. On the outskirts of Stockholm and
Copenhagen, most rail stations are physically and symbolically the hub
of the community. In master-planned new towns that orbit Stockholm,
notably Vällingby and Skarholmen, the rail stop sits squarely in the
town center (Cervero 1998). Upon exiting the station, one steps into a
car-free public square surrounded by shops, restaurants, schools, and
community facilities. The civic square, often adorned with benches,
water fountains, and greenery, is the community's central gathering
spot—a place to relax, socialize, and a setting for special events, whether
national holidays, public celebrations, parades, or social demonstrations.
Sometimes, the square doubles up as a place for farmers to sell their
produce or street artists to perform, changing chameleon-like from an
open-air market one day to a concert venue the next. The assortment of
flower stalls, sidewalk cafes, newsstands, and outdoor vendors dotting
the square, combined with the musings and conversations of residents
sitting in the square, retirees playing chess, and everyday encounters
among friends, adds color and breathes life into the community. Thus, a
community's rail station and its surroundings are more than a jumping
off point. As lively urban districts, they should be the kinds of places
people are naturally drawn to. If done well, TODs are "places to be,"
not "places to pass through" (Bertolini and Spit 1998).

First generation R+P projects built by MTRC were hardly pedestrian-
friendly TODs. Most featured indistinguishable apartment towers that
dumped the pedestrians onto busy streets and left them to their own
devises to find a way to a subway entrance. Growing public discontent
over sterile station-area environments and sagging real-estate market
performance of older buildings prompted MTRC to pay more attention
to principles of good town planning. Perhaps most notable was the establishment of a town-planning division within the corporation, charged

with pursuing land-development strategies that met corporate financial objectives while also promoting local land-use objectives and enhanced station-area environments. R+P projects from the early 1980s followed rather than anticipated development (Brownlee 2001). In keeping with the Hong Kong government's *Regional Development Strategy* to channel new growth along desired corridors through railway investment and enhance pedestrian environments, more railway investments and their associated R+P projects, such as the extension to the new international airport, have been in advance of market demand.

Recently built MTR stations and their associated R+P projects, notably Kowloon Bay and Tung Chung, embrace the Scandinavian model of TOD design, seeking to impart a sense of place. They do this in large part by creating a significant public space outside the station. Tung Chung station and its adjacent civic square is today the hub of Tung Chung new town and according to Tang et al. (2004) is poised to become Hong Kong's landmark gateway for visitors arriving at the airport. Compared to earlier R+P projects, Tung Chung is designed at a more human scale, featuring bright night lights, openness (much appreciated in a hyperdense city), vivid and coordinated urban designs, and through active pedestrian movements, the kind of natural surveillance that gives people a sense of comfort. A recent urban design audit found newer R+P projects like Tung Chung scored much higher than early-generation high-rise projects in terms of connectivity, comfort, aesthetics, public amenities, navigability, and natural surveillance (Cervero and Murakami 2008).

Occupying a 21.7 hectare parcel, Tung Chung was conceptualized and built along the lines of a master-planned new town, comprising predominantly residential housing intermixed with retail shops, offices, and a hotel next to the station. Tung Chung was also designed with TOD principles in mind. Several hundred meters from the station lies an arc of 30-plus story residential towers, connected to the town center by a network of covered walkways and footbridges. Upon exiting the station, MTR patrons are greeted by a spacious, attractively landscaped civic square dotted with public art. The "feel" of walking in and around the Tung Chung station is qualitatively different than that found at older MTR stations. If R+P projects built according to TOD models are beneficial, this should be reflected in ridership statistics and real-estate market performance. A recent statistical analysis found that each additional household built within 500 m of an MTR station added 1.75 transit trips per weekday (Cervero and Murakami 2008). If this housing unit part of a master-planned R+P project with a transit-oriented

design (e.g., grade-separated pedestrian access; mixed land uses, including retail shops, along pedestrian corridors; architectural integration;
and provision of public amenities like pocket parks), each new housing united added 2.84 daily rail trips. This relationship has not gone
unnoticed among MTRC's management: transit-oriented designs and
high-quality pedestrian environments can increase farebox income and
generate more walk-on traffic that purchases the many retail goods
and services at MTRC-owned shops in and around railway stations.

Equally important have been the price premiums recorded for R+P
housing projects designed according to TOD principles. A notable
example is the Hang Hau MTR station, built as a "new town/in town"
along the recently opened Tseung Kwan O (TKO) corridor. Hang Hau
station marks a strong departure in design practices and the relationship of the R+P project to the surrounding community. Notably, a
strong emphasis is given to "place-making." Owner-occupied apartments are directly tied to a nice landscaped garden and private club
house that sits above the station. Residents also have direct elevator
connections to the station concourse and lower level shopping mall. A
phalanx of second-level footbridges links the shopping mall and station to the surrounding neighborhood. Hang Hau's R+P project has
a comfortable, human-scale feel and a design that not only instills a
sense of place but also protects the financial investments of tenants.
These benefits have been capitalized into land prices. A recent hedonic price model study that controlled for building types and distance
to the subway entrance found that Hang Hau's condominiums built
under the R+P model with transit-oriented designs enjoyed average
rent premiums of 22 percent (Cervero and Murakami 2008). Overall,
the analysis found price premiums ranging from US$12 to US$36 per
square foot of gross floor area for housing estates built atop or adjacent to MTR stations.

While ridership and land-price premiums can be attributed to urban
design practices, it is likely that part of the explanation lies in the
institutional advantages of the R+P model. Tang et al. (2004) argue
that a single entity like MTRC is best suited to manage the complexity of land development and to leverage the opportunities to recapture
value created by rail investments. They attribute this to asset specificity
(allowing a professional focus on the intricacies of land development),
accumulated knowledge (among MTRC managers), reduced uncertainty
(owing to a disciplined approach to property development and accountability to equity shareholders), internalization of transit's value-added
(by maximizing ancillary development potential), and asset protection (through involvement in construction and property management).

As the master planner, master designer, and master architect, MTRC aligns the interests of different stakeholders. Importantly, it sets and enforces all development standards. For private developers, the "rules of the game" are clear at the outset. This reduces uncertainties and risks. One-entity oversight also allows strong transit/land-use linkages. In addition, MTRC acts as an intermediary between government and private developers—specifying site requirements, negotiating agreements, and balancing between competing public and private interests.

Transit Value Capture in Tokyo

Japan's form of privatizing railway construction and operations has mainly been in the form of metropolitan governments granting concessions and exclusive rights to companies to design, build, and operate transit services. During Japan's post–World War II era of rapid industrialization and suburbanization, private railway companies took advantage of these entitlements to bundle land development and other commercial enterprises with their transit businesses. In Tokyo and other large Japanese cities, regional governments write design, routing, and service requirements to assure privately built new towns comply with regional growth objectives.

Like Hong Kong's MTRC, Tokyo's railway companies have historically leveraged real-estate development to both pay for infrastructure and produce profits for shareholders. And they have similarly opened convenience stores and shopping malls within and adjacent to stations. What most distinguishes Tokyo's railway companies, however, is their construction of not just a handful of buildings but also veritable new towns on once virgin lands. West of central Tokyo, where many of the region's most upmarket suburbs are located, entire communities are today the domains of powerful conglomerates that are best known for their department store chains—Tokyu, Odakyu, Keio, and Seibu—but which first and foremost are in the business of railway and real-estate development. All started as private railway companies and over time branched into businesses closely related to the railway industry, including real estate, retailing, bus operations, and electric power generation. Such business expansion made perfectly good economic sense. Placing shopping malls, apartments, and entertainment complexes near stations generated rail traffic; in turn, railways brought customers to these establishments. During the 1980s at the height of railway/new-town co-development and a surge in Japanese real-estate prices, railway companies were earning investment returns on ancillary real-estate projects in the range of 50 to 70 percent (Cervero 1998).

Tokyu Corporation is greater Tokyo's largest private railway enterprise and was among the first companies to advance the business model of railway/new-town co-development. From 1960 to 1984, Tokyu Corporation's 23-km rail line transformed a vast, hilly, scarcely inhabited area into a planned community, called Tama Denin Toshi (Tama Garden City), of a half-million inhabitants. Tokyu used land-consolidation techniques to assemble farmland at cheap prices in advance of rail construction and to finance neighborhood infrastructure. Under this approach, landowners formed a cooperative that consolidated (often irregularly shaped) properties and returned smaller but fully serviced (and usually rectangular) parcels to landowners. Roads, drainage, sewerage, parks, and other infrastructure were funded through the sale of the "extra" reserved land contributed by cooperative members. Land consolidation relieved railway companies such as Tokyu from the up-front burden and risks of acquiring land and financing infrastructure.

The 1990s and onwards have marked a new era for Tokyo's private railway companies. For one, the bursting of Japan's real-estate price bubble saw the market valuations of rail companies' landholdings fall. In addition, powerful demographic trends like declining birth rates and an aging population, combined with a slowing of the economy, reduced the demand for new-town construction. To spread the risks of a shakier real-estate market, private railway companies have in recent years partnered with third parties to pursue large-scale development projects. Recent real-estate projects of Tokyu Corporation, for example, have relied on Real Estate Investment Trust (REIT) funding.

Changing traffic conditions have also had a hand in changing the portfolios of Tokyo's private railways. Greater Tokyo's rail-served new towns and subcenters featured housing and retail services while most white-collar jobs remained in the urban core (Cervero 1998, Sorensen 2001). This produced tidal, radial patterns of commuting thus worsening traffic congestion in the urban core. Lengthening commutes combined with crowded trains and roadways in turn triggered a return-to-the-city movement. Several large-scale redevelopment projects built as joint ventures between private railways and real-estate companies are today underway targeted at the market of young professionals, empty-nesters, and other less-traditional niche markets drawn to central-city living. In a break from tradition, what in the past would have been exclusively office-commercial projects built above major subway stations now features professional-class, high-end housing and consumer services. Residential and commercial districts around several central-city stations, notably Akihabara, Shinjuku, and Shinagawa, are today abuzz with activity, 24–7.

The redevelopment and infilling of strategic central-city land parcels is also being pursued by Tokyo's two former public railways, JR East and Tokyo Metro. In the case of JR East, mounting fiscal losses incurred by the former Japan National Railway (with an accumulated debt of US$300 billion) led to privatization in 1987. At the time, the national government gave JR East large developable land parcels around terminal stations, prime for commercial redevelopment. Borrowing a chapter from the practices of Tokyo and other long-standing private railway corporations, JR East and Tokyo Metro aggressively transformed these properties to high-rise commercial ventures. In 2006, real estate yielded more than 40 percent returns on investment for both former public railways.

JR East's showcase real-estate project is Tokyo Station City, jointly developed by the railway company and other private interests. Tokyo Station City features high-rise, class-A office buildings, retail centers, and hotels. Tokyo Station is well-suited for large-scale redevelopment owing to large amounts of buildable space above depots as well as high pedestrian traffic volumes. On a typical weekday in 2005, around half a million passengers passed through Tokyo Station each day (JR East 2005).

As in Hong Kong, Tokyo's private railways are clearly responding to market price signals, as indicated by an analysis of 2005 residential land prices along 16 mostly private railway corridors as a function of distance to central Tokyo. Within and along the Yamanote Loop where most large-scale redevelopment projects have been recently built on land owned by private railway companies, residential prices are generally double what they are 15–20 km from the center. Since 2000, the only area where residential land has gained value has been around terminal stations on the Yamanote Loop.

Lessons

Experiences in Hong Kong and Tokyo show that transit value capture, first introduced in the United States over a century ago, is still a viable model—not only for sustainable finance but also for sustainable urbanism. Both cases show it to be particularly suited for financing transit infrastructure in dense, congested settings where a high premium is placed on accessibility and the institutional capacity exists to administer the program. Even in ultra-dense, transit-friendly Hong Kong, the railway investment is not financially viable on its own. Property development has been MTRC's only source of return for meeting investors' equity demands. Through its R+P program, MTRC enjoys significant price premiums for housing built atop or adjacent to metro stations, making it the most profitable public-transit operation worldwide. Greater Tokyo's private railways have historically practiced transit value capture on an even grander scale, building massive new towns along rail-served corridors and cashing in the construction, retail, and household service opportunities created by these investments. In both places, rail and property development has created a virtuous cycle of viable railway operations and a highly transit-oriented built form.

Important to the success of transit value capture in both cities has been institutional adaptation and change. In Hong Kong, this has taken the form of MTRC's executives gaining an appreciation over time of the importance of urban design, pedestrian circulation, and public amenities, all particularly important in a dense, crowded city like Hong Kong, in creating financially successful R+P projects. Hong Kong's emergence as an international gateway combined with its economic transformation from traditional manufacturing to a service-based economy opened up new possibilities for R+P in both shaping growth and serving new market demands. To MTRC's credit, a conscious decision was made to build high-quality, mixed-use R+P projects on greenfields en route to the new international airport as well as on brownfields served by central-city railway extensions. These have proven to be wise investments: recent-generation R+P projects that functionally and architecturally blend well with surrounding communities have outperformed earlier projects in terms of both ridership gains and real-estate market returns.

Market adaptation has been just as pronounced in Tokyo in recent times. The region's real-estate market downturn, slowing economic growth, and changing demographic structure has prompted private railway companies—both new and old—to seek new market opportunities, most notably infill housing and mixed-use developments around major central-city railway terminals. Such redevelopment complements the earlier generation new towns built by private companies such as Tokyu Corporation. To appeal to professional class workers and a more youthful labor force, as in Hong Kong, a strong accent is being placed on creating high-quality urban spaces in and around joint development projects—a signature feature of Scandinavian-style TODs (Bernick and Cervero 1997).

Might these two East Asian models of transit value capture be applied elsewhere, particularly to other fast growing cities in Asia? One might argue that Hong Kong and Tokyo represent extreme cases and that the potential returns from transit joint development elsewhere will be modest. However, many coastal cities of mainland China are beginning to mimic Hong Kong's and Tokyo's development pattern (i.e., the emergence of high-rise, mixed use centers and suburban new towns). Today, urban passenger rail systems are found in ten mainland Chinese cities. Plans call for expanding and upgrading these current systems and building new in 15 other Chinese cities. Given the economic and spatial restructuring throughout urban China, there are tremendous opportunities to create sustainable urban forms and reliable funding source by bundling land development and railway investments.

A recent Asian Development Bank report (2005) suggests widespread interest in the People's Republic of China for the adoption of public-private partnerships for urban rail. As rapid urbanization continues to paralyze the streets of many cities in China as well as other parts of Asia with traffic and threatens environmental quality locally and on the global stage, it is imperative that arguably the most sustainable form of urbanism—the linkage of land use and public transport—be aggressively pursued. Hong Kong's and Tokyo's models of transit value capture are the best template available for sustainably financing transit and building cities.

Notes

I thank Jin Murakami, a doctoral student in the Department of City and Regional Planning at the University of California, Berkeley, for his assistance in carrying out this research.

1. The Hong Kong Special Administrative Region owns all land in the Hong Kong territory. Private individuals and organizations can purchase only 50-year leases that grant exclusive property development rights.

2. MTRC aims to set rents for its landholdings based on the WACC—the weighted average cost of capital—presently set at 9.5 percent (reflecting the value of borrowing capital) plus a rent premium of between 1.5 percent and 3 percent for equity shareholders, yielding a 11–12.5 percent return. The WACC fluctuates based loan rates charged by commercial banks. For riskier projects, the WACC might be set at 10 percent plus a 3 percent premium, yielding a 13 percent net return. Thus MTRC's economic rates of return on investments are not determined by the market. Rather, the company sets the

desirable rate of return and releases land to achieve this target. This is viewed by the populous as an appropriate strategy for a company whose majority ownership is the Hong Kong government. MTRC will invest in railway projects if these net rates of return (11 to 13 percent, depending on risks) are attained. This "WACC+premium" formula is used to guide not only railway investment but also MTRC's own real-estate investment, including shopping malls attached to stations.

References

Asian Development Bank. 2005. *Asian development outlook 2005*. Hong Kong: Asian Development Bank.

Bernick, M. and R. Cervero. 1997. *Transit villages for the 21st century*. New York: McGraw-Hill.

Bertolini, L. and T. Spit. 1998. *Cities on rail*. London: Spon Press.

Brownlee, J. 2001. Sustainable transport in Hong Kong: The dynamics of the transport related decision-making process. http://www.civic-exchange.org/publications/Intern/Sustainable%20Transport.pdf.

Cervero, R. 1998. *The transit metropolis: A global inquiry*. Washington, DC: Island Press.

Cervero, R. and J. Murakami. 2008. *Rail+property development in Hong Kong*. Hong Kong: MTR Corporation.

Estache, A. 1999. Privatization and regulation of transport infrastructure in the 1990s. Policy Research Working Paper No. 2248. Washington, DC: World Bank Institute.

Estache, A., J. Carbajo, and G. Rus. 1999. Argentina's transport privatization and re-regulation. Policy Research Working Paper No. 2249. Washington, DC: World Bank Institute.

International Association of Public Transport. 2002. *Mobility in cities database*. http://uitp.org/publications/Mobility-in-Cities-Database.cfm. JR East. 2005. Tokyo: JR East. Unpublished mimeo. http://www.jreast.co.jp/e/index.html

Lam, W.H.K. 2003. *Advanced modeling for transit operations and service planning*. Oxford, UK: Elsevier.

Rodriquez, D. 1999. Expanding the urban transportation infrastructure through concession agreements: Lessons from Latin America. *Transportation Research Record* 1659: 3–10.

Shaw, J. 2000. *Competition, regulation, and the privatization of British rail*. London: Ashgate.

Sorensen, A. 2001. Subcentres and satellite cities: Tokyo's 20th century experience of planned polycentrism. *International Planning Studies* 6(1): 9–32.

Tang, B.S., Y.H. Chiang, A.N. Baldwin, and C.W. Yeung. 2004. *Study of the integrated rail-property development model in Hong Kong*. Hong Kong: The Hong Kong Polytechnic University.

World Bank. 1996. *Sustainable transport: Priorities for policy reform.* Washington, DC: World Bank.

Zegras, C. 2004. Private sector participation in urban transport infrastructure provision. *Sustainable transport: A sourcebook for policy-makers in developing countries.* Eschborn, Germany: Deutsche Gesellschaft fur Technishe Zusammenarbeit (GTZ).

CHAPTER 7

Urban Reclamation and Regeneration in Seoul, South Korea

Robert Cervero

Since the turn of the twenty-first century, Seoul, South Korea, pursued a bold new experiment in urban regeneration. This has principally involved reclaiming urban space given to the automobile in the post–Korean War era. Through the leadership of Myung-Bak Lee, former mayor of Seoul and now president of South Korea, the city has sought to strike a balance between transport infrastructure as a mobility provider and public space as an urban amenity. In good part this has been motivated by a desire to be globally competitive with the likes of Hong Kong, Shanghai, and other tigers of East Asia's rapidly growing economy by emphasizing quality of life every bit as much as mobility and large-scale infrastructure development.

Like many modern metropolises of East Asia, over the past several decades Seoul has followed a pattern of American-style sprawl, fueled by steady economic growth and concomitantly the meteoric rise in private automobile ownership. However, population densities in the city of Seoul (presently 10.4 million inhabitants spread over a land area of 605 sq. km.) have historically been and remain quite high by global standards. The city of Seoul itself, along with the port city of Inchon to the west and surrounding Kyunggi Province, formally constitute the Seoul Metropolitan Area (also called the Seoul National Capital Area), with some 23 million inhabitants—the world's second largest urban agglomeration. In 2006, Seoul and Inchon combined had the sixth highest population density worldwide: 16,700 people per sq. km. Because of the city-region's historically high densities, the Seoul metropolitan government has over the years aggressively sought to decentralize growth, mainly in the form of building master-planned new towns sited on the region's periphery.

New Town Development

In all, 26 new towns have been built in the greater Seoul Metropolitan Area over the past three decades. The five most prominent ones— Bundang, Ilsan, Jungdong, Pyunchon, and Sanbon—lie within a ring of 20 to 28 km from Seoul City Hall (the heart of downtown Seoul). Most new towns were built in a modernist Le Corbusier style, as mid-to-high-rise "towers in the park." A serious housing shortage and rising housing rents (fueled mostly by land speculation) during the 1980s prompted the Korean government to build new towns quickly and as a mass-produced commodity. In 1987, then newly elected Korean president Tae Woo Roh promised the construction of 2 million new housing units in the Seoul Metropolitan Area during his tenure. The shortage of central-city land, combined with the presence of a protective greenbelt that collars the city of Seoul, resulted in most new towns being built on the region's far-flung fringes (Jun and Hur 2001).

Table 7.1 shows that the region's five largest new towns, built between 1989 and 1995, had population densities in the range of 18,600 to 41,000 per sq. km., between five and ten times denser than postwar new towns built in England. In all, 2 million people moved out to these five new towns between 1992 and 1999 at an average pace of 250,000 people per year (Lee 2003). As shown in figure 7.1, the impacts on the distribution of residents within the region was decisive: while the city of Seoul's population fell slightly during the 1992–2007 period, population in surrounding Kyunggi province jumped by more than 60 percent.

New town development achieved its goal of stabilizing housing prices, however at a price—notably dramatic increases in commuting traffic and the problems associated with auto-oriented development: extreme congestion on radial links to the urban center, rising tailpipe emissions and fuel consumption, and increased demand for expensive highway infrastructure. Between 1990 and 1996, the average commuting distance of new-town residents increased in the range of 12 to 70 percent (Jun 2000). Longer trips combined with rising car ownership has inevitably translated into steadily worsening traffic congestion: average speeds during evening hours in the Seoul Metropolitan Area fell from 24 kph in 1998 to 17 kph in 2003. Also, daily commuting expenses have risen sharply: one study pegged the total out-of-pocket

Table 7.1   Five Major New Towns in Seoul Metropolitan Area

Name	Distance to CBD (Direction)(km)	Construction Period	Project Area (sq. km)	Population Density in 1996 (per sq. km)
Bundang	25 km (SE)	1989–1995	20	18,621
Ilsan	28 km (NW)	1990–1995	16	22,267
Jungdong	25 km (W)	1994–1995	5	40,599
Pyungchon	20 km (SW)	1989–1995	5	31.911
Sanbon	25 km (SW)	1989–1995	4	41,067

Source: Jun and Hur (2001); population densities estimated by author.

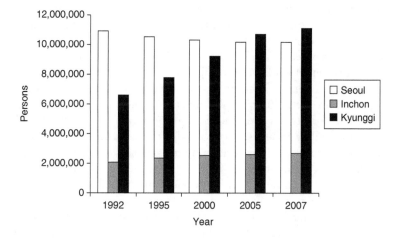

Figure 7.1   Population Changes in Seoul Metropolitan Area, 1992–2007

cost (ignoring the value of time and externalities) incurred by new-town residents living outside of Seoul's greenbelt at US$12 per commute trip (Jun and Bae 2000).

New Towns/In Town: Urban Reclamation

By the late 1990s, rumblings were starting to be heard within public policy circles that the region's new towns were a failed experiment, exacerbating traffic congestion and environmental quality. Some feared that such factors, along with the productivity losses from inordinately long commutes, would ultimately be a drag on economic growth, prompting disaffected companies and their workers to relocate elsewhere in the country and possibly even abroad. The idea of reurbanizing Seoul's central areas through "new towns/in town" began to surface.

The person who was in charge of reinvesting in the central city and regenerating Seoul city was Myung-Bak Lee. In 2001, Lee ran for mayor of Seoul, largely on a platform of reinvigorating Seoul's central city as means of creating a more sustainable yet productive city. Lee campaigned on the premise that Seoul could achieve a better balance between function and the environment by reordering public priorities so as to emphasize quality of place. Prior to becoming mayor, Lee founded and led the Hyundai Group, Korea's largest builder of public works and infrastructure projects, for three decades. During this time, he earned the nickname "Bulldozer" Lee, partly because of the company's legacy of constructing massive roadways throughout the country and partly because he reputedly once took apart a bulldozer to study its mechanism and figure out why it kept breaking down.

Lee won a decisive victory for the mayoral seat, and upon assuming office in early 2002, moved quickly on his campaign promises. His vision for Seoul's future urban transportation called for not only expanding public-transit services but also reducing the ecological footprint of the private car by reclaiming urban space consumed by roads and highways—notably, space used to funnel new-town inhabitants in and out of the central city. Why scar the interior of the city, he reasoned, to funnel suburbanites to good-paying white-collar office jobs in the core? A notable culprit was the network of elevated freeways that converged on central Seoul—facilities that severed long-standing neighborhoods, formed barriers and visual blight, cast shadows, and sprayed noise, fumes, and vibrations on surrounding areas. Though freeways provided important mobility benefits, Lee recognized that these have to be weighed against their nuisance effects, particularly in today's amenity-conscious workplace.

The removal of a six-kilometer elevated freeway in the heart of Seoul, Cheong Gye Cheon (CGC), and the restoration of urban stream and pedestrian-friendly greenway, was a natural choice to launch Lee's vision of a more sustainable urban landscape for the city. Change was swift. By February 2003, a plan for the freeway removal was completed, and five months later, the freeway was completely dismantled. Some two years later, in September 2005, the restored CGC stream and linear greenway was opened to the public following a major public celebration and ribbon cutting by Mayor Lee. The entire cost of the freeway demolition and stream restoration was US$313 million.

Though not as large and expensive, equally important in symbolic terms was the mayor's decision to convert a massive 1.3 hectare surface-street intersection to an oval-shaped grass park in front of Seoul's City Hall, the nerve center of the city. The huge swath of real estate devoted to car maneuvers in front of City Hall, an architectural icon and one of the busiest locations in the city, created an extremely pedestrian-hostile environment. Many residents en route to City Hall had to take a circuitous route in a car-dominated milieu. Today the former traffic circle is a popular leisure spot for Seoul residents, directly connected to City Hall and frequently used for public celebrations, cultural performances, and even student demonstrations. During winter months, a large outdoor ice rink occupies the oval, drawing thousands of Korean families and teens. Once populated by rows of cars, the entrance to Seoul's cherished City Hall is now populated by people.

Mayor Lee made his policy intentions clear when he publicly stated that the transformation of space for cars to space for people represented "a new paradigm for urban management in the new century" (Seoul Metropolitan Government 2003). His views were partly shaped by what was happening in several Latin American cities at the time. Echoing the sentiments of urban visionaries such as Jaime Lerner of Curitiba, Brazil, and Enrique Peñalosa of Bogotá, Colombia, both of whom staked their political careers on curbing the presence of cars in their own central cities, Mayor Lee defended the roadway removal projects on the grounds that "we want to make a city where people come first, not cars." The diminution of roadway capacity represents, in many ways, a recasting of public priorities. In Seoul's case, it marked a shift from building infrastructure that enhances automobility to infrastructure that enhances public amenities and quality of urban living. A longer-term objective was to encourage more and more households to settle in the central city and in redevelopment districts, thus reversing the centrifugal flow of residents to Seoul's outskirts and beyond—in effect, creating a new form of urban development, what Harvey Perloff, former dean of the urban planning program at the University of California at Los Angeles, coined "new towns/in town" (Perloff 1975).

Coping with Reduced Road Capacity

Of course, the withdrawal of road capacity in an increasingly automobile-dependent society, in and of itself, is unlikely to enhance urban living. Public opinion polls tell us that being stuck in traffic is among the most disliked aspects of urban living and traffic congestion tops the list of factors associated with a declining quality of life (Downs 2004). To Mayor Lee's credit, he understood that public transportation had to be substantially expanded and upgraded to absorb the traffic (169,000 daily cars in the case of the CGC freeway) displaced by large-scale reductions in roadway capacity. This was partly done through the extension of Subway Line 7 (28 km) and the opening of Line 6 (35 km). At least as important, however, was the 2004 opening of seven new lines of exclusive median-lane buses (stretching 84 km, later expanded to 162 km) and 294 km of dedicated curbside bus lanes. Such services go by the name Bus Rapid Transit, or BRT, because buses operate on their own rights-of-way, functioning like and enjoying the speed advantages of trains, albeit at a fraction of a railway's construction costs. In all, 74 lineal km of road lanes were expropriated to accommodate Seoul's BRT network. In addition, many regular bus routes were reconfigured to better feed into the city's extensive subway system and an integrated fare and transfer system between buses and the metrorail network was introduced (Pucher et al. 2005).

Seoul's BRT investments have paid off handsomely. Along BRT corridors, bus operating speeds have increased from an average of 11 to more than 21 kph, and have even increased on some passenger-car lanes. BRT buses, moreover, carry more than six times as many passengers per hour as buses operating on regular, mixed-traffic lanes. And because they are less subject to the vagaries of ambient traffic flows, buses operating in dedicated lanes have become more reliable—the travel-time variation of Seoul's BRT buses is, on average, one-fifth that of buses operating on nonexclusive lanes (Seoul Development Institute 2005). In addition, protective lanes have reduced accidents—down 27 percent one year after BRT services were introduced. Because of these service enhancements and safety improvements, ridership on BRT buses has increased 60 percent faster than on non-BRT buses over the past three years.

Transit service expansion was not the only relief valve that Seoul's transportation planners turned to. A real-time traffic information system with message boards and in-vehicle navigation aids was introduced to guide traffic flows and alert motorists to downstream hot spots. Several one-way arterial couplets were also created, and curbside parking was substantially curtailed to help expedite traffic flows. More draconian was the introduction of a license plate scheme that, based on the last number on their plates, required motorists to leave their cars at home once every ten days.

Cheong Gye Cheon Freeway-to-Greenway Conversion

The centerpiece of Mayor Lee's urban reclamation policy has been without question the Cheong Gye Cheon (CGC) freeway-to-greenway conversion. Cheong Gye Cheon, which means "clear valley stream," has long been a source of fresh water and "heart and soul" of urban life in Seoul, going back to the fourteenth century. During the Chosun dynasty (1392–1910), city dwellers did their laundry in the stream and frequently socialized on its banks. Following the Korean War (1950–1953), the stream's character quickly changed when temporary refugee housing was built along its banks. Untreated waste was dumped directly into the waterway, turning it into a veritable cesspool and eventually prompting city officials to cover the stream with an elevated freeway. The Cheong Gye Cheon freeway, 50 to 80 m in width and 6 km in length, opened in 1971 in the heart of central Seoul. Below the road were the running stream and a sewer trunk-line. The CGC freeway quickly became an important conduit for movement to and within central-city Seoul, gaining all the more importance as new towns began to populate the region's periphery in the 1980s and 1990s. However, time quickly took its toll on the facility. A 1992 study by the Korean Society of Civil Engineers found that more than 20 percent of the freeways steel beams were seriously corroded and in need of urgent repair (CGC Restoration Project Headquarters 2004). The Seoul Metropolitan Government immediately began repairing the road's understructure. However, due to concerns about the road's long-term safety and stability, this was seen as a stopgap measure compared to either totally reconstructing the freeway or tearing it down altogether.

At roughly the same time the CGC freeway was being repaired and facing increased scrutiny, calls for urban regeneration were starting to be heard, reflecting growing dissatisfaction with the suburban new-town model of urban planning and growth management. In midst of the debate about the CGC freeway's future, its outright removal was a perfect platform for incoming mayor Myung-Bak Lee to advance his vision of a greener, more livable, and pedestrian-friendly city. The rapidity of the freeway-to-greenway conversion was impressive by any standard. Mayor Lee took office in mid-2002 and by February 2003 a Master Plan for the project was completed. Less than six months later the entire freeway had been completely removed and on September 2005—26 months after the freeway had been razed—the linear park and restored stream was open to the public. By comparison, the time between initial planning and projection completion for the US$15 billion "Big Dig" freeway burial megaproject in Boston was 25 years. A combination of environmental reviews, legal challenges, cost overruns, and delays in securing land entitlements delayed the conversion of San Francisco's Embarcadero Freeway to a tree-lined surface boulevard by more than a decade.

The restoration of the CGC stream has proven to be far more than the greening of central-city Seoul and a political commitment to urban regeneration. For many local residents, it has marked a rediscovery of the city's past. Hidden by the freeway were a number of long-forgotten treasures, including 22 historical footbridges as well as myriad stone carvings and relics. Today, the CGC stream and greenway is Seoul's second most popular tourist draw. On weekends and summer evenings, thousands of residents and tourists can be seen strolling along the flowing stream's banks, enjoying a small slice of tranquility in an otherwise dense, bustling city.

The CGC project has not been without controversy. Besides concerns over possible increases in traffic congestion, many small shopkeepers and merchants were against the project out of fear of losing business. Alongside the former elevated freeway was an assembly of small-scale shops and markets selling shoes, apparel, tools, electronic goods, and appliances. In 2000, more than 200,000 merchants and 60,000 shops were within 2 km of the freeway. To some, the freeway-to-greenway conversion threatened to alter the existing tradeshed and disrupt the flow of customers and logistics. Informal vendors, moreover, would lose their spots under the freeway, in the past an unwanted place where they, and they alone, could ply their trade, rent-free (Hwang, Byun, and Nah 2005). Following intensive negotiations, the Seoul Metropolitan Government was able to head off opposition by financially compensating merchants and relocating a number of shops to a newly constructed market center south of the Han River that was easily accessible by highways and public transit.

Impacts of the CGC Greenway

In general, past research shows that freeways increase land values for nearby commercial properties due to the accessibility benefits conferred. However, residences within an impact zone—often 0.5 to 1 km away from the facility—are worth less due to the noise, fumes, and other nuisances (Boarnet 1997). What about urban amenities, like a greenway? Empirical evidence on their land-price impacts is slimmer.

Open space can increase land prices not only by its intrinsic qualities (e.g., greenery, spaciousness) but also by reducing the amount of developable land available. However, the noise and foot traffic generated by nearby popular parks and open areas might be viewed as a nuisance by some residential property owners (Frech and Lafferty 1984). A study in the United States showed that average land prices were no different in nicely landscaped districts than in less lavish ones with similar levels of traffic congestion (Polinsky and Shavell 1976). The benefits of open space are most capitalized in residential property values in areas that are denser, have higher household incomes, and are closer central business areas (Anderson and West 2006, Dehring and Dunse 2006). The impacts of open space and public amenities on nonresidential properties are less clear. Urban economists such as Glaeser, Kolko, and Saiz (2001) contend that urban parks, open space, and waterfront improvements can help cities attract skilled workers and knowledge-based industries in addition to stabilizing declining neighborhoods. One study in greater Los Angeles found that public amenities like parks did influence the location patterns of firms (Sivitanidou 1995).

Even less is known about the land-price impacts of converting from one form of public amenity to another, such as replacing an elevated freeway with a linear parkway. A study of Boston's notorious "Big Dig" project (wherein an elevated freeway was replaced by a tunnel and a linear park) found that proximity to open space had a positive impact on both residential and commercial property values (Tajima 2003).

According to the Seoul Development Institute (2005), the CGC conversion to greenway resulted in property price gains. From 2003 to 2005, office rents went up by an average of 10 percent while land prices jumped by nearly 40 percent within the CGC impact zone (approximately 2 km in each direction from the corridor). The number of businesses and mixed-use buildings within the zone also rose. So did mean condominium prices. A more recent, in-depth analysis of the land-price effects of the CGC freeway-to-greenway conversion was carried out by Kang and Cervero (2009), using multilevel hedonic price modeling. For office, commercial, and other nonresidential uses, land-value premiums were found for parcels within 500 m of the corridor for both the former freeway and present-day urban greenway (figure 7.2). However, premiums were notably higher for parcels within the 500-meter walkshed of the urban greenway entrance points than the freeway on-ramps.

For residential properties, figure 7.3 reveals that housing had been worth less, all else being equal, within 3 km of the elevated freeway, reflecting a dis-amenity; however the opposite held once the corridor

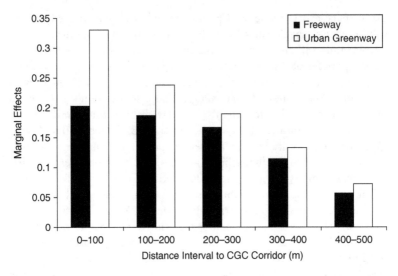

Figure 7.2 Marginal Effect of the CGC Freeway and Urban Greenway on Nonresidential Property Values by Distance Intervals (2001–2006)

was transformed to a greenway: homes within 2 km were worth as much as 8 percent more. Clearly, Seoul's unique freeway disinvestment/ greenway investment scheme conferred net benefits to both residential and nonresidential property owners. From the standpoint of land market performance, one could argue that an urban amenity, and specifically quality of urban space, was more highly valued in central Seoul than a significant component of urban infrastructure, namely a freeway. That is, quality of place has won out over automobility as a desirable urban attribute.

Besides the attractions of greenery and open space, part of the land-value gains conferred by the freeway-to-greenway conversion were likely also because of indirect environmental benefits. For one, air pollution levels along the CGC corridor have fallen since the stream restoration and greenway conversion. Concentrations of fine-grained particulate matter (PM_{10}) along the CGC corridor were 13 percent higher than Seoul's regional average before the conversion; afterwards, it was 4 percent below the region's average (Seoul Development Institute 2005). In the case of nitrogen dioxide (NO_2), a precursor to the formation of photochemical smog, concentrations went from 2 percent above the regional average when the freeway was in operation to 17 percent below when the greenway was in place.

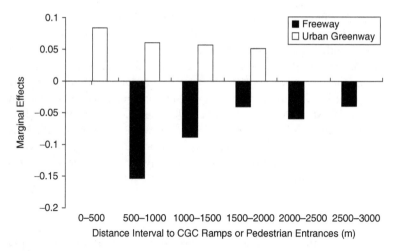

Figure 7.3 Marginal Effects of the CGC Freeway and Urban Greenway on Residential Property Values by Distance Intervals (2001–2006)

Many urban centers suffer a heat island effect, with temperatures higher than surrounding suburban/rural areas due to greater surface-area coverage, and Seoul is no exception. The spillover "cooling" benefits from the CGC transformation are revealed by a heat-island study that found ambient temperatures along the central-city stream and greenway were 3.3° and 5.9°C lower than along a parallel surface arterial 5 blocks away (Hwang 2006).

In sum, the evidence to date suggests that Myung-Bak Lee's bold experiment with land reclamation and urban transformation has been an unqualified success. Land prices have risen and traffic conditions have not materially changed—thanks in good part to vastly expanded public transit services that absorbed some of the former car traffic. The Cheong Gye Cheon running stream and pedestrian promenade has become an attractive tourist draw and while statistics are hard to come by, anecdotally a considerable amount of new construction can be seen today within a block or two of the greenway. It could very well be the case that Seoul's focus on beautification and greening of urban environments creates a virtuous cycle: improved environmental conditions, including cleaner air and cooler climes, could draw more businesses, residents, and tourists to the center, prompting the investment in more urban amenities that further spawn private investment in the central city and reverse past trends toward exurbanization and new-town expansion.

Myung-Bak Lee's unwavering commitment to sustainable urbanism has paid off in personal ways. In May 2006, the *Times Asia* reported that "Seoul, once a symbol of concrete jungle, has achieved successful transformation of its face into a green oasis and now it is inculcating upon other Asian cities with the love of environment," inserting the picture of Lee standing ankle-deep in the waters of Cheong Gye Cheon stream (Walsh 2006: 1). In October 2007, Lee was chosen as the "Hero of Environment" in *Time* magazine along with the former U.S. Vice President Al Gore. The Cheong Gye Cheon stream restoration cata-pulted Lee to national prominence, and many local observers credit this with helping him win the presidency in 2007.

Conclusion

The forces toward rapid-pace suburbanization—rising incomes, rapid population growth, the location-liberating influences of information technologies, and so on—are universal but have been particularly pro-nounced in East Asia's megacities. Such trends certainly characterize the past three decades of unfolding settlement patterns in the one of the world's largest urban agglomeration, Seoul, South Korea. In the tradi-tion of British town planning, policy-makers at both the central and metropolitan government level embarked upon an ambitious campaign over the last quarter of the twentieth century to create a protective green-belt around Seoul and building large-scale, master-planned new towns on virgin lands beyond the greenbelt. While these new towns achieved their intended objectives of accommodating newly formed households and moderating housing price increases, with time the cumulative social costs began to rear their ugly head—notably, ever-worsening traf-fic conditions and environmental degradation. As often the case, bold, new urban visions require bold, new visionaries. In Seoul's case, this was in the person of Myung-Bak Lee, who oddly enough made a career of building mega-scale infrastructure projects throughout South Korea as the head of Hyundai Group. Yet once he retired from Hyundai and entered public life, he "found religion," as they say. When running for Mayor of Seoul in the early 2000s, Lee recognized that the daily tidal pattern of moving large segments of Seoul's workforce in and out of new towns to the core city was unsustainable—not only in terms of worsen-ing traffic and air quality, but also "time pollution," a term coined by British planners that recognizes time stuck in traffic is time robbed from one's personal life, whether being with one's family, for leisure, or civic engagement (Whitelegg 1993, Putnam 2000).

Mayor Lee's vision involved redefining the link between public infrastructure and community living. Long considered a public asset, land-hungry freeways and roadway interchanges can over time become a public liability. Mayor Lee and his contemporaries in a handful of other global cities have in recent times turned to a different kind of public asset to grow local economies—notably public amenities, urban parks, and other civic functions that enhance aesthetics and quality of life. These civic leaders have embraced a postmodern vision of how cities should look and function. In an increasingly competitive, knowledge-based global marketplace, improved civic spaces and expansion of the arts and cultural-entertainment offerings, proponents contend, appeal to highly sought professional-class workers, Richard Florida's (2002) so-called creative class. The economic dividends from civic investments, some contend, can be appreciable. Preliminary doctoral research at UC Berkeley suggests this is being borne out in Seoul: the fastest employment growth since CGC was converted from a freeway to a greenway has been in professional-class fields such as architecture, financial consulting, and engineering.

The longer-term consequences of Seoul's bold experiment with urban land reclamation are yet to be seen. The hope and expectation of many urban planners and political greens is that it will slow the pace of new town development, reduce the spatial mismatch between development north (primarily employment) and south (primarily housing) of the Han River, and spur redevelopment of former industrial land. More balanced, infill development, planners hope, will make Seoul an attractive city on the global stage that appeals to international finance and businesses as well as tourists, professionals, and foreign investors.

Experiences not only in Seoul but in other global cities that have opted to dismantle freeways and expropriate road space—San Francisco, Boston, Paris, and New York, among others—suggest that the era of indiscriminate large-scale infrastructure construction and a blind devotion to mobility-based planning is over. The urban footprint of the transport sector—freeways, interchanges, surface roads, and parking—is immense, consuming as much as half of all land area in many First-World cities (and in so doing, separating activities and thus creating greater demands for motorized transportation as well as roadway infrastructure). Whatever freeways and mega-scale urban infrastructure projects are built in coming years will have to be strategically sited and designed to pass a stricter litmus test of contributing to larger urban-development objectives of the cities and neighborhoods they serve. In Seoul and elsewhere, freeway deconstruction and land reclamation is tied to the reordering of urban priorities that gives preference to planning for people and neighborhoods, not just mobility. Experiences in Seoul suggest that the provision of high-quality public transport services and nicely designed pedestrian-friendly greenways can diminish the necessity for high-capacity elevated freeway structures. And in so doing, Seoul and similarly adventuresome cities are likely to find themselves on a far more sustainable pathway—not only in terms of environmental quality but economic prosperity and quality of life as well.

Note

I thank Chang Deok Kang, a doctoral student in the Department of City and Regional Planning at the University of California, Berkeley, for his assistance in compiling information and data used to carry out this research.

References

Anderson, S.T. and S.E. West. 2006. Open space, residential property values, and spatial context. *Regional Science and Urban Economics* 36: 773–789.

Boarnet, M. 1997. Highways and economic productivity: Interpreting recent evidence. *Journal of Planning Literature* 11(4): 476–486.

CGC Restoration Project Headquarters 2004. CGC restoration. Seoul: Seoul Metropolitan Government.

Dehring, C.and Dunse, N. 2006. Housing density and the effect of proximity to public open space in Aberdeen, Scotland. *Real Estate Economics* 34(4): 553–566.

Downs, A. 2004. *Still stuck in traffic: Coping with peak-hour traffic congestion.* Washington, DC: Brookings Institution Press.

Florida, R. 2002. *The rise of creative class.* New York: Basic Books.

Frech III, H.E. and R.N. Lafferty. 1984. The effect of the California Coastal Commission on housing prices. *Journal of Urban Economics* 16: 105–123.

Glaeser, E.L., J. Kolko, and A. Saiz, 2001. Consumer city. *Journal of Economic Geography* 1: 27–50.

Hwang, K. 2006. *Cheong Gye Cheon restoration & city regeneration: Cheong Gye Cheon, urban revitalization and future vision.* Seoul: Seoul Metropolitan Government.

Hwang, K., M. Byun, and T. Nah. 2005. *Project Cheong Gye Cheon.* Seoul: Nanam Publishing House.

Jun, M.J. 2000. Commuting pattern of new town residents in the Seoul metropolitan areas. *Journal of Korean Regional Development Association* 12(2): 157–170.

Jun, M.J. and C. Bae. 2000. Estimating commuting costs of Seoul's Greenbelt. *International Regional Science Review* 23(3): 300–315.

Jun, M.J. and J.W. Hur. 2001. Commuting cost of leap-frog newtown development in Korea. *Cities* 18(3): 151–158.

Kang, C.D. and R. Cervero. 2008. From elevated freeway to linear park: Land price impacts of Seoul, Korea's CGC Project. Working Paper. Berkeley: UC Berkeley Center for Urban Future Transport.

Lee, K.S. 2003. Seoul's urban growth in the 20th century: From a pre-modern city to a global metropolis. In *Seoul, 20th Century: Growth & Change of the Last 100 Years*, ed. K.J. Kim. Seoul: Seoul Development Institute.

Perloff, H. 1975. *Modernizing the central city: New towns intown…and beyond.* Cambridge, MA: Ballinger Publishing Company.

Polinsky, M. and S. Shavell. 1976. Amenities and property values in a model of an urban area. *Journal of Public Economics* 5: 119–129.

Pucher, J., H.Y. Park, M.H. Kim, and J. Song 2005. Public transport reforms in Seoul: Innovations motivated by funding crisis. *Journal of Public Transportation* 8(5): 41–62.

Putnam, S. 2000. *Bowling alone: The collapse and revival of American community.* New York: Simon & Schuster.

Seoul Development Institute 2005. *Toward better public transport.* Seoul: Seoul Development Institute.

Seoul Metropolitan Government 2003. *CGC Restoration Project.* Seoul: Seoul Metropolitan Government.

Sivitanidou, R. 1995. Urban spatial variation in office-commercial rents: The role of spatial amenities and commercial zoning. *Journal of Urban Economics* 38: 23–49.

Tajima, K. 2003. New estimates of the demand for urban green space: Implication for valuing the environmental benefits of Boston's Big Dig Project. *Journal of Urban Affairs* 25(5): 641–655.

Walsh, B. 2006. Saving Seoul. *Time Asia*, May 8, pp. 1–2. http://www.time.com/time/asia/covers/501060515/story.htm

Whitelegg, J. 1993. *Transport for a sustainable future: The case for Europe.* Belhaven Press: London.

CHAPTER 8

Electrifying Rural Areas: Extending Electricity Infrastructure and Services in Developing Countries

Corinne Krupp

Introduction

Electricity is an important part of the modern infrastructure of any country. It is taken for granted in developed countries that nearly every household has access to dependable electricity services; yet in many developing countries it is a luxury reserved mainly for wealthier households and businesses in urban areas. There are also problems with uneven coverage, unreliable service, and frequent breakdowns, and in some cases, the public sector ownership and provision of electricity has resulted in a huge budget burden, a failure to invest adequately in the generation, transmission, and distribution infrastructure, and the inability to expand electricity provision to rural areas.

This chapter discusses the problems of electricity provision in developing countries, focusing more on the issue of access in rural areas, and the inherent difficulties associated with designing a regulatory regime that promotes an efficient, sustainable, and equitable provision of electricity services. Several papers discuss the challenges associated with electricity provision in developing countries: private participation vs. public ownership, capital investment and maintenance of the infrastructure, ways of introducing competition into the generation and transmission sectors of the electricity market, and applying innovative approaches to spurring the spread of electricity to the poor living in remote areas. The focus of this chapter is to examine this literature, and to draw some general insights about the best ways to regulate and structure the electricity market to ensure equitable provision and reach to the rural poor.

The chapter is organized as follows: in the section titled The Economics of Electricity, I describe the basic economics of centralized electricity provision, including the traditional economies of scale and natural monopoly aspects of this service.[1] I examine the way electricity regulation has developed over time in developed countries, and explore the rationale for some of the recent deregulation and restructuring plans that have been proposed.

In the section titled Rural Electrification, I identify the problems inherent in providing electricity to rural customers and analyze ways in which this problem was addressed historically in several countries, including the United States and China. This section analyzes the evolution of electricity regulation, with a focus on relatively recent pro-market reforms that many countries are considering, or are in the process of adopting. I also briefly discuss a few other developing country case studies of electricity reforms that were promoted in India, Bolivia, and Ghana, and their outcomes.

In the section titled Pro-Market Reforms in Other Countries, I present several innovative approaches to solving the rural electrification problem, including a discussion of new technologies and possible regulatory designs that can address the challenge of making electricity more widely accessible in developing countries. In the penultimate section titled Innovations and Regulatory Designs, I briefly cover some of the chief problems in designing rural electrification systems that target the poor, and discuss how technology change is likely to affect the cost of provision. Finally, in the section titled Conclusion—Lessons Learned, I offer concluding remarks.

The Economics of Electricity

Flip a switch and instantly, the room is full of light. How does this happen? There are essentially three separate parts of the provision of electricity: *generation* of electric power, most often by using turbines powered by natural gas, hydropower, coal, or other fuels; *transmission* of the electric power from the generation station to smaller substations across the grid; and, the *distribution* of the electric currents to individual households and businesses.

Electricity, once generated, cannot be stored (except in limited amounts using batteries), but it can be sent long distances across the grid. A given electricity generation facility has a maximum capacity that cannot be breached, given the risk of dangerous overload that can lead to explosions and electric surges. Demand is uneven, dependent on the weather and time of day.

The infrastructure required for centralized electricity provision includes major capital investment in generation facilities, transmission lines and substations, the grid across which the power is transmitted, and individual distribution lines to link households and businesses to the power network. Given that power can be generated in a location far from the end users, there is less of a need to build dedicated generation facilities in each town, but the transmission and distribution infrastructure must be built to enable each customer to gain access. As more users are attached to the distribution network, the per-customer cost of power provision drops, given that the initial capital investment required to build the transmission and distribution infrastructure is fixed. Thus, there are significant economies of scale associated with attaching more paying customers to the electricity network. Currently, in many countries, this kind of centralized generation and distribution of electricity is the most common type of network used.[2] One of the primary ways in which electricity is generated is by spinning giant turbines, powered either by pressurized steam or through harnessing the mechanical energy of hydropower, where the turbines are connected to an electric generator. Various fuels can be used to produce steam (e.g., coal, natural gas, nuclear power, etc.), or the turbines can be spun through the use of water (hydropower), wind, geothermal energy, or solar energy. Once the electricity is generated, it must be transmitted from the power plant at very high voltages over long distances to reach substations where it is "stepped down" and distributed to customers.[3]

In developing countries, especially in rural areas, there is a chicken-and-egg problem inherent in connecting rural customers to the grid. That is, the up-front capital investment costs of building the transmission and distribution network to provide rural access to electricity is extremely high, especially if the customers are diffused through mountainous terrain and/or across long distances. Given the previous lack of electricity, these communities initially have little demand for it, and have not pursued income-generating activities that involve the use of electricity. The trick: how to justify the large up-front capital costs of providing electricity to rural areas by encouraging income-generating activities that make use of the electricity once it is provided? In order for such an investment to be profitable over time, rural dwellers will need to learn about electric appliances and machinery that can be used to improve their living conditions, as well as increasing productivity in many activities.[4]

Because demand is unpredictable and the initial capital investment to bring electricity to unserved communities is high, under what circumstances can this service be provided? What kind of regulatory environment must exist to encourage service provision?

The private market may be responsive if companies can reliably collect payment for services provided (i.e., electric meters must be installed and monitored) and if uncertainty is minimized about the rates companies can charge to cover not only marginal costs, but also the sunk investment costs of setting up the network, as well as the ongoing costs of maintaining the grid and investing in upgrades to accommodate demand growth. Thus, one key to successful provision is reducing uncertainty about the ability to set rates to cover these costs. The state is in a position to provide a regulatory environment that fosters competition while promoting transparency, consistency between costs and rate-setting, and minimizing the uncertainty firms face about future demand and the ability to recoup capital investment.

A stable regulatory environment can provide the incentive for private firms to pay for the initial investment. Alternatively, the state can finance the capital investment and contract for the electricity services to be provided once the infrastructure is in place. Continued investment and expenditures on upkeep and maintenance of the network must be incurred, and the state must either provide these, or they must be included in the contract provisions with the private firms. As with anything else in economic policy, the incentives must be structured correctly to ensure sustainability.

Since parts of the centralized electricity system retain elements of natural monopoly, given the significant economies of scale associated with transmission and distribution, pricing in this market is frequently regulated to prevent monopoly pricing and to ensure adequate service provision. The regulation of electricity in developed countries like the United States is currently conducted both at the state level, usually through public utility commissions that determine both rate levels and the rate structures utilities can use, and at the federal level, which regulates interstate wholesale pricing of electricity, and maintains the national grids. In the United States, this division of regulatory power evolved over time because fragmented community-based regulation became too difficult when the population grew and electricity demand increased.

While it used to be true that electricity was essentially a local, natural monopoly, technological and legal changes have made selling electricity across long distances possible, and this has implications for increasing customer choices of supply from the generators. Thus, the market has the potential to become more competitive and less monopolistic. Economists argue that competitive markets lead to lower prices and more efficient production than do markets dominated by monopolies, and so, they have led the push to deregulate electricity markets to the extent that is feasible.[5]

Many developed countries are pursuing various deregulation programs in order to increase the competitive pressure on electric utility companies to cut costs, lower prices, and improve service provision. In the United States, these changes have come about because of technology changes and the passage of the Energy Policy Act of 1992, which "gave the Federal Energy Regulatory Commission (FERC) the right to order utilities to 'wheel' power over their transmission lines, making transmission of electricity over long distances possible."[6] In addition, the 2005 Energy Policy Act "offers incentive mechanisms to overcome problems with insufficient investments in transmission to ensure reliability and to minimize congestion costs."[7] Clearly, the restructuring of electricity markets in the United States is far from complete, and given the 2000 crisis in California and the 2003 blackout in the Midwest, politicians' appetites for more reforms have been dulled.

There are wide differences between the social, political, and economic environments in developed and developing countries that have a major influence on the success or failure of electricity reform programs. Unfortunately, much of the policy advice given by many economists and policy-makers has been standardized, and the result has been uneven reforms and disappointing results. Several recent papers document the types of electric power sector reforms undertaken in both OECD and non-OECD countries, and the results of these well-intentioned reforms.[8] I summarize the basic thrust of these reforms, and discuss the intended and actual impact on the rural poor in various developing countries. My ultimate goal is to be able to offer some fundamental lessons we can draw from these reform attempts in order to improve the outcomes in the next round.

Rural Electrification

In this section, I briefly review how large-scale electricity generation was developed and adopted, and how two countries, the United States and China, solved the problem of supplying electricity to rural areas. It is my hope that some of the insights drawn from this analysis may inform policy advice for developing countries struggling with rural electrification issues. Rural electrification doesn't necessarily imply the provision of services to the poor, so we have to separately consider the impact of these reforms on the poor.

History of the U.S. Experience

Harnessing electric power for consumer and business use was made possible through the research and inventions of many men in the mid-1800s, principally, Thomas Edison, Nikola Tesla, and George Westinghouse. The development and adoption of alternating current technology and the invention of large turbines has enabled the large-scale electricity generation and distribution system used in most countries today. When electricity was first made available, it was in the form of direct current (DC) generators sold to individual businesses and customers, a rather expensive proposition. Tesla championed the use of more powerful alternating current (AC) power that could be sent over longer distances and generated in a large, central facility more cheaply, taking advantage of scale economies.[9] Samuel Insull, a former secretary to Thomas Edison, also saw the promise of a profitable business in the centralized generation and distribution of electricity by noting that different customers had different demands over the day, and that he could generate power at a large centralized generation plant more cheaply on a 24-hour per day basis and sell it at different prices based on peak and off-peak demands. Insull was successful in building an electricity empire in Chicago and the Midwest. He also successfully lobbied for the establishment of state utility commissions to set rates based on a fair-rate-of-return pricing, similar to that used in the gas industry, which not only protected his firm from potential competitors, but also ensured a profitable return.[10]

Given the economies of scale and the high fixed costs of building the transmission and distribution networks for centralized electricity provision, urban areas initially achieved higher rates of electrification than did rural areas. The United States adopted specific programs in order to promote widespread access to electricity in rural communities. The Rural Electrification Administration (REA) was created by the Roosevelt administration in 1935, with the express goal of enabling farmers to obtain electricity at low cost. Low-cost loans from the REA were made available to nonprofit organizations, farm cooperatives, and through state and local governments to finance rural electrification, so that groups of farmers could finance the construction and operation of their own local electricity generation facilities. The program was very successful: by the early 1970s, 98 percent of American farmers had electricity.[11]

Regulation of the electric utilities largely took the form of state-run public utility commissions (thanks to lobbying by Insull, especially in the Midwest). These boards protected the market from new entrants, and enabled the vertically -integrated monopolies to set rates that covered the full average total cost of provision, including an allowance for future investment. This kind of pricing was known as "rate-of-return pricing," and a variant of it is still in common use by most state regulatory commissions in the United States.[12]

The federal government also plays an important role in regulating the electricity industry in the United States. Since the 1930s, there have been three major Federal Acts passed that shaped the structure of the industry. They were: (1) The Public Utility Holding Company Act of 1935 [PUHCA], (2) The Public Utility Regulatory Policies Act of 1978 [PURPA], and (3) The Energy Policy Act of 1992. The PUHCA sought to break up the concentration of the industry due to the formation of large trusts as holding companies and the abuses in which they had engaged, including manipulation of subsidies, improper accounting practices, watering-down of their stock values, and capital inflation.[13] Through this Act, the Securities and Exchange Commission (SEC) had the power to break up these large holding companies, requiring them to divest their asset holdings until they were of a size "appropriate to operate a single utility in a specific, limited geographic area."[14]

This law essentially prohibited utilities from diversifying into nonutility businesses, and it blocked nonutilities from participating in the wholesale market for electricity. These provisions were later modified in the Energy Act of 1992 "to permit both utilities and nonutilities to build, own, and operate power plants wholesaling electricity in more than one geographic area."[15]

The National Energy Act, of which PURPA is a part, was passed in the wake of rising oil prices because of the Organization of Petroleum Exporting Countries (OPEC) oil embargo in the mid-1970s, and it was designed to encourage conservation and improved efficiency in the operation of U.S. energy markets. PURPA specifically *required* electric utilities to buy whatever amount of capacity and energy were offered wholesale by "qualified facilities,"[16] and that the price for this power be set at the in-house cost to the utility had it generated that power itself. This was known as the "avoided cost" of production.

Qualifying facilities wishing to enter the wholesale market were exempted from rate and accounting regulation by the Federal Energy Regulatory Commission (FERC), SEC regulation under PUHCA, and from state regulations on rates, finances, and the way in which they were organized. In essence, this Act opened the electricity market to entry from smaller generators who faced fewer restrictions and regulations, and since this "avoided cost" price wasn't linked at all to the actual cost of production, it saddled electric utilities with long-term power contracts, requiring them to buy more expensive electric power even if they had an adequate supply to meet demand at the time.

Important changes in the competitive landscape of the U.S. electricity market really began in early 1992 with the passage of the Energy Policy Act. Major modifications in PUHCA were made which enabled non-utility generators to sell into the wholesale market. These new exempt wholesale generators (EWG) were not subject to PURPA's restrictions, and utilities weren't required to purchase from EWGs. There were also transmission provisions that enabled FERC to require utilities to "wheel" or transmit power across their lines.

Independent system operators (ISOs) and regional system operators (RSOs) were created to monitor and facilitate open, nondiscriminatory access of the grid to all power producers, so that electricity could be traded across the country. This meant that the wholesale electricity market opened substantially to competition in the generation sector, and it pushed producers to cut costs and increase efficiency.

Given the interstate nature of the market, the federal government was in charge of regulating access to the grids and to ensure the rates charged were "appropriate to permit the utility to recover all legitimate, verifiable economic costs incurred with transmission services."[17] At that time, the political winds were blowing in the direction of a market-based, competitive system; however, because state regulators still monitored and set retail distribution rates for in-state utilities, the regulatory system remained fragmented.

Within the United States, the movement toward a more competitive electricity market has been far from smooth. We have witnessed the failure of Enron—the largest bankruptcy in U.S. history; the California electricity crisis in 2000; and an enormous regional (Mid-Atlantic) blackout in 2003 due to cascading failures in an antiquated transmission structure that continues to face problems with overloading and the use of old mechanical switching technologies.[18]

Several states have continued to experiment with various electricity market reforms, and many have been successful in that prices have fallen and efficiency has increased. Others have seen few or no gains from painful restructuring, and are moving back toward the old regulation models. According to Munson (2005), some of the lessons learned from these restructuring efforts include the following:

1. Utility sales of power plants have shown that nuclear plants are worth far less than their book values, but conventional natural gas- and coal-fired plants sell for more than their book values, indicating that past investments by utilities were certainly not evaluated correctly when they were made."
2. Much of the new construction of power generation plants is focused on smaller capacity plants, indicating a shift away from centralized power generation and distribution, and toward "distributed generation."
3. The deals that monopoly utilities made to have their "stranded costs" covered allowed them to shirk responsibility for bad investment decisions, leaving consumers holding the bag.[19]

These findings clearly indicate that the U.S. electricity market is still a long way from being competitive, and that the monopoly utilities still have tremendous influence on the process and outcomes. In addition, the promises of lower prices and costs and increased efficiency through deregulation may not be as dramatic as initially believed. Trading in the deregulated markets is vulnerable to manipulation and distortion, resulting in even worse outcomes for consumers compared to a more concentrated vertical monopoly structure.[20]

Rural Electrification in China

The Chinese government has been particularly successful in recently achieving nearly universal access to electricity (98 percent according to the International Energy Agency).[21] This achievement is mostly due to the huge commitment by the central government to mobilize financial contributions and commitments at the local level. The central government directly financed infrastructure investment, with local governments implementing the plans, including several huge dam projects (e.g., Three Gorges Dam). In some rural communities, the government introduced mini-hydropower plants that utilize the annual run-off of local rivers for hydropower generation. In order to ensure year-round reliability, these communities still need to be connected to the grid, but this innovation enables the production of cheaper hydropower especially during certain seasons. Government subsidies paid for half of the total investment in each plant, and the local governments contributed the remaining share.[22]

The central government maintains central control over pricing, but this has evolved to a more market-based system through corporatization of the state-owned enterprises in which the SOEs are responsible for managing their costs and output decisions, while also being allowed to retain part of their profits.[23]

China has struggled with capacity expansions as demand has grown, alternating between supply gluts and shortages. There are also problems with corruption and political control, as well as many layers of management. There is a huge bureaucracy associated with electricity provision and pricing: power is sold from the provincial level to the county; then to the township level, and from there, to the village level; and finally, reaches the households. This layered structure increases management costs and drives prices up. While some changes have been made, the cost of electricity in China is still higher per kilowatt hour (kWh) than in many developed countries.[24] The government increased electricity prices in the summer of 2009 to reflect rising costs of coal.

Pro-Market Reforms in Other Countries

In many other developed countries, similar pro-market electricity reforms began in the late 1980s, when economists and policy-makers became convinced that deregulation would lead to lower prices for consumers, faster innovation, more efficient and better service provision, and less pressure on government budgets. Changes in technology made it possible to unbundle electricity generation from transmission and distribution, and the belief in the efficiency of competitive markets led policy-makers to advocate reforms that would deregulate the market. Of course, deregulation meant moving away from monopoly and toward competitive markets, but not the end of regulation. For the market to work well, it still had to be subject to regulatory oversight to prevent abuses, along with the rule of law, the ability to enforce contracts, monitor usage, and to be able to collect payment for usage.

It is hard to believe that any of the economists saw the electricity market as having the potential to be perfectly competitive, with numerous small producers selling at marginal cost, earning zero economic profits, behaving atomistically, and with free entry and exit. The current centralized supply reality of electricity provision, as discussed in the previous chapter, flies in the face of such a naive belief. Even if power generation can become a more competitive market, the power still has to flow over the grid, and the grid has many characteristics of a public good.

The transmission and distribution infrastructure must be maintained and expanded as demand rises; yet no firm has the wherewithal or the incentive to make these investments if power can be wheeled over the grid without sharing these costs. Since electricity, once produced, cannot be stored, this also implies that this market would remain imperfectly competitive, even if deregulated. Thus, the importance of maintaining a strong role for the government in regulating and monitoring this market remains. This does not suggest that there is no room for introducing more competition into this market, but that the utopia of perfect competition does not exist here.

The driving forces behind electricity reforms were numerous, depending on the country in question. For OECD countries, the main reason for reform was improvement in the functioning of the market through more competition, and the hoped-for efficiency gains, cost savings, and lower prices that such reforms were expected to bring. By introducing competition, policy-makers believed that prices would fall to long-run marginal cost, and that the market would reward the more efficient and innovative producers with higher profits. The government would act more as a "referee" in ensuring that the market functioned smoothly, but it would get out of the business of setting rates and deciding where and how to invest in capital projects.

Since the technology of electricity provision was available to all countries, the belief in the gains from increased competition led to the push for the same kinds of policy reforms in developing countries, too. The World Bank, in 1992, changed its lending focus for electricity sectors in developing countries away from specific project lending, and toward policy lending. According to Wu, "Any country borrowing from the Bank on power projects would have to agree to move away from a 'single national electricity utility as a public monopoly' and adopt ownership, structural, and regulatory reforms."[25] In many cases (e.g., China, India), increasing demand for electricity and the poor performance of state-owned firms created pressure for reforms, and in other countries (e.g., Thailand, Bolivia, etc.), budget pressures and macroeconomic crises precipitated the push for reforms.

The "standard prescription" for electricity reforms in non-OECD countries included the following:[26]

1. Corporatization (separate the utility from the government ministry, install private managers, and adopt a clear accounting system);

2. Commercialization (use cost recovery in setting rates, reduce or eliminate subsidies, enforce collection);
3. Legal framework (adopt energy laws to mandate restructuring, permit private ownership, including foreign participation);
4. Regulatory framework (remove regulatory function from the ministry, create an independent regulator, legally define the scope, methods, and authority of the new regulator);
5. Independent power producers (create by privatizing state utility generation, greenfield development, power purchase agreements);
6. Restructuring (vertical and horizontal unbundling, create independent transmission company, separate profitable services for sale to private buyers);
7. Privatization (outright sale of state-owned firms, stock sale, joint ventures); and
8. Competitive markets (single buyers, bilateral forward contracts, cost-based pool, bid-based pool).

The World Bank promoted a set of key reform steps that focused on the financial aspects of power reform, neglecting issues of access, equity, and environmental issues in the initial design of the reforms. While it is true that many of these issues should have been addressed at the state and local levels, it soon became clear that they were neglected, and this contributed to the uneven results and, in some cases, the failure of the reforms to achieve their expected goals. In addition, the Asian financial crisis in 1997–1998 and the California electricity crisis in 2000 also had a major negative impact on the willingness and the ability to implement the reforms as planned.

To what extent were these reforms implemented, and how were the rural poor largely affected? To answer these questions, I will now turn to some specific developing country case studies, done by Xu, and Williams and Ghanadan, as noted.[27]

1. *Bolivia:* In Bolivia, one company, Empresa Nacional de Electricidad (ENDE), controlled 80 percent of power generation and operated the grid. While ENDE self-financed its day-to-day operations, it relied on public debt to finance capital investment. Generation and distribution were already partly unbundled when reforms began in the early 1990s, and Bolivia privatized its energy assets by selling 50 percent of its state-owned electricity shares through competitive bidding to international investors. The new owner retained these proceeds in order

to finance future capital investment. The remaining shares were invested in an old age pension fund in order to finance employee retirements. This enabled the reformers to convince the labor unions, industry, and citizen groups, who were opposed to the sale of Bolivian assets to foreign investors, to support the privatization reforms.

Poor households in Bolivia had been receiving subsidized rates on electricity prior to the reforms, and a gradual phase-out of these subsidies was part of the reform package. Rural access to electricity remains limited, although it rose from 16 to 25 percent of the rural population between 1992 and 2001.[28] On the positive side, the reform program resulted in complete privatization of the electric power sector, significant investment increases in distribution, transmission, and generation, and an improvement in the Bolivian government finances.

However, access for the rural poor has remained relatively sparse. As it was never an explicit goal of the reforms, the reforms cannot be blamed for the lack of progress in this area. The political winds have recently shifted in Bolivia, and the current government looks less kindly on foreign investment and control of Bolivia's infrastructure (witness the recent decision to renationalize the natural gas fields in Bolivia and to renegotiate all of the natural gas supply contracts with foreign investors), so it is unclear what will happen next in the electricity sector.

2. Ghana: Prior to the reforms undertaken in 1993, Ghana's generation and transmission of electricity was handled by the Volta River Authority (VRA), a monopoly that sold power in Ghana to the Electricity Corporation of Ghana (ECG) for distribution, and also directly to large industrial customers and those in nearby countries who paid in hard currency. While the VRA was profitable, the ECG lost money (both were state-owned), and did not offer reliable service. The reforms aimed to diversify the source of Ghana's electricity generation, away from hydropower and toward thermal generation, with the help of a World Bank loan. Competition in generation was also supposed to have been introduced, with the proposed unbundling of the VRA and a reorganization of the transmission and distribution networks into segments by geographic location.

Unfortunately, the reform plan was never implemented, and Ghana continues to suffer from supply shocks due to drought, the loss of its biggest customer (Kaiser Aluminum), and excess capacity made worse by the expensive commitment to purchase thermal power generated by natural gas. More recently, Ghana has improved its energy outlook by diversifying its energy sources (including access to the West African Gas Pipeline and participation in the West African Power Pool), implementing changes in its pricing structure, retiring debt, and undertaking several restructuring reforms. Ghana currently has a relatively high rural access rate (averaging 50 percent or more) compared to its other African neighbors.[29]

3. *India:* India's electricity sector was formerly state-owned, with the ownership divided between the central government and the states. While about 30 percent of electricity generation is seen as a well-run and profitable part of the business (run by the National Thermal Power and National Hydropower Companies), the State Electricity Boards (SEBs) are in dire financial straits given their poor management and failure to meter and charge many of their customers. These are vertically integrated state-run entities that generate about 60 percent of India's electricity and also handle distribution. Poor service and the use of cross-subsidies to the poor give large industrial customers the incentive to generate their own electricity, and this worsens the finances of the SEBs. Rural access is very limited, with only 46 percent of the population connected to the grid in India, including only 33 percent of rural residents (compared to 82 percent of urban residents).[30]

India's initial reforms addressed capacity expansion, through the encouragement of independent power producers (IPPs). The government received proposals for 190 projects which would have increased electricity availability by 75GW and cost more than US$100 billion, but only 15 of these proposals made it through the final approval process. Of those that were ultimately built, several were mired in controversy. Enron built a 26 GW gas-powered plant in Dabhol, but the state did not honor the financially unsustainable take-or-pay contract, and the plant sat idle.[31]

Not all of the reforms were national; states began to initiate their own reforms to address the supply shortage. Orissa was the first state to unbundle and privatize services, including generation and distribution, provided by the SEB. Transmission was still in state hands, and tariffs were raised; subsidies were cut, and assets were sold. Unfortunately, not many private investors were interested, and some who did invest eventually pulled out, complaining of government interference. Tariffs were increased even though service quality remained low, and little new investment in distribution was made, so access was not improved. An independent electricity regulator was created, and this concept was copied by other states, with some success.

After little effective reform occurred at the state level, the central government passed the Electricity Act of 2003, in which a uniform national framework was constructed, requiring metering, the payment of subsidies from state budgets, and punishments for electricity theft. The bill also included consumer protections and mandated rural electrification, but without funding for these mandates, little has happened. In fact, farmers were offered free electricity after the election in 2004, another setback to promoting financial sustainability in the electricity sector.

These case examples demonstrate several different attempts to change the nature of the electricity market in both developed and a sample of developing countries. Clearly, no country has found an easy way to do this, and all have experienced setbacks and crises. In the next section, I pull together what the deregulation experiments have taught us, with a specific focus on the access of electricity to the rural poor.

Innovations and Regulatory Designs

There is a difference between the questions of how to best achieve rural electrification in developing countries and how to best ensure that the poor have access to electricity services. The two concepts have become synonymous in many discussions, but they do not necessarily mean the same thing. Rural electrification in some countries has meant electricity access for the wealthiest rural residents, while the poor remain marginalized. The focus of this section is on assessing some of the shortcomings in the regulatory structure that need to be addressed in order to achieve sustainable rural electrification that specifically focuses on access for the poor.

The economics of electricity have been changing with technology, and as governments respond by deregulating markets. Unfortunately, some of these experiments in deregulation have been disastrous in developed countries, so the path forward to advising developing countries on how to promote electrification, and how to regulate it, is mixed. There are some basic principles that must be borne in mind when designing an electricity reform program. Here are some of the problems that arise from well-intentioned aid and expenditures on electricity infrastructure, taken from a recent Global Network on Energy for Sustainable Development study on renewable energy technologies and the poor:[32]

- Equipment failures due to inappropriate technology, installed without training or support to ensure sustainability;
- Too high cost of initial investments in renewable energy technologies (RETs) for the poor individuals and communities to afford;
- Mismatch between the energy provided and what is needed (e.g., type and, affordability) due to a lack of understanding about community needs;

- Focus on providing big, centralized grid-based electricity systems, which may make sense for large urban communities, but are too expensive and difficult to install for dispersed rural communities, especially those that are poor;
- Financing for and a lack of ongoing R&D that focuses on the environment and resources in poor communities for RETs has been spotty and sparse;
- Inadequate development of income-generating uses of RETs by poor households has limited the RET sellers' ability to obtain financing, given high risk and low profitability perceptions; and,
- Case studies show that the real barriers to adoption of RETs in developing countries are not technological, but they are attributable to the absence of an enabling environment that allows the customers to communicate what they really need with those who can provide it (holistic link between donors, RET providers, and local users), along with the training and education necessary to operate the RETs and to maintain them.

From this list, it is clear that providing electricity access for the rural poor in developing countries is much more a problem of information and creating an enabling environment, rather than just attracting donor funds to build centralized generation and distribution facilities and networks. Certainly, it is useless to build an expensive network if individuals lack the ability to make use of it, or cannot afford the services provided, or lack the ability to maintain it once donor support is withdrawn.

Conclusion—Lessons Learned

It is clear that centralized electricity production, transmission, and distribution cannot be treated as a truly competitive market, given the capital-intensive nature of production, the huge sunk costs, and ongoing investment requirements involved. Thus, while technology enables generators to wheel power across long distances, the transmission and distribution segments are networks that have high fixed costs, implying that the market will still be dominated by relatively few, large firms.

It is also true that there is a public goods nature to electricity provision, in the sense that maintaining the grid cannot be profitable for one firm given that all firms use it, and that regulation of pricing, upkeep and maintenance of the grids, and oversight of the system must stay in some kind of central authority's hands. Of course, it is preferable that this oversight authority be independent from the central energy authority in the government to avoid politicization of the decision-making.

The crux of the rural electrification problem in developing countries is linked to the ability of the rural poor to pay for electricity and the sunk cost of extending the grid, and the relative lack of demand for electricity initially. If we consider electricity a fundamental need in a developed society, then the investment must be undertaken. Paying for it, especially in a poor country whose budgets are already under strain, is only part of the problem. Ensuring adequate ongoing investment in the grid, building excess capacity as the population and demand grows, and determination of local needs and growth projections are all critical issues to address.

Some basic lessons:

- *Metering and Payment.* Establishing a link between usage and payment is essential. If customers do not pay for the electricity they use, then the power must be shut off. Prevention of electricity theft is important for establishing a profit motive for provision and continued investment.
- *Understand the Crux of the Failure to Connect to the Grid.* Is it a supply side problem (lack of local infrastructure that makes connection possible?), or is it a demand side problem (infrastructure is adequate, but some households choose not to connect?). These problems have very different solutions, so it is important to know why rural electrification is less than complete.[33]
- *Local Buy-in and Training.* Plans that involve local citizens in delivering and maintaining local electricity provision can help to promote protection of the system, increase the likelihood of payment, and enable the villagers to increase their skills and competency in maintaining electricity services. An innovative project in the Lao PDR features a hire-purchase mechanism for small villages, choices of supply technology, and the training of a village electricity manager to provide sales and maintenance of local equipment.[34]
- *Flexible Arrangements.* Permitting a wide variety of private, commercial, joint ventures, and public-private partnerships in the generation, distribution, and transmission segments of electricity markets is key to ensuring adequate capital investment and reliable supply. There is no "perfect" competitive structure that fits every country. The structure of ownership and the degree of competition to introduce depends on the level of development, the quality of the central and

local institutions, and the ability to enforce contracts, collect tariffs, punish electricity theft, and to repatriate profits.

- *Regulation.* An independent power authority should be created, with the power to ensure that open access to the grid is maintained; that power providers do not charge monopoly prices; that competition is introduced, where possible; and, that adequate tariffs are collected to ensure new capital investment to accommodate demand growth and maintenance of the infrastructure is ensured.

- *Make the Reforms Specifically "Pro-Poor."* One suggestion is to introduce a "social tariff," or a much lower electricity rate for households using a small amount of electricity (e.g., monthly use of 100 kWh or less), as well as for the government to pay for the initial connection of these households to the grid. Poor households tend to use much less electricity compared to wealthier households, so targeting the social tariff to those households using an amount at or below a relatively low threshold specifically targets the poor.[35] This would encourage poor households to connect to the grid, and it would improve the efficiency of power provision. Typical sources of heat, light, and cooking fuel for the poor include candles, burning wood or other biomass, and kerosene lamps, which yield much less illumination and heat, and create more indoor air pollution than electricity. Given their low relative efficiency, the implicit cost of power provision is substantially more expensive per kilowatt hour than electricity. Thus, by encouraging the poor to switch to electrification, several other problems can also be addressed: improved health (less indoor air pollution), time savings (less need to collect firewood or other biomass), and cleaner, more efficient power for multiple uses, including more productive microenterprises.[36]

It is interesting to note that as pressure on the grid increases in developed countries and as fuel costs rise, resulting in rising costs of electricity, there are incentives to investigate on-site electricity production alternatives for large consumers of electricity. These alternatives include cogeneration plants and the use of small gas-fired generators. For example, Dow Chemical Company in the United States uses its own cogeneration plants to source 95 percent of its power, saving the company US$40 million annually.[37] On the supply side, a new service market is developing that involves energy service companies (ESCOs) installing and maintaining energy-efficient systems in buildings and facilities, shopping for the best energy deals, and saving their customers' money on their energy bills while creating a profit for the ESCOs. Technological changes may make the notion of a centralized transmission and distribution system obsolete in the future.

This has major implications for developing countries and especially rural electrification. It is not a foregone conclusion that electricity provision to remote locations involves connection to a central grid. On-site, stand-alone generation facilities located in rural areas may be able to provide electricity more cheaply and more efficiently than connection to a centralized system. In some climates, solar and wind-powered generators may be feasible and cost-effective.

Given the technological advances in electricity generation, there may be many lower-cost options for supplying power to customers that do not involve an enormous capital investment in a comprehensive transmission and distribution infrastructure. Let the innovative entrepreneurs gain access to these markets, and by ensuring that the rule of law is applied, contracts made enforceable, and a transparent and fair regulatory structure is in place, maybe the lights will come on in the rural areas.

Notes

1. I recognize that the market is changing, and that distributed generation is becoming more common as countries experiment with deregulation and technology changes. This may have major implications for rural electrification in developing countries, and I discuss these issues in the section titled Innovations and Regulatory Designs .
2. Technological change is making micropower possible, meaning that individual firms and villages can supply their own electricity by building and maintaining a local source of power generation. More on this later in the chapter.
3. For an interesting primer on how electricity is generated and distributed, see Marshall Brain's website: http://people.howstuffworks.com/power.htm.
4. As will be discussed in the case of China, the time lag between making electricity available and adoption is extremely short in many rural communities.
5. Of course, this is a very much an unsettled issue. There are many voices on the other side of the debate who argue that electricity restructuring should be carefully reconsidered and planned. For a recent discussion, see Van Doren and Taylor (2004).
6. Viscusi, Harrington, and Vernon (2001: 388).
7. Performance-based regulation is discussed in an interesting article by Nieto (2006). The quote is from page 1 of the article.
8. See Williams and Ghanadan (2006) and Xu (2006).
9. The battle between Tesla and Edison over the adoption of AC or DC current is legendary. See Munson (2005) for a full discussion.

10. Munson (2005).
11. This historical background on U.S. rural electrification was taken from National Academy of Engineering (2003).
12. There have been changes in how prices are set that employ more incentive-based methods to encourage firms to lower costs, improve quality, and innovate. See Viscusi, Harrington, and Vernon (2001: 436–442).
13. See U.S. Department of Energy (2004: Chapter 4).
14. U.S. Department of Energy (2004: 1).
15. U.S. Department of Energy (2004: 3).
16. Qualified facilities had to either be cogeneration plants (those producing electricity and another form of energy [heat or steam usually] from a single source of power) or renewable energy producers (using biomass, solar, wind, waste, geothermal, or hydroelectric power to product electricity).
17. U.S. Department of Energy (2004: 6).
18. See Anonymous (2003).
19. Munson (2005: 131).
20. See Trebing and Voll (2006).
21. International Energy Agency (2002: Chapter 9, p. 1).
22. Chao (2004).
23. Xu (2006: 6).
24. Anonymous (2002).
25. Xu (2006): 2.
26. This list and the term "standard prescription" are taken directly from Williams and Ghanadan (2006: 5–6). I have paraphrased their terms and discussion.
27. In this section, I am summarizing the findings of these authors, but not offering any of my own analysis.
28. Williams and Ghanadan (2006: 10). The authors note that rural access rose from 16 to 25 percent between 1992 and 2001, but that these gains were due to infill of the existing grid near urban areas rather than rural area grid extensions.
29. World Bank (2005). According to this project update from the World Bank, rural access has increased considerably, thanks to a community-focused project called Self-Help Electricity Program (SHEP) started in 2005.
30. Williams and Ghanadan (2006: 11). It is important to note that rural electrification and access to electricity for the poor are not necessarily synonymous. Not all who live in rural areas are poor, nor do the poor only live in rural areas. In a World Bank working paper by http://siteresources.world-bank.org/PROJECTS/537857–1134770349044/20760161/EDAP-PID-Nov-11–2005.pdf, the authors specifically analyze coverage, availability, and take-up rates. They find that the coverage and take-up rates can differ widely.
31. Williams and Ghanadan (2006: 11).
32. Global Network on Energy for Sustainable Development (2006).

33. This interesting issue is discussed in the context of Guatemalan infrastructure reforms in the late 1990s. See Foster and Araujo (2004).
34. Harvey (2004).
35. The idea for this social tariff came from Foster and Araujo (2004), as it was used in Guatemala.
36. It is clear that changing energy sources will require new investment in appliances that utilize electricity. This may open up vistas for small business opportunities (i.e., individual or group investments in washing machines, dryer, televisions, etc. that may be made available to multiple families on a user fee basis).
37. Munson (2005).

References

Anonymous. 2002. Power politics. *The Economist*, June 6.

———. 2003. America's electricity crisis: Bring me your powerless masses. *The Economist,* August 21.

Brain, Marshall. n.d. How power grids work. http://people.howstuffworks.com/power.htm

Chao, Ling. 2004. Electricity scheme lights up the lives of rural residents. *China Daily*, May 12.

Foster, V. and C. Araujo. 2004. *Does infrastructure reform work for the poor? A case study of Guatemala.* Washington, DC: World Bank.

Global Network for Energy and Sustainable Development. 2006. Poverty reduction: Can renewable energy make a real contribution? May. http://www.gnesd.org/Downloadables/PovertyReductionSPM.pdf

Harvey, Adam. 2004. Village electricity in Lao PDR. *Renewable Energy for Development* 17(2): 1–4.

International Energy Agency. 2002. Energy and poverty, Chapter 9 in *World energy outlook 2002*. Paris. http://www.iea.org/textbase/nppdf/free/2002/energy_poverty.pdf.

Munson, Richard. 2005. *From Edison to Enron.* Westport, CT: Praeger Publishers.

National Academy of Engineering. 2003. Rural electrification. In *A century of innovations*, Chapter 2. http://www.greatachievements.org/?id=2990.

Nieto, Amparo. 2006. Performance-based regulation of electricity transmission in the U.S.: Goals and necessary reforms, *Energy Regulation Insights*, NERA Consulting, March. http://www.nera.com/NewsletterIssue/NL_ERI_EN454_0603_FINAL.pdf

Trebing, H. and S. Voll. 2006. Infrastructure deregulation and privatization in industrialized and emerging economies. *Journal of Economic Issues* 60(2): 307–315.

U.S. Department of Energy. 2000. The federal statutory background of the electric power industry. In *The Changing Structure of the Electric Power Industry 2000:*

An Update, p. 1. http://www.eia.doe.gov/cneaf/electricity/chg_stru_update/update2000.html.

Van Doren, Peter and Jerry Taylor. 2004. Rethinking electricity restructuring, *Policy Analysis* 530, Cato Institute, November 30.

Viscusi, W. Kip, Joseph E. Harrington, and John M. Vernon. 2001. *Economics of regulation and antitrust*. Cambridge, MA: The MIT Press.

Williams, J.H. and R. Ghanadan. 2006. Electricity reforms in developing and transition countries: A reappraisal. *Energy* 31(6–7): 815–844.

World Bank. 2005. Project information document: Ghana: Energy Development and Access Project. Washington, DC. http://siteresources.worldbank.org/PROJECTS/537857–1134770349044/20760161/EDAP-PID-Nov-11–2005.pdf.

Xu, Yi-Chong. 2006. The myth of the single solutions: Electricity reforms and the World Bank. *Energy* 31(6–7): 802–814.

CHAPTER 9

Infrastructure and Inclusive Development through "Free, Prior, and Informed Consent" of Indigenous Peoples

Rosemary Morales Fernholz

Introduction

Overall, the aim of major infrastructure projects to exploit natural resources, such as large dams and extractive industries for hydrocarbons and hard minerals, is to improve economic growth and well-being in a country or region. Yet, many studies show that the people living in the proximate areas frequently do not share in these benefits, and often suffer major economic, health, and cultural losses. This chapter focuses on these kinds of major infrastructure projects in developing countries, considered important and beneficial nationally, yet disruptive and even detrimental in the remote areas that are home to indigenous peoples and their communities.[1] It is important to review the social impacts of these projects because world trends indicate that infrastructure development will reach practically all remote areas, communities, and peoples in the twenty-first century, and global demands for energy and natural resources will require a major expansion of large-scale infrastructure projects. With current global concern for the environment and the social condition of vulnerable people, there are opportunities and new approaches to improve distributional impacts of major infrastructure projects. This chapter shows the positive developments in this regard and issues that still need to be addressed.

This chapter begins with the factors that drive development in remote areas, considering location aspects of natural resources such as water and minerals, growing demand for and competition over these resources, and the pressures to expand coverage of services to local citizenry. The next section introduces the numbers, conditions, and concerns of indigenous peoples who live in the areas where infrastructure expansion is taking place. This is followed by examples of major infrastructure projects to identify features in their design and execution that impact local peoples. In particular, the issues of building large dams and the expansions of extractive industries, specifically hydrocarbon and hard mineral industries, are reviewed because they are the most "potentially invasive" development projects in remote areas, and with a high probability to affect indigenous peoples and their communities (Asian Development Bank 2007: 8).

The third section analyzes key issues that include asymmetry of power, rights of indigenous peoples, and the challenge to address social impacts such as displacement and resettlement due to major infrastructure projects. The section identifies traditional and contemporary actors and their interests on these issues. It will also discuss the evolution and adequacy of social safeguards used in development agencies, financial institutions, and donor agencies. It considers new financing arrangements that support major infrastructure projects and the role of local, national, and international enforcement agencies and agreements.

The fourth section assesses the importance of information and participation in decision-making, and summarizes the issues and concludes with the theme of "Development with Dignity" related to infrastructure. Given that the main actors for sustainable development are governments, citizens, and the private sector, how can the concepts of "free, prior, and informed consent" for infrastructure development be made more meaningful? This section ends with viewpoints on infrastructure that indigenous peoples have expressed in their statements and declarations, including the 2007 United Nations Declaration on the Rights of Indigenous Peoples (United Nations General Assembly 2007). This is followed by a broad summary of the issues and dilemmas of balancing the national benefits of development and the well-being of the indigenous people impacted by development. Finally, the chapter summarizes the recommendations flowing from the analysis.

Infrastructure and Development in the Territories of Indigenous Peoples

The Location Aspects of Major Infrastructure Development

What drives the big infrastructure projects to the remote areas is the nature and location of the natural resources such as major rivers and hard mineral or hydrocarbon deposits. The existence of rich metal ores generally makes soils unfit for agriculture, so they are often found in forested or desert areas of low human population density. The expansion of hydroelectric capacity is now taking place in more remote areas because the developments in heavily settled areas either are already in place or are prohibitively expensive.

One might think that major infrastructure expansion into remote areas would benefit the local inhabitants by bringing goods, services, and access to them. However, the implications are mixed, depending on the type of infrastructure and the conditions associated with it. Roads provide greater access to economic opportunities, health services, and educational services. A joint Asian Development Bank and World Bank survey found that low-income rural people in China, India, and Thailand typically believe that the expanded transport opportunities are to their benefit (Cook et al. 2004), in terms of both access to services and enhanced social capital through greater opportunities for contact among community members. However, appreciation of the access benefits cannot incorporate the risks of loss of land, user rights, cultural integrity, or other potential longer-term consequences. Expanded electricity generation will provide greater residential and industrial opportunities in the affected areas, but this is not a gain for the people who are displaced from the area; this is an especially serious problem with major hydroelectric projects.

The capacity of the local people to take protective actions is typically very limited. Private companies, particularly the multinational corporations engaged in mining or energy development, may engage in careful exploration and planning in their quest for profits and supply of product, but the timing and magnitude of exploitation depends on the complex mix of political opportunity, favorable financing, and market conditions. Government officials, whether committed to the nation's well-being or their own self-enrichment, often have much higher priorities than the protection of the local people who are in the path of infrastructure expansion.

An example is the development of energy resources in the Philippines. In the 1930s, the commonwealth government, through the newly established National Power Corporation, undertook studies to assess the power potential of the country and prepared the first map-based comprehensive report on the potential of water, coal, and other power sources, titled *Power and Fuels of the Philippines*. This was followed a decade later by economic and investment studies of these resources. In 1963, the UN Special Fund provided assistance for more in-depth studies to evaluate the energy resource potential in the country of water, coal, geothermal, oil, and gas. Although the national agency identified the location of potential major hydro development in 1948 and undertook more detailed studies in the 1960s, the government did not inform the indigenous peoples in the Cordillera mountain region that imminent plans to construct dams on the Chico River would flood part of their territory and ultimately displace some 100,000 people. Despite the analytical work that went into the decision to proceed with the dams, the local people learned of this only when they encountered survey teams in their area in 1970 (Fernholz 2002). This caused much violence in the region and anger toward the government and the World Bank as a potential funder of the project[2].

More of this type of major infrastructure development is expected in remote areas and territories of indigenous peoples. A map prepared by the International Forum on Globalization in 2003 for their Indigenous Peoples' Project lists 19 globalization-related factors that impact indigenous peoples. Of these, dams, water, mining, and various energy projects are directly linked to the location of the resource; other projects such as roads, land conversion into plantations, and logging often complement or follow major infrastructure development (International Forum on Globalization 2003). The International Forum on Globalization lists 96 situations in which indigenous groups face threats from oil exploitation, 55 threats from expanded mining, and 27 threats from the development of new dams.

Consideration for the welfare of indigenous peoples and other vulnerable rural residents has largely been swamped by the allure of taking advantage of the dramatic increase in the demand for natural-resource exports. Despite the periodic recessions that have occurred over the past several decades, the rapidly growing demand for energy and raw materials has made it very difficult for governments to resist the political and economic pressures to press forward with extractive industries and expanding energy for both domestic use and export. In the 1995–2006 period, the annual increases in the value of oil exports exceeded 14 percent, natural gas exports at a rate of nearly 16 percent, and iron ore and copper ore at rates of 11 percent and 13 percent respectively.[3]

To meet the demand for raw materials, developing countries need massive infrastructure investments to extract and transport these materials. Whatever domestic economic growth arises from export expansion also generates demand for energy and transport expansion. The World Bank estimate, as stated in the introductory chapter, is that investment in infrastructure in the developing world needs to at least double and increase from 6.5 to 7.7 percent of GDP over the period from 2005 to 2010.

The result, thus far, is an inexorable encroachment into more remote areas, by both governments and the private sector, to exploit more natural resources, giving rise to varying and evolving kinds of competition and conflict over land, water, timber, and other resources. In the current biofuel versus food debate, for example, a concern expressed in a 2008 Asian Development Bank study on Laos and Cambodia is over the environmental and social consequences that result when financial or other policy incentives encourage land conversions. Forestlands that have been the basis for survival among many indigenous groups are rapidly transformed into plantations by big corporations. This study states, "Indeed, the broader goals of poverty reduction through rural development, promoted by both governments, may be undercut by the resultant surge in land conflict and the scramble for natural resources" (Setboonsarng and Markandya 2008: 18). This same kind of conflict occurs when big infrastructure development projects undermine the land security of local peoples, limit their access to productive resources, or displace them arbitrarily, whether it is by corporations seeking to exploit hard mineral or hydrocarbon energy resources, or governments approving construction of large-scale dams.

The combination of location aspects and demand to exploit and profit from natural resources has led in the past to schemes to take over ownership of land resources and to disregard claims of local peoples over their territories. Some forms of expropriation have been through government policies that disregard or deny alternative forms of land claims that are held by indigenous peoples—such as collective forms of ownership versus individual or ancestral claims and understandings versus written titles. Some governments have used coercion or even violence to displace indigenous peoples. And, in specific instances, corporations or their corrupt officials acting in collusion with corrupt public officials have used various means to gain control over natural resources for their personal gain. As a result, indigenous communities in general have remained relatively poor and marginalized, and in some cases, highly distrustful of government and mainstream society.

Thus when local villagers are expected to "make way" for the projects, conflicts emerge with governmental authorities, the personnel involved in infrastructure construction or operation, or even with other local groups. For example, plans to build dams in the Changuinola-Teribe watershed of Panama have built up tensions with the Ngobe and Naso people. Although the Changuinola River area is in a buffer zone of a recognized UNESCO World Heritage Site and the local people are fearful of the negative impacts of the plans to build dams on them, the central government is pursuing the projects as part of a national strategy to reduce dependence on oil. Ellen Lutz (2008: 1) points out that "electricity from the dams will supply the ever-expanding appetite of Panama City, which today is a modern First-World city. About 3,500 indigenous people will be affected by the dams." In some cases, and to the frustration of local people, the hydro-generated electricity is made available to the cities years before the nearby towns.

Expanding coverage of social services to national populations

As pressure grows on the governments of developing countries to provide wider coverage of social services to their populations, these governments are expected to expand infrastructure in the form of roads and transport, electricity and water provision, schools and clinics to remote villages and towns. The Millennium Development Goal agreements, targets, and scorecards are effective measures for motivating countries to achieve significant social development improvements, and infrastructure development helps make this possible.

Therefore it is important to understand that the impact of infrastructure development on the indigenous communities in remote areas is mixed; some development, such as building rural roads, bridges, schools and clinics, is sought by the indigenous communities and the impact of these projects on the people tends to be favorable. In other cases, and especially for large-scale infrastructure projects such as dams, however, many local people face displacement or loss of livelihood sources, and the impact can be unfavorable (Colchester 2000).

Indigenous Peoples in the Path of Development

There are approximately 370 million indigenous peoples, or 5 percent of the world's population, who live in 5,000 distinct indigenous societies in 70 countries. Indigenous communities claim as territories some 20 percent of the world's land surface. Since they often have close cultural affinity to the land and natural resources around it, they use the term "territory" rather than simply land, and often have ancestral claims to tracts of land and resources that are managed in a communal way. Ancestral claims, however, can be insecure claims because many governments are reluctant to consider communal ownership forms over large tracts of land and to redress past land abuses, and country constitutions or laws consider natural resources as property of the state.

About 15 percent of indigenous peoples live in the tropical rainforests. In all, the areas they occupy harbor 80 percent of the world's biodiversity. They are widely considered responsible stewards of their environments or environmental defenders,[4] hence many environmental organizations support causes of indigenous peoples. Many indigenous peoples live in areas that are remotely situated in mountains or jungles where watersheds, timber, or mineral resources are found. Therefore these are prime areas for the location of large dams or mineral exploration. For example, in the Philippines, almost all large dams are located in or close to territories claimed by indigenous peoples (United Nations 2006, Asian Development Bank 2007, WCD Dams and Development 2000). Hence, social and environmental issues are intertwined when development impacts are considered in their areas.

Despite progress made in some countries, indigenous peoples tend to be among the poorest in terms of human development and other socioeconomic indicators. They account for 15 percent of the world's poor, although, in number, they are roughly 5 percent of the world's population. In the Latin American region, for example, the indigenous population is estimated at 28 million, 80 percent of whom live in poverty. Indigenous peoples in this region tend to have low levels of education and assets (Patrinos and Skoufias 2007).

Many countries have had discriminatory policies against "native people" and these have taken different forms. Indigenous peoples historically have had minimal participation in policy- or decision-making about these resources or factors affecting their livelihoods. Yet in many countries, this has been changing in recent years, with more political participation and leadership from indigenous peoples locally, nationally, and internationally. Hence, national constitutions or laws are being rewritten to simplify rules for land ownership, remove discriminatory laws, and to allow for communal ownership and/or autonomy. This is illustrated by the case of *comarcas* in Panama, which are areas predominantly populated by Indians. The area has the status equivalent to a province or municipality, the *comunidades campesinas* in Peru, and the administrative and autonomous regions in the Philippines including the Cordillera Administrative Region with a big indigenous population and the Autonomous Region in Muslim Mindanao, that have much greater autonomy to plan and manage regional affairs, than most other Philippine regions are granted.

Changing the Rural Village and Indigenous Peoples' Lives: Impacts of Large Dams and Hydrocarbon and Hard Mineral Extractive Industry

Dams

Large dams are likely to be a major form of infrastructure development worldwide in the future, despite the problems and the reluctance of international organizations to finance them without strong assurances that affected people will be protected. Many developing countries are looking to their watersheds and rivers as sources for hydropower, irrigation, and water storage, or as resources that can generate foreign exchange, as in the case of the Nam Theun II dam in Laos that will be the source of energy export to Thailand. In the most populous region of the world (Asia has almost 40 percent of the world's large dams), it is perhaps not surprising that the demand for the services that dams can offer (such as irrigation, hydropower, water supply, etc.) would be high, and therefore, the potential impact on large numbers of local peoples is also high. The International Commission on Large Dams[5] has listed 50,000 large dams[6] in their Register of Dams in the World (International Commission on Large Dams 2007). Khagram (2005) notes that the majority of the big dams, operating in about 140 countries, were built in the past 50 years.

In principle, large dams could provide advantages for local people, bringing the benefits of increased energy, irrigation, and increased land values. However, although the farmers receiving a steadier water supply will benefit, displaced families will not have the land to benefit from irrigation, and ironically the rise in land prices will often put nearby land out of reach for the displaced families. When displaced families are resettled to other areas, often to towns and cities where their skills and ways of life are incompatible, they become excluded from whatever benefits accrue to residents in the area where the infrastructure has been developed.

The trend in construction has not been upward always, however, one reason being that negative social and environmental impacts caused fierce opposition from local peoples and international environmental and human rights organizations, affecting financial support for and slowing down the construction of big dams in the 1980s. Only in the early 2000s has there been a resumption of interest in these projects.

Despite the potential role of large dams in addressing development needs stated earlier, persistent objections have centered on environmental and social impacts, such as the short- and long-term negative effects on the ecosystem and aquatic resources as well as impacts on local people's lives and livelihoods. A review of the experiences of 1,000 dams in 79 countries concluded that "while dams have made an important and significant contribution to human development, and the benefits derived from them have been considerable, in too many cases, an unacceptable and often unnecessary price has been paid to secure those benefits, especially in economic, social and environmental terms, by people displaced, by communities downstream, by taxpayers and by the natural environment" (Moore and Scudder 2008: 23). Unfortunately, the past history of dams has been painful for many indigenous peoples and their communities in areas around watersheds and major rivers.

Displacement. The main issue related to large dams that have a significant impact on indigenous peoples is displacement due to flooding of big areas for the reservoir and to land acquisition for the areas needed for other related infrastructure and protection. The World Commission on Dams in 2000 estimated that some 40 to 80 million people have been displaced by dams worldwide, and these dams along with other diversions, have affected 60 percent of the world's rivers (WCD Dams and Development 2000). Scudder (2005) quotes World Bank advisors on social policy and the environment who pointed to forced or involuntary population displacement caused by dam projects as a very serious, if not the most serious impact of water resource development. Literature on infrastructure cite two prominent displacement examples: the Sardar Sarovar (Narmada) project in India that displaced almost a quarter million, mostly tribal, people, and the Itaparica project in Brazil that resettled or otherwise affected more than 150,000 indigenous peoples. These are projects that have had strongly adverse social and environmental effects and that led to the rise of scrutiny of these projects by civil society organizations (Infrastructure Network 2006). More recent examples of displacement are "the Three Gorges Dam on the Yangtze River in China, due for completion in 2009, will displace some 1.3–1.6 million people from 320 villages and 140 towns, and destroy very many ancient and historic sites" (World Wildlife Fund 2007: 1). The Nam Theun II hydroelectric project in Laos requires the relocation of more than 2,000 households of indigenous peoples to other areas (Hirsch 2002). The Theun Hinboun Dam Expansion Project in the same country is expected to displace almost 5,000 people and ultimately affect more than 50,000 people in downstream areas and host villages (Imhof 2008, Imhof and Preston 2008).

Relocation and Resettlement. The relocation and resettlement of people resulting from displacement required for major infrastructure projects is a very complex and difficult challenge. In the past, this was mainly forced or involuntary resettlement, meaning that local people were often not given information or choice in the process, their claims to their land were not respected, and they were denied legal recourse. For indigenous peoples who have strong spiritual connections to their territory, and whose claims to the territories have been controversial, this has proven a very high cost and a cause worth fighting for, as discussed in subsequent sections of this chapter. De Wet (2006: 1) points out that "in the overwhelming majority of cases, most of the people displaced or resettled by development projects are still left worse off than before and suffer socio-economic impoverishment." Displacement due to large dams further means that massive numbers of people and communities have to be relocated and resettled in a fairly short period of time, posing an enormous challenge. In effect, this may mean the creation of "villages" with supporting infrastructure, services, and livelihood, and may take years to implement. Experience has shown many other losses can lead to impoverishment of people who are relocated, including loss of access to productive factors such as sources of firewood or grazing land; loss of traditional employment; loss of access to support systems; and insecurity arising from lack of food and water, exposure to disease, and so on.

The Inter-American Development Bank, despite its involvement in major infrastructure projects requiring displacement, acknowledges the difficulty of preserving the well-being of displaced people (Inter-American Development Bank 1998: 27) and notes that resettlement of indigenous peoples is complex:

> The resettlement and rehabilitation of indigenous and other low-income ethnic minority communities living in rural areas is particularly difficult. The identity of many of these communities is closely tied to the land, which often has a significant spiritual and emotional importance, as well as providing the economic basis for the livelihood of the community. Indigenous people also tend to be more vulnerable than other sectors of society as they often lack formal rights to the areas on which they depend for their subsistence. Even when they hold legal title to the lands they use most intensively, they often depend on much larger areas

for their subsistence. In addition, indigenous peoples generally are at a disadvantage in pressing their claims for fair compensation. Living in remote rural areas, they often do not have any formal education, and may face language barriers, cultural obstacles and racial prejudice as well as a lack of financial resources and the social and political contacts necessary to influence the decisions that are made in the national or regional capitals.

There are several other issues related with large dam projects that impact local people and these include (1) adequacy of compensation, (2) impacts on livelihood, and (3) social, environmental, and cultural impacts on people and communities directly affected and in nearby areas. These are discussed below:

Adequacy of Compensation for Land and Other Physical Resources. One key issue related to displacement and resettlement is *adequacy of compensation* for displacement, property appropriation, or reduced livelihood opportunities. Even establishing a level of compensation that leaves people no worse off is a very complex issue, because values of locale and property can be very different from the perspectives of different stakeholders. This is expressed succinctly by de Wet (2006: 5):

> One area in which local complexity is misunderstood and misrepresented is in the area of compensation, where a value is attached to local resources in order to be able to compensate affected people for losses arising from displacement. To calculate compensation, resources are evaluated in terms of assumed uses, productive value and apparent patterns of access. However, resources have multiple uses, both more directly economic and otherwise, and patterns of access to resources are notoriously complex, ambiguous and dynamic. What the outside implementers think they are taking away and compensating for may bear little resemblance to the multiple uses and meanings the affected people see themselves as losing, and to whether they consider such loss can in principle be made good through compensation. The attempt to secure and impose a process of commensurability of evaluation necessarily requires a process of simplification, which is likely to give rise to confusion, anger and resistance.

Negative Impacts on Livelihood. Livelihood changes can be significant for those who remain in areas close to the dam or who live or work in upstream or downstream areas close to dams. While employment may increase in dam-related construction or maintenance work, studies of changes in ecosystems caused by dams note the effects on the lifestyles, livelihood, and health of local peoples. These can include impacts on fishing potential as dams change fish migratory patterns or water flows, loss of navigability in the rivers, pollution of various kinds, and health issues. In many cases, the area around the watershed is declared a protected area and indigenous peoples who depended on minor forest products for their subsistence or livelihood may have to find alternative sources of employment, supplementary income, or food.

For resettled people, the result is often loss of income sources, especially the loss of traditional forms of employment known to the indigenous peoples. In some cases, people who have been traditional fisher folk get moved to inland areas or people who rely on nearby forests are moved to barren areas. Often there is a lack of support services for basic needs such as water in the new areas leading to a deterioration in health and well-being, and hence productivity. Ironically, quality of life of poor people in a country can be adversely affected by the very development projects that aim to improve quality of life. In the study earlier referenced of 1,000 large dam projects, "(t)hose who were resettled rarely had their livelihoods restored, as resettlement programs have focused on physical relocation rather than the economic and social development of the displaced. The poor, other vulnerable groups, and future generations are likely to bear a disproportionate share of the social and environmental cost of large dam projects without gaining a commensurate share of the economic benefits" (Moore and Scudder 2008: 24).

Loss of Cultural Resources and Identity. Indigenous peoples often place high value and sense of identity in their social networks and in their relationships to natural objects or phenomena. This is disrupted when there is displacement and shattered when their areas, sacred shrines or monuments, burial sites, or symbols are inundated. Often, dams affect areas with cultural treasures or protected forests. The Ilisu Dam reservoir under construction in Turkey, for example, will submerge the town of Hasankeyf that dates back to the Middle Ages.

Resettlement typically changes important social networks that had existed in the villages prior to resettlement. People are divided both physically in the new areas and politically over differences toward the projects. In addition, resettled people have often faced problems with host communities, resulting in competition and friction, since large numbers of displaced people tend to put pressure on existing resources and services. Disputes over land as well as cultural differences between the newly relocated people and the host communities often result in violent confrontation.

To try to protect displaced families, the World Bank developed a doctrine that required borrowing governments to guarantee that families displaced by hydroelectric dam projects would be left no worse off than they were before the displacement. The difficulty of keeping governments to this commitment was one of the factors that led the World Bank to suspend its financing of large dams for more than a decade, resumed only with the enormous oversight effort with the "experiment" of the Nam Theun II Dam in Laos.

It is worth noting the social impact of this project:

> The 2005 Nam Theun II Hydroelectric Project in Lao PDR flooded 45,000 hectares of land of the tribes of the Nakai Plateau (Brou, Tai Bo, Upland Tai, Vietic, and Sek) displacing more than 1,000 ethnic households due to the reservoir and another 1,000 due to land acquisition. Other difficulties facing the local people include the loss of traditional and culturally significant structures, and archeological and historical artifacts. Some of the risks identified for ethnic minorities in the surrounding areas were:
> resettlement of tribes in the Nakai Plateau
> changes in livelihood
> loss of access to resources (herbs and roots) for traditional medicine practices, hence affecting culture and wellbeing.
> These losses and risks have been addressed in the planning of the project and mitigation measures were drawn up. The project is ongoing and environmental and social effects are monitored by various agencies. (Excerpted from Asian Development Bank 2007: 75,76)

Yet even with the heavy oversight of the Nam Theun II project, currently underway, it has provoked strong criticism in light of the risks to affected families (Mydans 2006).

Extractive Minerals and Energy Resources—the Indigenous Peoples' "Resource Curse"

The Human Development Report of 2004 points out that it is mostly in the historical territories of indigenous peoples where watersheds and rich resources of minerals exist, increasing the likelihood that extractive industry expansion will impact indigenous groups and "the potential for conflict between promoting national economic growth through extractive industries and protecting the cultural identity and economic livelihood of indigenous people" (UN Development Programme 2004: 91). The relevance for physical infrastructure is that the expansion of extractive industries requires transportation expansion, both for the extraction itself (e.g., logging roads) and to bring the material to ports or processing facilities. The expansion of extractive industries often requires the construction of energy-generation facilities, telecommunications networks, and on-site processing facilities. The causal chain works in the opposite direction as well: the expansion of infrastructure requires quarrying for road building, extraction of hydrocarbons to fuel vehicles on the expanded transportation system, uranium for nuclear power plants, and the like.

Investments in extractive industries are increasing rapidly. Data compiled by the UN Conference on Trade and Development (2008a: 227; 2008b) show a big increase in estimated world inward foreign direct investment flows to mining, quarrying, and petroleum in developing countries from US\$3.2 billion during the 1989–1991 period to US\$15.0 billion during the 2003–2005 period.

Activities of extractive industries threaten the well-being of indigenous peoples through (1) displacement of populations, though usually on a smaller scale than for large dams; (2) environmental degradation and resource depletion, often without inadequate compensation; (3) negative impacts on local livelihoods; and (4) loss of cultural resources and identity. In general, the issues that arise are similar to those associated with large dams, though there are some distinctions.

Displacement and Inadequate Compensation for Environmental Degradation and Resource Depletion. Extractive industry opportunities often attract domestic and multinational corporations that use various kinds of pressure to obtain land, though not in the magnitude of the large dam projects, and to secure access rights from the local people. In countries with high levels of corruption, pressure is often exerted with the collusion and support of public officials with minimal compensation or regard for local people. There is, therefore, a sense of injustice among the local peoples when they perceive, correctly or not, that "enormous" profits are being made from natural resources. Even when royalty funds are earmarked for the local communities, corruption and bureaucracy often combine to deny the local people access to these funds. Examples include the funds from gold mining in the Cajamarca region of Peru[7] and a special Amazon development fund from Ecuadorian oil revenues that largely bypassed the indigenous peoples they were promised to help (UN Development Programme 2004). The health costs of environmental degradation, which are extremely difficult to measure or to attribute to particular polluters, typically goes uncompensated, or compensated minimally.

Negative Impacts on Local Livelihoods. The stakes that indigenous peoples have in their territories include not just the land, but also the air, water, and natural resources that provide them their lives and livelihoods. Extractive industries undermine livelihoods of local people through environmental degradation of soil and water, and by exclusion of local people from areas appropriated for resource extraction. For example, the Tuareg are restricted from using pastureland in Niger near Agadez because the government has given the concession to mining companies (Wessal 2008). Although extractive industries do offer some employment, most extractive industries are capital intensive, and the jobs are often low-paying and hazardous.

Loss of Cultural Resources and Identity. Control over territory and its natural components is a concept that is deeply linked to the cultural identity and belief systems of many indigenous peoples. In many instances, the cultural attachment to the land is a sacred trust or stewardship. A well-known speech that underscores the deep cultural affinity of indigenous peoples to the environment is attributed to the Chief Seattle of the Suquamish Native American tribe:

> Our dead never forget this beautiful earth, for it is the mother of the red man. We are part of the earth and it is part of us. The perfumed flowers are our sisters; the deer, the horse, the great eagle, these are our brothers. The rocky crests, the juices in the meadows, the body heat of the pony, and man—all belong to the same family... For this land is sacred to us. This shining water that moves in the streams and rivers is not just water but the blood of our ancestors... The water's murmur is the voice of my father's father.[8]

Such sentiments are by no means unique to North America (Mander and Tauli-Corpuz 2006). Similar spiritual sentiments are behind the resistance to mineral extractive industries by the Lihirians in Papua New Guinea and the San in Botswana (UN Development Programme 2004: 92).

Information and Participation in Decision-Making

In many cases, indigenous peoples and other rural communities have not been informed or consulted about plans for large-scale infrastructure development in their areas or on issues that affect them directly, such as land acquisition or confiscation, resettlement and relocation, or compensation. Even when they are consulted, their resistance to engaging constructively with government agencies promoting or regulating infrastructure expansion is often heightened by a lack of information about successful cases and the notoriety of reports of projects that were social and environmental disasters. Hence, opposition to the development of large dams or mines in their territories is very strong, as reflected in the campaigns and movements of indigenous peoples and their supporters.

However, changes are occurring at various levels that can alter this dynamic. International norms are slowly changing, to require participatory processes as part of development planning. National governments and international organizations are increasingly cognizant of the importance of including indigenous leaders and other representatives of civil society in participatory planning. This involves, among other things, sharing information and recognizing the customary rights of indigenous peoples which in turn empowers indigenous groups in the stakeholder negotiations. This can lead to rebuilding of trust in societies and a rewriting of "social contracts" between governments, indigenous peoples, project proponents, and other stakeholders. More flexibility in approaches to security in property rights and user rights is being promoted. For example, in Latin America and the Caribbean, since 1997 the Inter-American Development Bank has underscored the need to respect communal land tenure systems in relevant projects involving indigenous communities (Plant and Hvalkof 2001).

What Do Indigenous Peoples Want?

For broad participation to be embraced by all relevant stakeholder groups, clarity regarding the goals of each group must be understood, lest others balk at participating out of fear that the participation process will only heighten the conflicts. Because only the most contentious (and often violent) confrontations over infrastructure expansion between indigenous groups and government or private sector personnel tend to be highly publicized, the perception that indigenous groups are "antidevelopment" is often exaggerated. Various declarations initiated by indigenous groups and their advocates reveal a very different orientation. The United Nations Declaration on the Rights of Indigenous Peoples, prepared with the participation of indigenous leaders from different parts of the world and approved in 2007, states very clearly that indigenous peoples want development, but it must be development that respects their identity and rights as citizens. The Declaration, approved by 143 of the 158 voting members of the UN General Assembly, affirms the rights of indigenous peoples to participate in decisions affecting their lives, and their land, territories, and resources. Article 5 links political, legal, economic, social, and cultural rights:

> Indigenous peoples have the right to maintain and strengthen their distinct political, legal, economic, social and cultural institutions, while retaining their right to participate fully, if they so choose, in the political, economic, social and cultural life of the State.

Reflecting prior experiences of forced assimilation or displacement, Articles 8, 10, and 11 affirm the rights of indigenous peoples to their lands and cultural heritage, and to just recourse and compensation in case of displacement.

Article 8
1. Indigenous peoples and individuals have the right not to be subjected to forced assimilation or destruction of their culture.
2. States shall provide effective mechanisms for prevention of, and redress for:
   a. Any action which has the aim or effect of depriving them of their integrity as distinct peoples, or of their cultural values or ethnic identities;
   b. Any action which has the aim or effect of dispossessing them of their lands, territories or resources;
   c. Any form of forced population transfer which has the aim or effect of violating or undermining any of their rights;
   d. Any form of forced assimilation or integration;
   e. Any form of propaganda designed to promote or incite racial or ethnic discrimination directed against them.

Article 10
Indigenous peoples shall not be forcibly removed from their lands or territories. No relocation shall take place without the free, prior and informed consent of the indigenous peoples concerned and after agreement on just and fair compensation and, where possible, with the option of return.

Article 11
Indigenous peoples have the right to practice and revitalize their cultural traditions and customs. This includes the right to maintain, protect and develop the past, present and future manifestations of their cultures, such as archeological and historical sites, artifacts, designs, ceremonies, technologies and visual and performing arts and literature...States shall provide redress through effective mechanisms, which may include

restitution, developed in conjunction with indigenous peoples, with respect to their cultural, intellectual, religious and spiritual property taken without their free, prior and informed consent or in violation of their laws, traditions and customs (UN General Assembly 2007).

Previous declarations made in various assemblies of indigenous peoples—national and international—support the provisions of the UN declaration. A statement issued at the 2003 International Cancun Declaration of Indigenous Peoples during the 5th WTO Ministerial Meeting in Mexico gives examples of what the international representatives of indigenous peoples consider to be adverse impacts of globalization and some international trade agreements, such as "the increasing conflicts between transnational mining, gas and oil corporations and Indigenous Peoples in the Philippines, Indonesia, Papua New Guinea, India, Ecuador, Guyana, Venezuela, Colombia, Nigeria, Chad-Cameroon, USA, Russia, Venezuela, among others, and the militarization and environmental devastation in these communities due to the operations of these extractive industries" (Indigenous Peoples Council on Biocolonialism 2005: 1). The facilitation of the entry of such corporations are made possible because of liberalization of investment laws pushed by the TRIMS (Trade-Related Investment Measures) Agreement and World Bank-International Monetary Fund conditionalities, regional trade agreements like North American Free Trade Agreement, and bilateral investment agreements (International Cancun Declaration of Indigenous Peoples 2003).[9]

Similar sentiments are reflected in declarations such as the Baguio Declaration of the 2nd Asian Indigenous Women's Conference in the Philippines (2004), the Indigenous Peoples Kyoto Water Declaration at the Third Water Forum in Japan (2003), the Kimberley Declaration at the International Indigenous Peoples Summit on Sustainable Development Khoi-San Territory, South Africa (2002), the Declaration of Civil Society and Indigenous Participants of the Regional Workshop of the World Bank's Extractive Industries Review in Brazil (2002), and various national and subnational level conferences and workshops.

Issues, Challenges, and Dilemmas

One fundamental question is development for whom? This hinges on the roles of the various actors and their interests to protect or disregard the rights of indigenous peoples relevant to major infrastructure, and the current and emerging initiatives to address the social impacts of the major infrastructure projects.

Power, Rights, and Development

The main issues that arise in the debate over the treatment of indigenous peoples impacted by major infrastructure projects are the "ownership" of land and natural resources, and the distribution of costs and benefits when development projects come in. The World Commission on Dams (2000: xxxiii) recognized the importance of "reconciling competing needs and entitlements [a]s the single most important factor in understanding the conflicts associated with development projects and programmes—particularly large-scale interventions such as dams."

As pointed out in earlier sections, the identities of indigenous peoples are closely linked to their territories—and their concept of territory includes not just the land, but also the natural resources below or on the land, and the air above it. This is a complex and highly debated issue, because many national constitutions enshrine the principle that while land can be individually titled and owned, the subsoil natural resources, water, and air belong to the state. In countries such as Ecuador, specific constitutional provisions deny indigenous peoples the rights to oil and gas within their territories (UN Development Programme 2004: 93). In contrast, a provision in the 1987 Philippine Constitution recognizes indigenous peoples' claims for ancestral rights to land and natural resources. Thus each nation's basic principles of property rights establish the legal framework to determine whether and how indigenous peoples' claims are recognized, on what basis compensation or resettlement benefits can be based, and whether indigenous peoples have legal recourse in case of conflict. Principles of property rights also determine the legal standing of individual versus collective claims, encompassing land alone or including the natural environment. Aside from laws, however, there are often difficulties and long delays in making rules operational and in implementing, monitoring, and enforcing them. In some countries, the rulings on ancestral claims are linked to a bigger set of national policies that discriminate or discourage expressions of cultural diversity. Meanwhile, many indigenous leaders demand secure rights over the territory they claim and respect for their forms of ownership and management.

There is much need for negotiation, therefore, when it comes to major development projects. However, asymmetry of power and information, as well as negative past experiences, typically make indigenous peoples distrustful and fearful of public or private sector initiatives with major infrastructure projects. This is clearly shown in the various declarations in the previous section. Yet new approaches, emphasizing consultation and participation, initiated by infrastructure proponents are changing the relationships among stakeholders in the direction of more equitable sharing of the costs and benefits of the development projects. This has been reinforced by the growing strength of civil society organizations to promote coalitions, information sharing, and accountability. Compared to the long history of development projects with widely publicized negative impacts, this changing environment is fairly recent; hence it will take time and much sincerity and consistency among the different actors for trust to be established.

Negotiations over the land and natural resources that are needed for sustainable operation of dams or mines take much time and skill because worldviews are divergent and causes deeply held. Experience shows that for equitable and sustainable development, the negotiation must be guided by a sense of respect for territorial rights and values of indigenous peoples. This is the basis for the concept of *free, prior, and informed consent*.

It should be noted here that while most developing countries approved the UN Declaration on the Rights of Indigenous Peoples where the term "free, prior and informed *consent*" was used, many development finance institutions use the term "free, prior and informed *consultation*." Although the UN Declarations are not legally binding, these provisions reflect the implicit approval of the states to move in the direction of an international legal norm. There are various examples of consultation going on in various countries, as shown in the reports of international financial institutions. If a major infrastructure project would impact indigenous peoples, development finance institutions are typically willing to provide funds only if free, prior and informed consultation is done. Several mineral extraction projects in Latin America have set up "dialogue tables"; others use voting to determine whether a community supports an incoming project or activity. Whether and how negotiation can solve a possible impasse, or whether alternative methods will need to be devised, is part of the ongoing international debate. It should be noted that the formal legal regimes in most countries dictate that when government needs to take privately owned land for development purposes, there are mandatory processes of information gathering, hearings for stakeholders, and objective determination of compensation.

Actors, Institutions, and Interests

Many stakeholders are involved in the planning, design, construction, implementation, and management of large-scale infrastructure projects.

This section discusses the interests and influence of the four main stakeholder groups in major infrastructure projects that affect indigenous communities in the rural areas: government agencies, development and financial institutions, the private sector (including multinational corporations), and civil society organizations including international, national, and local actors. The most serious concern arises when infrastructure projects are sponsored by "a powerful coalition including heads of state, multinational corporations of consulting engineers, contractors and suppliers, and multilateral and bilateral donors"[10] (Dorcey et al. 1997: 63).

Government Agencies. The national-level government agencies involved in infrastructure development are typically the national planning agency, the finance ministry, and some combination of the ministries of energy, mines, industry, and development. The subnational scene is typically a complex web of regional, provincial, district, and municipal policy-makers. Even when the overriding interest of the top-level national leaders is to develop revenues and capacity for economic growth and national well-being, the difficulties of coordinating and controlling agencies, financial agents, developers, designers, legal and scientific experts, engineers, managers, and contractors often leaves the national leaders with tenuous control.

Private Sector. The private sector is most prominent stakeholder in extractive industries and large dam projects. They are supported by host governments or have public financial agencies as partners. A 2002 study by the British development agency found that roughly 70 percent of recent of infrastructure-related programs worldwide had been undertaken by states (from own resources or nonconcessional borrowing) and about 27 percent by the private sector, rather than by development aid agencies (Department for International Development 2002). Because of the level of financing and technical skill required, the private sector firms are often multinational corporations that work with international and local teams of consultants, project managers, suppliers, and the like. The overriding goal of corporate investment is profitability for the shareholders, balanced in some cases by a sense of corporate social responsibility. Among the many risks faced by infrastructure and extractive industry corporations (ranging from governments reneging on royalty arrangements when initiatives are more profitable than originally expected, to requirements that the corporations provide social services for which they have no particular expertise), the most relevant for this analysis is the potential that local communities will obstruct construction or extraction. One reason why corporations seem to demand such high profits is that the corporations must hedge against the possibility that their operations will be stalled or even aborted because of clashes with local communities. Therefore governments have a strong financial interest in fostering more amicable relationships among the government, corporations, and indigenous groups.

Development Banks and Other Financial Institutions. The financial demands of multimillion dollar infrastructure projects typically require funds from international sources. Often these sources include intergovernmental financial institutions, such as the World Bank, the regional development banks, and bilateral foreign assistance agencies of wealthier countries.[11] They provide the financing, guarantees, and some technical support that enable planning, construction, and implementation. Policies in these agencies have evolved partly as a response to concerns about adverse social and environmental impacts of large-scale infrastructure projects in the 1970s and 1980s. The World Bank was the first multilateral financial institution to establish a safeguard policy on indigenous peoples in 1982: a "do no harm" policy requiring sufficient attention and compensation to leave displaced people no worse off. Subsequently the World Bank strengthened its guidelines to "doing good" in its attempts to address directly the needs of vulnerable groups in World Bank-funded development projects (Bridgeman 2001, World Bank 2008).This policy is put into effect if indigenous peoples are present in or have collective attachment to a proposed project area. The regional development banks and other development finance agencies have also developed their parallel policies. The International Finance Corporation (IFC) also modified its Policy on Social and Environmental Sustainability in 2006 to introduce results-based requirements and best practices. The new IFC Performance Standards are now used by over 60 large commercial financial institutions for project finance (IFC 2008).

There are many times in a project cycle that reviews of projects are done to ensure compliance with the operational safeguard guidelines. Starting early in the project proposal stage, for example, the World Bank requires an environmental assessment of the potential environmental impacts of a project, including impacts on the natural environment, human health and safety, social aspects, and transboundary and global environmental aspects. On the basis of the environmental assessment, different safeguard policies are put into effect. The Indigenous Peoples Safeguard Policy requires assessments performed with the help of social scientists. These assessments evaluate the impacts of a project on indigenous peoples, and these assessments form the basis for consultation with the affected indigenous peoples, sharing of information, preparation of specific plans and a planning framework to ensure local people affected have a share in potential benefits and/or are compensated for potential adverse impacts. Under the Indigenous Peoples Safeguard (OP 4.10 of the Operations Manual July 1005), the bank requires the borrower to engage in a process of free, prior, and informed consultation to ensure that there is broad community support from the affected Indigenous Peoples. The intention is to (1) avoid potentially adverse effects on the Indigenous Peoples communities; (2) when avoidance is not feasible, minimize, mitigate, or compensate for such effects; and (c) ensure that the Indigenous Peoples receive social and economic benefits that are culturally appropriate and inclusive. Depending on the type of project, the environmental assessment is more intensive—for example, for Category A (potentially high impact) projects, the borrower is required to consult the project-affected groups at least twice prior to approval, and, once approved, throughout project implementation.

The mind-set over the social impacts of development has changed over time. The Asian Development Bank included in the rationale for its Involuntary Resettlement Policy in 1995 that "Until recently, development-induced displacement of population was considered a "sacrifice" some people have to make for the larger good." However, as this same document notes, "Resettlement is viewed increasingly as a development issue" (Asian Development Bank 1995: 8). Hence, the changes in perception have guided changes in development bank policy; impacts of major infrastructure projects on local and particularly indigenous peoples would be considered in all aspects of planning and implementing a project supported by the development bank. The World Bank (2006) has claimed that its safeguard, transparency, and accountability policies have shown positive results in the design, decision-making, and implementation process of World Bank–funded projects.

In many instances these institutions have sufficient leverage to require that the loan or grant agreements include provisions for consultation and other participatory processes for affected groups, environmental safeguards, and compensation for anyone facing displacement. While the application of safeguard policies have increased the up-front costs and complication of financing through the development banks, the requirements have provided more opportunities for active participation and involvement of local peoples in the planning of the projects.

When these provisions are honored, they can avoid or minimize negative social and environmental impacts of the projects. However, compliance with such provisions has been very spotty. Daniel Gibson (1993) documented the discrepancies during the 1980s between the agreements and practices in the cases of World Bank–funded dams in

India and Indonesia, with respect to the commitments to compensate displaced people. An especially troubling aspect of these interactions was the apparent willingness of the national government of India to comply with the provisions, but the failure of the state governments to implement them. Such cases were important in the World Bank's decision to withdraw from funding large dam projects. As multilateral financial institutions resume their funding of very large projects, the critical question is whether local people's participation will be genuine, and whether the doctrine of full compensation will be honored. Because of these concerns, the funding for the big dam and extractive industry projects from the multilateral development-oriented financing agencies has declined over recent years, even though total investments in extractive industries have increased.[12]

However, with the emergence of rapidly developing economies in such countries as Brazil, India, and China, with both capital and huge appetites for energy and materials, the national credit agencies of these countries have become important agencies that finance infrastructure. China, for example, is supporting infrastructure projects such as mineral extraction projects in Africa (Davies 2008). China is financing Cambodia's hydroelectric Kamchay Dam as part of a US$600 million aid package announced in 2006, to be constructed by China's largest hydropower developer. At least six more potential large dams in the country are being evaluated with support from the Chinese agency. What has not been demonstrated so far is whether these projects will have the umbrella of safeguard policies or transparency that allows monitoring by institutions beyond the Cambodian government (International Rivers 2008, Middleton 2008).

Other International Agencies. Agencies of the United Nations have been at the forefront of agreements and conventions to support the rights of indigenous peoples. The International Labor Organization Convention 169, which came into force in 1991, is considered a milestone in defining who indigenous peoples are and in identifying their basic needs. Other UN organizations have promoted policies in support of indigenous peoples' rights and well-being. The Permanent Forum on Indigenous Issues is now a part of the United Nations system, actively working on behalf of indigenous peoples, and provides a forum for their leaders to meet and speak.

Civil society organizations. The motivations of the international, regional, and national civil society organizations involved with these projects include concerns for the environment and concerns for the rights of the indigenous and other vulnerable peoples. These concerns are sometimes compatible, sometimes not, depending on the organizations' views on whether they see indigenous peoples as environmental defenders. Some environmental groups oppose both major infrastructure projects and the extractive activities of rural peoples, seeing both as threats to ecosystems. In contrast, other organizations combine environmental and human rights concerns, combining the commitments to environmental protection and environmental justice. The latter organizations provide support locally to indigenous groups and causes, or they work in the global arena to inform and advocate. National organizations such as the Movement of Dam-Affected Peoples in Brazil have developed around the issue of displacement and anti-dam activism.

International and local academic, research, and professional organizations play or can play an important role. As independent institutions, they can conduct research, monitor, and evaluate potential projects to give timely and long-term feedback to stakeholders including the indigenous communities (in local languages and appropriate communication forms). They can also play significant roles in negotiation and mediation. The media and investigative journalists are important in raising public awareness about impacts of projects on local people and the environment. In many cases in the past, it was church leaders who worked as credible sources of information and support, or bridging partners to local communities especially during disputes.

Modes of Cooperation. The coalitions that have formed among the different stakeholders are important. Private financing agencies adopted safeguard guidelines after a conference hosted by the International Finance Corporation (World Bank Group's facility that lends to the private sector), and the World Bank's main facility (which lends to governments) partnered with NGOs to sponsor the World Commission on Dams that developed criteria and guidelines, including standards and codes of conduct (World Commission on Dams 2000, Moore and Scudder 2008), for large dam projects.

Through these interactions, the safeguards for indigenous peoples developed by the international agencies have been widely disseminated.

Newer Forms of Participation, Mitigation, and Broader Based Development

Globalization and advances in science and information technology are changing how indigenous peoples can react to major infrastructure initiatives. Indigenous peoples are less isolated because of the formation of worldwide NGOs and coalitions that address their concerns and provide them low-cost access through cell phones, computers, and various kinds of forums. The availability of expertise is a parallel development. For example civil society organizations such as the Environmental Defender Law Center (established in 2003) can overcome indigenous groups' relative lack of technical or legal expertise by providing pro bono legal assistance. The center assists in conducting local votes on mines and dam projects. The center's philosophy is that these votes will ascertain community sentiment on infrastructure or extractive initiatives, thereby reducing the likelihood of violence if the developers take these results into account (Environmental Defender Law Center 2008a, 2008b). This electoral innovation has been used successfully to assess whether there was indigenous community support for mining activity in Peru (more than 90 percent of the local residents opposed the Rio Blanco project in 2007), Guatemala (more than 97 percent of the villagers in the municipality of Sipacapa opposed the Marlin Mine Project in 2005), and Mexico (97 percent of the residents rejected the San Xavier Mine initiative in Cerro de San Pedro in a 2006 vote). These votes resulted in series of complicated legal decisions regarding the status of these votes, appeals by the mining companies or the indigenous groups, and a mixed record in terms of whether, and at what pace, the mining initiatives would proceed. Community voting has also been conducted to gauge support for dam projects. In 2007, in the municipality of Ixcan, 90 percent of the Mayan indigenous people in Guatemala voted against proposed dams in the Chixoy and other rivers and against potential oil exploration in their area. Although the contested legal standing of these votes limits their force, they do provide a channel for community sentiment about development projects (Environmental Defender Law Center 2008).

Equator Principles

Some international private sector financial institutions have embraced the set of safeguards patterned after the International Finance Corporation safeguards and growing out of a sense of corporate social responsibility, which they have called the Equator Principles (Equator Principles Financial Institutions 2006). The bulk of these financial institutions, numbering more than 65 by early 2009, are large banks such as Citigroup, ABN AMRO, HSBC, and Barclays.[13] In conditioning the lending that these financial institutions make to state or private borrowers undertaking expansions in infrastructure or extractive industries, the Equator Principles bind the financial institutions to (1) categorize the magnitude of risks and impacts; (2) undertake social and environmental impact assessments; (3) adhere to International Finance Corporation social and environmental standards; (4) develop and apply an action plan to monitor and mitigate negative impacts, to be overseen by a "social and environmental management system; (5) engage in serious consultation and disclosure; (6) institute a grievance procedure; (7) arrange for independent review; and (8) imbed the borrower's commitment to these principles within the loan covenants, providing an opportunity for the lender to suspend the loan or to take other actions either to pressure the borrower into compliance or to withdraw financing (Equator Principles Financial Institutions 2006). The commitment of these institutions is to apply the principles on projects costing US$10 million or more.

Conclusion and Summary of Recommendations

Many factors have been changing the way stakeholders in infrastructure expansion and extractive industries interrelate. Some of these changes could improve the condition of local peoples affected by large-scale infrastructure development in projects such as large dams and extractive industries. Many steps can be taken to ensure that net positive social benefits reach indigenous peoples in rural communities and safeguard their environments:[14]

1. *Explicitly recognize indigenous peoples' rights over their physical and intellectual property.*

   More countries are taking steps to include specific provisions in their laws that provide for rights to be respected and legal recourse to be provided. This should be incorporated in a country's national policies and legal framework. Global and local information sharing, monitoring technologies such as periodic reports in local language, and scorecards that are objective and openly available should be required. This ensures that indigenous peoples can be "at the table" as active participants in the development and monitoring of infrastructure projects. Anguelovski in O'Faircheallaigh and Ali (2008: 218) argue that "respecting the traditional organizations of indigenous peoples and their communication channels is an essential prerequisite to getting the 'social license to operate' extractive ventures. It also ensures that local people can negotiate with new actors and on evolving schemes on infrastructure projects that affect them."

2. *Consult with indigenous communities and invite their participation for the use of any resource.*

Many new technologies can be used to ensure that local communities can participate effectively in decisions about potential infrastructure development in their areas. Involvement of local communities should be done as a matter of course and from the start. In Peru, for example, more recent development of zinc and copper mines started with the involvement of indigenous communities in decision-making. Safeguard policies and processes evolving at the development agencies should be highly simplified and disseminated widely so that governments, emerging country leaders, universities, NGOs, and communities can adapt and use them both for planning and monitoring.

3. *Empower communities by developing strategies to share benefits.*

The many benefits that development can bring should be shared with local communities. Displacement should be avoided when possible or minimized when necessary, and adequate compensation negotiated and given. The choice of resettlement areas should improve, not worsen, the well-being of displaced people, in terms of both socioeconomic and political conditions, taking into account the risks of clashes between the old and new residents of the areas. In case of mining ventures, effective support can come from the establishment and good management of trust funds sourced from royalties or taxes. Innovation in approaches to sharing the benefits from infrastructure development and the use of new technologies should be incorporated into strategies to make infrastructure part of shared development (O'Faircheallaigh 2002).

4. *Encourage international agencies to review ways of increasing the transparency of the multidimensional social and environmental costs and benefits of major infrastructure development.*

This is crucial to the objective of having these values guide decision-making, and to ensure that adequate forms and amounts of compensation will be provided when needed. In addition, analysis should be done to determine how much compensation is necessary to leave impacted people at least as well off as they were prior to the impact.

5. *Build the capacity of local people to participate effectively in stakeholder negotiations.*

Capacity building among indigenous leaders should be encouraged as part of the funding for the projects. To support these leaders, project planning and implementation should involve local professionals to provide reliable, independent analysis, information dissemination, feedback, and monitoring. This can be incorporated into the safeguard policies with funding provided through the financing entities. There is a need to improve the capacity of independent monitoring agencies to use new technologies in providing information, analysis, and feedback to local peoples. Effective monitoring and corrective actions can rescue the success of resettlement projects (World Bank 2006).

6. *Promote research to document the successful methods used in large-scale development projects involving indigenous peoples, and the dissemination of this research.*

Too few of the successes have been documented and circulated, accounting for the largely negative view of the social impacts and processes involving indigenous peoples. Such accounts by indigenous people themselves would be particularly credible.

7. *Include indigenous communities in "Development with Dignity" processes regarding major infrastructure projects and industrial development.*

At a minimum, "free, prior and informed consultation" must be observed. Yet it is very important to evolve to the doctrine of "free, prior and informed consent" where indigenous people have long-established customary property rights, even if these had been customary rights rather than formal legal rights.

Notes

1. "Indigenous peoples" is a generic concept that includes cultural minorities, ethnic minorities, indigenous cultural communities, tribal people, natives, and aboriginals, distinct from dominant or mainstream society. Often these peoples have an ethnic identity, historical continuity in their society, their own social, economic, cultural, and political institutions, and their ancestral territories that may be communally shared.
2. The World Bank later withdrew from the project. Around this time and faced with mounting global pressures due to negative environmental and social impacts, development finance agencies such as the World Bank started a review of their involvement in large dam projects.
3. UN Conference on Trade and Development (2008 : Table 3.2.B).

4. Of course, this broad statement does not hold for all cases. There are circumstances in which indigenous people degrade the ecosystem, especially when defending their property rights requires it. For example, Godoy, Kirby, and Wilkie (2001) cite the forest clearing of Bolivian Amerindians as an effort to secure property rights.

5. The International Commission on Large Dams (ICOLD) is an international nongovernmental organization founded in 1928. The goal of the organization, which has National Committees from 88 countries and approximately 10,000 individual members, is to provide a forum for the exchange of knowledge and experience in dam engineering. In recent years, it has included as subjects, cost studies, environmental issues, international river issues, and provision of public information.

6. ICOLD defines large dams as those rising 15 m or more from the foundation or having 3 million cubic meters of water reservoir capacity.

7. See, for example, Anguelovski (2008).

8. This is one of several versions of a speech supposedly given by Chief Seattle in 1854 after receiving a U.S. government offer to purchase Indian land. This version can be found at http://www.kyphilom.com/wwwseattle.html.

9. Unlike the earlier stated declaration, this declaration was aimed at addressing globalization and world trade. International Cancun Declaration of Indigenous Peoples (2003).

10. Thayer Scudder, cited in Dorcey et al. (1997: 63).

11. See, for instance, World Bank (2005).

12. In the case of extractive industry projects, although investment has been increasing overall from 1990 to 2002, data show that funding from the World Bank's International Finance Corporation for these projects has been decreasing (Liebenthal, Michelitsch, and Tarazona 2005). See also the World Bank's extensive report on extractive industries (World Bank Group 2004).

13. The remainder of the institutions consists of a few regional development banks.

14. Several of these recommendations are elaborated in UN Economic Development Programme (2004).

References

Anguelovski, Isabelle. 2008. Environmental justice concerns with transnational mining operations: Exploring the limitations of post-crisis community dialogues in Peru. In *Earth matters: Indigenous peoples, the extractive industries and corporate social responsibility*, ed. Ciaran O'Faircheallaigh and Ali Saleem.UK: Greenleaf Publishing, Ltd.

Asian Development Bank 1995. *Operations manual: Involuntary resettlement.* Manila: Asian Development Bank, August.

_____. 2007. Indigenous peoples safeguards. Special Evaluation Study. Manila: Asian Development Bank, February.

Bridgeman, Natalie L. 2001. World Bank reform in the "post-policy" era. *Georgetown International Environmental Law Review* 13(4): 1013–1046.

Colchester, Marcus 2000. Forest Peoples Programme: Dams, indigenous peoples and ethnic minorities. Thematic Review 1.2 prepared as an input to the World Commission on Dams. Capetown. http://www.dams.org. Accessed December 18, 2008.

Cook, Cynthia, Tyrrell Duncan, Somchai Jitsuchon, Anil K. Sharma, and Wu Guobao. 2004. Assessing the impact of transport and energy infrastructure on poverty reduction. Manila: Asian Development Bank Regional Technical Assistance Report 5947, June.

Davies, Martyn. 2008. How China delivers development assistance to Africa. Centre for Chinese Studies, University of Stellenbosch. http://www.dfid.gov.uk/Pubs/files/china-dev-africa.pdf. Accessed December 18, 2008.

Department for International Development (DFID). 2002. Making connections: infrastructure for poverty reduction. http://www.dfid.gov.uk. Accessed December 18, 2008.

De Wet, Chris, ed. 2006. *Development-induced displacement: Problems, policies and people.* New York: Berghahn Books.

Dorcey, Tony, Achim Steiner, Michael Acreman, and Brett Orlando, eds. 1997. *Large dams: Learning from the past, looking at the future. Workshop proceedings.* Gland, Switzerland: The World Conservation Union and the World Bank Group.

Environmental Defender Law Center. 2008a. Local votes on mines and dams. http://www.edlc.org. Accessed December 18, 2008.

_____. 2008b. Who are environmental defenders? http://www.edlc.org. Accessed December 18, 2008.

Equator Principles Financial Institutions. 2006. The Equator Principles. http://www.equator-principles.com/documents/Equator_Principles.pdf. Accessed January 20, 2009.

Fernholz, Rosemary Morales. 2002. Indigenous land rights: Who controls the Philippine public domain? In *Sovereignty under challenge: How governments respond*, ed. John D. Montgomery and Nathan Glazer. pp. 321–343. New Brunswick, NJ: Transaction Publishers.

Gibson, Daniel. 1993. The politics of involuntary resettlement: World Bank-supported projects in Asia, Duke University Ph.D. dissertation. Durham, NC.

Godoy, Ricardo, Kris Kirby, and David Wilkie. 2001. Tenure security, private time preference, and use of natural resources among lowland Bolivian Amerindians. *Ecological Economics* 38: 105–118.

Hirsch, Philip. 2002. Global norms, local compliance and the human rights-environment nexus: A case study of the Nam Theun II Dam. In *Human rights and the environment: Conflicts and norms in a globalizing world*, ed. Lyuba Zarsky. London: Earthscan Publications, Ltd.

Imhof, Aviva. 2008. Review of draft final resettlement Action plan for Theun-Hinboun Expansion project. http://www.internationalrivers.org/en/node/2710. Accessed December 18, 2008.

Imhof, Aviva and Andrew Preston. 2008. Theun-Hinboun Dam nightmare revealed: Resettlement plan and EIA riddled with flaws. http://www.internationalrivers.org/en/southeast-asia/laos/theun-hinboun. Accessed December 18, 2008.

Infrastructure Network. 2006. Infrastructure: Lessons from the last two decades of World Bank engagement. Discussion Paper, January 30.

Inter-American Development Bank. 1998. Involuntary resettlement operational policy and background paper. Washington, D.C.

International Cancun Declaration of Indigenous Peoples. 2003. http://www.treatycouncil.org/section_21171111.htm. Accessed December 1, 2009.

International Commission on Large Dams 2007. Dams and the world's water. http://www.icold-cigb.org. Accessed December 18, 2008

International Finance Corporation 2008. Creating opportunity: 2008 annual report, http://www.ifc.org/ifcext/annualreport.nsf/AttachmentsByTitle/AR2008_English/$FILE/AR2008_English.pdf. Accessed December 18, 2008.

International Forum on Globalization 2003. http://www.ifg.org/programs/indig.htm. Accessed December 18, 2008.

International Rivers. 2008. Southeast Asia. http:// www.internationalrivers.org/en/southeast-asia. Accessed December 18, 2008.

Khagram, Sanjeev. 2004. *Dams and development: Transnational struggles for water and power.* New York: Cornell University Press.

Liebenthal, Andrés, Roland Michelitsch, and Ethel Tarazona. 2005. *Extractive industries and sustainable development: An evaluation of World Bank Group experience.* Washington, DC: World Bank Group.

Lutz, Ellen. 2008. Dam nation. *Cultural survival.* http://www.internationalrivers.org/en/print/3617. Accessed December 18.

Mander, Jerry and Victoria Tauli-Corpuz, eds. 2006. *Paradigm wars: Indigenous peoples' resistance to globalization.* San Francisco: Sierra Club Books and University of California Press.

Middleton, Carl. 2008. New report urges better energy planning in Cambodia before hydropower dams are developed. http://www.international rivers.org/en/way-forward/world-commission-dams. Accessed December 18, 2008.

Moore, Deborah and Thayer Scudder. 2008. The World Commission on Dams framework: solutions for managing dams, water and energy in international rivers 2008. New financiers and the environment: Ten perspectives on how financial institutions can protect the environment. http://www.internationalrivers.org/files/NewFinanciers_Eng.pdf. Accessed December 18, 2008.

Mydans, Seth. 2006. A massive dam, under way in Laos, generates worries, *New York Times,* June 26. http://www.nytimes.com/2006/06/26/world/asia/26laos.html. Accessed January 31, 2009.

O'Faircheallaigh, Ciaran. 2002. *A new approach to policy evaluation: Mining and indigenous people.* Vermont: Ashgate Publishing, Ltd.

O'Faircheallaigh, Ciaran and Salim Ali 2008. Understanding corporate-aboriginal agreements on mineral development. In *Earth matters: Indigenous peoples, the extractive industries and corporate social responsibility*. ed. Ciaran O'Faircheallaigh and Salim Ali. pp. 67–82. London: Greenleaf Publishing.

Patrinos, Harry Anthony and Emmanuel Skoufias. 2007. Economic opportunities for indigenous peoples in Latin America. Washington, DC: World Bank.

Plant, Roger and Soren Hvalkof. 2001. Land titling and indigenous peoples. Washington, DC: Inter-American Development Bank. http://www.iadb.org/sds/IND/publication/publication_133_1635_e.htm. Accessed December 18, 2008.

Scudder, Thayer. 1997. Social impacts of large dam projects. In *Large dams: Learning from the past, looking at the future. Workshop proceedings*, ed. Tony Dorcey Achim Steiner, Michael Acreman, and Brett Orlando. pp. 41–68. Gland, Switzerland: The World Conservation Union and the World Bank Group.

_____. 2005. *The future of large dams: Dealing with social, environmental, institutional and political costs*. London: Earthscan.

Setboonsarng, Sununtar and Anil Markandya. 2008. Organic crops or energy crops? Options for rural development in Cambodia and the Lao People's Democratic Republic. Discussion Paper No. 101. April 11, 2008. Manila: Asian Development Bank Institute.

United Nations. 2006. Brief overview of the current situation facing indigenous peoples. http://www.un.org/esa/socdev/unpfii/en/mdgs.html. Accessed December 10, 2008.

UN Conference on Trade and Development. 2008a. *Handbook of statistics 2008*. Geneva. http://www.unctad.org/Templates/Page.asp?intItemID=1890&lang=1. Accessed December 1, 2008.

_____. 2008b. *World investment report*. Geneva. http://www.unctad.org/Templates/webflyer.asp?docid=10502&intItemID=2068&lang=1. Accessed December 1, 2008.

UN Development Programme. 2004. Human development report 2004. New York. http://hdr.undp.org/en/reports/global/hdr2004/. Accessed December 18, 2008.

UN General Assembly. 2007. The United Nations Declaration on the Rights of Indigenous Peoples. http://www.un.org/esa/socdev/unpfii/en/declaration. Accessed December 18, 2008.

Wessal, Arianne. 2008. Providing basic education for the migrant groups of Mali and Niger: A case study of the Tuareg. Unpublished Master's Project. Durham, NC: Duke Center for International Development.

World Bank. 2005. Infrastructure and the World Bank: A progress report. Washington, DC, September. http://siteresources.worldbank.org/DEVCOMMINT/Documentation/20651863/DC2005–0015(E)-Infrastructure.pdf. Accessed December 1, 2008.

_____. 2006. Infrastructure: Lessons from the last two decades of World Bank Engagement: A discussion paper. Washington, DC.

World Bank. 2008. Implementing the extractive industries transparency initiative: Applying early lessons from the field. Washington, DC: World Bank. http://www.eitransparency.org/document/validationguide. Accessed December 18, 2008.

World Bank Group. 2004. Striking a better balance: The World Bank Group and extractive industries: The final report of the extractive industries review. Washington, DCC: World Bank, September. http://www.ifc.org/ifcext/eir.nsf/AttachmentsByTitle/FinalMgtResponseExecSum/$FILE/finaleirmanagementresponseexecsum.pdf. Accessed December 18, 2008.

World Commission on Dams. 2000. *Dams and development: A new framework for decision-making*. London: Earthscan. http://www.dams.org//docs/report/wcdreport.pdf. Accessed December 1, 2008

World Wildlife Fund 2007. Dam good plans do not always make good practice. http://www.panda.org/what_we_do/knowledge_centres/freshwater/our_solutions/policy_practice/dams_initiative/problems/social/. Accessed December 18, 2008.

Index

CPSIA information can be obtained
at www.ICGtesting.com
Printed in the USA
LVHW10*1339060918
589346LV00009B/36/P